WHOSE BUSINESS VALUES

Some Asian and Cross-Cultural Perspecti

The editors dedicate this book to
their families with great affection

WHOSE BUSINESS VALUES ?

Some Asian and Cross-Cultural Perspectives

edited by Sally Stewart and Gabriel Donleavy

Hong Kong University Press
香港大學出版社

Hong Kong University Press
139 Pokfulam Road, Hong Kong

© Hong Kong University Press 1995

ISBN 962 209 386 8

The editors would like to express their thanks to the Lee
Hysan Foundation whose support made this book possible.
We are also grateful to Susan Makowski for her invaluable
contributions; to Kathryn Wolfendale for her excellent
editorial assistance and to the staff of the Department of
Management Studies at the University of Hong Kong with
whom it has been a privilege to work.

Printed in Hong Kong by ColorPrint Production Co.

CONTENTS

CONTRIBUTORS

Robert E. Allinson has authored or edited four books, including *Global Disasters: Inquiries into Management Ethics* (Prentice-Hall), and *Understanding the Chinese Mind* (OUP), and written more than 80 articles for such journals as *The Academy of Management Executive* and *Philosophy East and West*. He sits on the editorial boards of eight journals, including the *Journal of Chinese Philosophy* and *Asian Philosophy*. He has been invited to teach senior executives in programmes sponsored by MITI in Japan, the Pacific Asian Management Institute in Honolulu and the Helsinki School of Economics. His work has been translated into Italian and Chinese and has been abstracted in Japanese, French and German.

Anne Carver is a solicitor of the Supreme Court of England and Wales and of the Supreme Court of Hong Kong. She is the author of *Hong Kong Business Law* and *The Guide to Insolvency Law in Hong Kong* and has contributed articles and chapters to books on Hong Kong trade union and employment law. She is currently co-authoring a book *What Lawyers Do: A Theory of Legal Practice*. She has been a lecturer in the Department of Professional Legal Education, Faculty of Law, the University of Hong Kong since 1984.

Stewart Clegg researches and teaches at the University of Western Sydney Macarthur (UWSM), where he is Foundation Professor of Management. Previously he has been professor at the Universities of New England and St Andrews. He is the author of about 100 articles and books. Among his better-known volumes are *Power, Rule and Domination; Organization, Class and Control* (with David Dunkerley); *Modern Organizations*; and *Frameworks of Power*. His current research interests are in the field of 'embryonic industries', an area that he has been researching for the Australian Federal Government Task Force into Leadership and Management Skills for the twenty-first century, and high technology product innovation, which he is currently researching with colleagues at UWSM, as part of an international comparative project. He is editor (with Cynthia Hardy and Walter Nord) of the new and definitive *Handbook of Organization Studies*, to be published in 1996 and is also working with Gill Palmer (University of Wollongong) on two other edited volumes on management.

Gabriel Donleavy graduated from Cambridge in Economics and obtained his Ph.D. from Glasgow in Accounting. He taught the first MBA business ethics course in Hong Kong and has done a number of pieces of research for the ICAC. He has published over 50 articles on accounting, ethics and regulatory matters, more than three-quarters of them being written since he came to Hong Kong in 1986.

Georges Enderle is Professor of International Business Ethics at the University of Notre Dame, Indiana. His books include *Handlungsorientierte Wirtschaftsethik* [Action Oriented Business Ethics] (1993); *Lexikon der Wirtschaftsethik* [Encyclopedia of Business Ethics] (coeditor: 1993); and *People in Corporations: Ethical Responsibilities and Corporate Effectiveness* (with B. Arlnond and A. Argandona: 1990). He is co-founder of the European Business Ethics Network (EBEN).

Paul A. Fadil is a Ph.D. student at Florida State University.

Klaus M. Leisinger was born in Lorrach, West Germany in 1947. He studied Economics and Social Sciences at the University of Basel, Switzerland. He received his doctorate degree in business problems and technology in the Third World. From 1974 to 1977, he was a scientific employee of the staff 'Relations to Third World Countries' with Ciba-Geigy Ltd., Basel. He spent four years in sub-Saharan Africa as Manager of Ciba Pharmaceuticals, then from 1982 to 1989 he headed the staff 'Relations to Third World Countries'. Since 1990 he has been Vice President and Delegate of the Advisory Board of the Ciba-Geigy Foundation for Cooperation with Developing Countries. In addition to his position at Ciba, Dr Leisinger is Professor of Developmental Sociology at the University of Basel. He has advisory functions in different national and international organizations dealing with development issues, e.g. the Committee for International Development Cooperation of the Swiss Federal Council and the Expert Group of the Swiss National Science Foundation. Other affiliations include membership of the following: the board of trustees and managing committee of SWISSCONTACT (Swiss Foundation for Technical Cooperation); the scientific board of the Swiss Academy of Development; the liaison group of the Business Council for Sustainable Development; and the international editorial board of the *Cambridge Quarterly of Healthcare Ethics*.

Jack Mahoney was appointed in 1993 as the first Dixons Professor of Business Ethics and Social Responsibility at London Business School. He was born in Scotland in 1939 and is a graduate of Glasgow University and of the Gregorian University, Rome, as well as being a Jesuit priest and former Principal of Heythrop College, University of London. From 1986 to 1993 he was F.D. Maurice Professor of Moral and Social Theology at King's College, University of London, where he was also, from 1987, founding Director of King's College Business Ethics Research Centre. From 1987 to 1993 he developed the subject of business ethics in the City of London as the Mercers' School Memorial Professor of Commerce at Gresham College, London. Professor Mahoney is the author of several books, including *Teaching Business Ethics in the UK, Europe and the USA: A Comparative Study* (Athlone, London 1990), and coeditor of *Business Ethics in a New Europe* (Kluwer, Amsterdam 1992). He is also a founding editor of the quarterly publication *Business Ethics: A European Review* (Blackwells, Oxford) which first appeared in January 1992. He is a Fellow of the Royal Society of Arts, a Member of the European Academy of Sciences and Arts and a Companion of the Institute of Management.

John F. Quinn completed his doctoral studies in ethics and logic at the University of Washington and Juris doctorate in Law at the

University of Dayton, USA. He is Associate Professor of Business Ethics and Business Law at the University of Dayton. He has published various articles on applied ethics. His book on *Managerial Ethics* will be published in 1996 by Sage. It will include academic perspectives of law, philosophy and management, as well as some practical results from his ethics consulting practice, Organizational Ethics Associates.

David A. Ralston is an Associate Professor of Management at the University of Connecticut. He has led management development and corporate enchancement programmes in Hong Kong, China and Russia. His research interests focus upon cross-cultural management issues regarding work values, influence strategies, and stress. This research has concentrated on Asia and the Pacific-Rim nations. His most recent research has been published in the *Journal of Applied Psychology, Journal of International Business Studies, Asia Pacific Journal of Management,* and *Journal of Business Ethics.*

David M. Reid lectures in marketing at the University of Hong Kong. Previously he was MBA Director and Lecturer in Business Policy and Marketing at the University of Edinburgh, and he has also lectured in marketing and international business at the Chinese University of Hong Kong. He trained as a mechanical engineer, then, after obtaining a Master's degree in Management Sciences from the University of Manchester Institute of Science and Technology, he worked in marketing in Europe and the USA. He has carried out research on strategic management and published a number of articles on this topic and on strategic marketing. He also acts as a strategic consultant to major corporations and advertising agencies.

Robin Snell directs the MBA programme at the City University of Hong Kong, where he is a senior lecturer. He came to Hong Kong in 1992, after many years at Lancaster University. He edits the journal *Management Learning,* formerly *Management Education and Development.* His book *Developing Skills for Ethical Management* was published by Chapman & Hall in 1993.

Lee P. Stepina is an Associate Professor of Management at Florida State University. His research concentrates upon issues of equity theory.

Sally Stewart is Head of the Department of Management Studies and specializes in international marketing at the University of Hong Kong. Her degrees are from Oxford University and she has had 30 years of research experience in Asia. She has published her research on the PRC and its neighbours in many journals, including *International Studies of Management and Organization, Columbia Journal of World Business, the International Journal of Advertising,* as chapters in books and elsewhere. Her recent work has focused on the role of the Overseas Chinese in the development of southern China. She is the founder and acting Chairman of the University of Hong Kong's Centre for the Study of Business Values.

Robert H. Terpstra is an Associate Professor at the University of Macau. He has consulted on management development in Russia, the People's Republic of China, and other Asian nations. He has published numerous articles on various issues ranging from the 'Accuracy of Financial Analysts' Forecasts of EPS' to 'The Influence of Culture on Risk Taking' in the following publications: *Financial Review, California Management Review, Journal of International Business Studies, Journal of International Management, Pacific Basin Finance Journal, Asia-Pacific Journal of Management, Journal of Applied Psychology* and *Journal of Business Ethics.* He also edited the *Manual of the Hong Kong Securities Industry* published by the Stock Exchange of Hong Kong and the Chinese University's Asia Pacific Institute of Business. Dr Terpstra holds a Bachelor's and a Master's degree in Business Administration from the University of Michigan and a Doctorate in Finance from Florida State University.

William White was a research assistant in the Department of Management Studies at the University of Hong Kong before going to Exeter College, Oxford.

Arthur Yeung is an Associate Professor at San Francisco State University and the Executive Director of the California Strategic

Human Resource Partnership. He is the author of three books and an active management consultant. He received his doctorate from the University of Michigan and his Master's and Bachelor's degrees from the University of Hong Kong.

Jenny Yeung is a Lecturer in the Department of International Business, San Francisco State University. She has worked as a management consultant assisting foreign companies to conduct business in China and as a research associate at the University of Michigan. She received her BSocSc from the University of Hong Kong and her MBA from CERAM (France).

Yu Kai-Cheng is professor of Organizational Behavior and Human Resources Management in the School of Management of the Dalian University of Technology, and Dean of the National Center for Management Development at Dalian. His research interests focus on China's employees' organizational commitment, motivation, particularly sense of fair allocation, power mentality, work values, innovative HRM techniques and cross-cultural interactions. He has been involved in consulting activities with a variety of Sino-Western joint ventures, e.g. Tianjin OTIS Elevator, Shanghai Xerox Copier, GAMECO.

PREFACE: TRADING VALUES

Gabriel Donleavy

This book is the result of Asia's first international conference on business values held in June 1994 in Hong Kong. It was hosted by the newly launched Centre for the Study of Business Values in the University of Hong Kong.

Business values are manifested in business conduct and/or strategy, depending whether they are terminal or instrumental values (Rokeach 1973). They include business ethics but are distinguishable from them in that ethics are by definition prescriptive and carry an implication of an a priori judgement of rightness. Studying business values includes the study of profit maximizing behaviour as well as the study of green issue management by firms and carries no implication that the scholar espouses any particular position in the various ethical continua. In particular s/he is not committed to any one ethical philosopher's views, to any one approach to ethical relativism, to any one answer to the question of the moral substantiality of the business corporation. Nor, however, is the scholar working on business values a mere *tabula rasa*, or posing as being in Rawls's 'original position' or, in some rarefied way, value free. Rather, the scholar is in the business of comparing theory with praxis, words with other words and with actions to see if they mutually reinforce or reciprocally deconstruct. The researcher examines what business people believe and explores the gap between ideals and actualities.

Being human, it is inevitable that the researcher into business values will make value judgements even if they are not voiced. Some judgements may be held so strongly that only a partisan type of scholarship is felt to be honourable. In this book are included pieces all along the spectrum from explicit partisanship (e.g. Mahoney against bribery) to extreme ethical relativism (as in Reid's discussion of Japanese gift giving). Although ethics are a focus for most authors in this collection, some papers are about values without being centred on ethics. Clegg is concerned with values as facilitators of innovation, Donleavy with feudalism as an ideational reservoir of trust building mechanisms and Quinn is concerned with the interplay of economy and ecology. The contrast of West and East is frequently addressed in the assembled articles, but some authors, such as Stewart, discern that converging or universalist tendencies underlie the contrast.

In Chapter 1, Sally Stewart points out the reluctance of Hong Kong business academics hitherto to address business values for fear of being accused of ethnocentricity or special pleading. This fear may be exaggerated, she argues, given the remarkable overlap between Aristotle's and Confucius's prescriptions for virtuous conduct.

Allinson, in Chapter 2, argues there is no special science of business ethics, as ethics is extrinsic to a whole range of disciplines. Such disciplines absorb ethical dimensions more readily whenever ethics is incorporated at the design stage of their conceptual framework rather than being grafted on after construction. As a discipline, business has a minimum ethical content in order for business trading to be possible at all. The act of assessing whether a market exists for the products or services of a new firm entails the act of considering whether an unfilled social need exists. There is no such thing as a business completely divorced from the production of some social value. Finally, Allinson reminds us that credit trading involves trust. Since the conference in June and the compilation of this book in December 1994, Lehman Brothers have proceeded to issue writs in the Chinese courts against two state owned subsidiaries for non-payment of debts. In the commentaries by the parties and the media, one can be forgiven for gaining the impression that both sides in this dispute operated from a basis of trust. The Americans trusted the PRC firms would pay but the PRC firms trusted the Americans would not make insensitive demands.

Carver, in Chapter 3, considers ethical codes and the freedom of the individual under the law, revisiting jurisprudence's famous Hart–Devlin debate on the matter following England's 1957 Wolfenden Report recommending the decriminalization of homosexuality. Devlin (1958) held that society has a right to outlaw practices it finds so intolerable that their performance erodes the social fabric itself. Hart (1959) held no such right could be validly extruded from the generally accepted libertarian right of individuals to be secure from the violent or otherwise harmful conduct of their fellow members of society. Carver mentions Dworkin's (1971) criticism of the Devlin position; namely that Devlin wants to have society's self protection as reason enough to interfere with individuals 'without vouching for the morality' that holds that society together. This introduces a theme that recurs throughout the book; whether ethics is coterminous with the culture of a society or whether extrinsic ethical perspectives on a society can exist other than ethnocentrically.

Reid, in Chapter 4, asserts 'what is ethically correct is largely culturally determined' and in this he echoes Peter Drucker (1981). Whereas Drucker used nepotism's different ethical overtones on either side of the Pacific, Reid illustrates his claim with the experience of gift giving and joint venture breakdowns in Japan. What is unethical corruption in many western cultures is polite and respectable gift giving in cultures such as Japan. When De Beers introduces to the Japanese the notion that men and women should give each other diamond jewellery especially at Christmas, is this reprehensible exploitation or is it admirable adaptation to an innocent local custom? Westerners have had problems with Japanese joint venture partners underwhelming energy in pursuing the joint venture's business interests inside Japan, failing to appreciate the primary motive on the Japanese side for entering joint ventures with foreign multinationals is often to contain foreign competition not to facilitate it. Is this fair or is it dishonest? Are universal ethics really applicable to these situations? Reid is unsure, Drucker (1981) was not. He was quite sure that claims for ethical universalism, especially in a business context was a modern resurrection of seventeenth-century casuistry with its subordination of ethics to politics. Be that as it may, we can all agree with Drucker (1981: 19) when he reminds us that stupidity is not a court martial offence, even if his demonized business ethicists would, as he claims, so make it.

Ethical relativism continues to occupy centre stage in Chapter 5, where Ralston et al. ask whether western theories apply abroad, again focusing on Japan but this time on perceptions of fairness in reward systems. Westerners tend to see fair rewards as grounded in equity theory wherein reward is proportional to input, while Easterners are said to prefer equality of reward within the work group as more comfortable for all. Studies of Chinese, Japanese and Koreans relative to Americans and Australians have lent empirical support to this view. Recent work by Schwartz (1992, 1994) has built up instruments and topologies for multicultural analysis which Bond (1994) expects to take the whole field forward in a quantum leap from Hofstede sourced studies. Meanwhile, Ralston et al. deem it likely that greater collectivism à la Hofstede may be responsible for the difference, especially since such a difference was not found in studies of Indonesians whose culture is said to be less collectivist than the Japanese, Chinese and Koreans. However, when the rewards of someone inside an Eastern membership group are compared by a member with someone outside that group, it would seem that the member then uses equity rather than equality in the evaluation of fairness. This makes the issue of inclusiveness an ethical issue.

Inclusiveness is a central theme in Chapter 6 by Enderle. He sees the morality of inclusion as a key underpinning of the East Asian economic miracle. By inclusion he means the inclusion of all citizens in the economy and its benefits with no marginalized underclass, but not the inclusion of prospective immigrants for they face stiffer barriers than they would encounter around most western jurisdictions. Enderle cites Buchanan (1993: 223) whose morality of inclusion explicitly targets the obligation to include in our states and economies other people based on their personal characteristics rather than on any notion of self-interested reciprocity. Thus the importation of skilled labour is not the performance of any obligation to include but simple economic self interest. Conversely the granting of political asylum or the issuing of full passports to one's otherwise stateless descendants of one's ancestors' indentured labourers is the recognition of just such an obligation.

Enderle notes that workers in East Asia are apt to be seen as assets to invest in rather than costs to be minimized, but it is perhaps open to debate as to how accurate this distinction between East and West still is. Equally debateable is his distinction between the continuous improvement philosophy of *Kaizen* which is encouraged of everyone in a Japanese firm, in contrast with the allegedly sporadic and top-down driven efforts at innovation in the West.

Returning to the question of inclusiveness Enderle asks some questions derived from Rawls's attribution of such an obligation not only to liberal democratic societies but also to so-called well-ordered hierarchical societies. Rawls (1993) expresses his views in his writing on the law of peoples. Rawls (1993: 59) sees human rights as having a role that transcends culture and geography: 'They set a limit to pluralism' among peoples. It is the notion of justice that he sees as universal in its essence and entirely compatible with, indeed a prerequisite of, a hierarchical society that is well ordered.

A well-ordered, hierarchical society is a description not only of a few countries but also of many companies, perhaps even most companies. Donleavy in Chapter 7 introduces a framework for considering companies as micro-societies where trust is built up in ways similar to how allegiance was built up in the feudal systems of medieval Europe and Shogunate Japan. There are useful parallels between vassalage and employment, between the ancient fief and the modern office, between the ancient troth and the modern contract. Of potential significance is the comparison between the medieval Church's attempts to civilize warlordism through the codes of Pax Dei and of chivalry and the modern state's attempts to regulate business warfare through corporate codes of conduct. Any parallels and analogies can be overstated but, in this case, Donleavy is only starting a project of comparison so all claims are but preliminary and tentative. As the present age is as often deemed post-Fordist as postmodern, and given that Ford's most famous dictum is 'history is bunk', perhaps it is appropriate that postmodern business scholarship should include a repositioning of the value of studying history.

Another representation of a well-ordered, hierarchical society is taken by Snell in Chapter 8 who paints a picture of four types of psychic imprisonment manifested by Hong Kong managers confronted with ethical dilemmas. These are limited ethical reasoning capacity, stereotyped assumptions about organizational structures and power relationships, stunted organizational responsibilities or powers, and a confining moral ethos. These are all adumbrated and exemplified. In the course of the chapter Snell also exemplifies Jackall's (1988) notion of a moral maze as a firm playing its own language games the resultant mazes from which are negotiable only by knowledgeable insiders whose expertise is acquired at the cost of losing sight of wider ethical landscapes. Snell also sounds a cautionary note about the facile application of Kohlberg's paradigm of individual ethical development to organizations. The Kohlberg paradigm was developed only for individuals and is in any case not grounded in empirical evidence.

Inapplicability of individual paradigms to corporate analyses also concerns Leisinger in Chapter 9. He advocates meeting the challenge of corporate ethics with moral common sense, corporate codes of conduct and holistic management development, all of which he analyses. Echoing Snell's 'psychic imprisonment' is Leisinger's use of the notion of structural violence, a concept coined by Galtung (1971) and indicating the prevention of a person's development by the contextual social system. Lay (1993: 21) attributes the dehumanizing influence of organizations to the necessarily amoral nature of any collectivity given that ethics solely concerns human individuals. Hoesle (1991: 21) characterized this malign influence in the words of Bundeskanzler Helmut Schmidt thus: 'Naked lies are recognisable—skilful rationalization, levelling down and trivialization are more efficient'. To combat malevolent institutional pressure, Leisinger advocates civil courage, which should be nurtured within firms by including it and other ethical dimensions in regular staff performance appraisals.

Yeung and Yeung in Chapter 10 warn us that business values should not be eclipsed by process re-engineering and organizational learning on the research agenda as if they were just another ephemeral fashion in the business media. Shared business values within an organization enable staff better to handle complex decisions like those associated with globalization, fussier customers, mapping the information highway network and managing knowledge workers. Case studies of American Express and Levi Strauss are used to illustrate how firms manage and render effective their value systems. These cases provide good evidence that values can be managed and manifested effectively in large classical corporations without incurring stockholder displeasure. Evans (1992) is cited for his very evocative notion of business values as a glue technology or strategy to enhance corporate cohesiveness— something which can be overdone with harmful effects on adaptability and agility.

Mahoney in Chapter 11 condemns bribery as a distortion of markets, a non-productive use of resources, and an addictive catalyst of suspicion and deceit in general. Some bribery is a response to extortion, so some may see it as merely a transaction cost if the business it facilitates is socially desirable. Italy's recent history shows how endemic bribery can be purged, as exemplified by Fiat's strict anti-bribery code. The Chinese Prime Minister, Li Peng, has said the abuse of power for personal gain, graft and bribery must be punished unsparingly (Poole 1994). Mahoney lists a series of internal control procedures to minimize prevalence of bribery, including the frequent transfer or rotation of officials to prevent corrupt long term relationships developing. He agrees with De George (1993: 111) in seeing moral courage as central to acting ethically in difficult situations, no matter how good the internal control system may be.

Clegg in Chapter 12 is concerned with values as distinct from ethics in his discussion of embryonic industry. In Australia incoming cultures can mix with local culture to create a new coherent subculture such as 'Mediterrasian cuisine'. The facilitation of new economic activity is a function of a firm's technical competence and its cultural competence. The former includes learning aspects, cultural embeddedness and locale (Gattiker and Willoughby 1993). The latter is the ability to harness symbols, rituals, norms and myths in such a way as to add value to the firm's activities. No doubt the latter is assisted by multiculturalism and the associated pluralism which has been found to encourage innovation in organizations (Perry and Sandholtz 1988). Clegg offers several prescriptions to educators for promoting innovation in industry, noting that non-agile firms will not survive in competitive markets so the traditional advocacy of strong unitary culture has become pedagogically misleading. Management is becoming feminized in the Hofstede sense as greater recognition is given to relational rather than competitive values and to alliances and bridge building rather than to pure rivalry. Clegg also holds that green values have marketing advantages for Australian exporters to 'polluted and dense overseas markets'.

Quinn in Chapter 13 regards green issues and economic development as being within the ambit of ethics and views sustainable development as an ethical imperative requiring the co-operation of government and industry across the developed and less developed worlds. The UN Conference on Environment and Development (UNCED 1992) recognized that sustainable development was needed to maintain human survival as well as to promote Third World economic growth. Industrialized countries have to help the Third World restructure its debts to halt the practice of plundering natural resources just to pay interest bills. Ramphal (1992: 128) blames the need for food among ever increasing numbers of the poor in the Third World as the major cause of tropical deforestation. Quinn concludes with a description of the major strategies involved in sustainable development, emphasizing the role of local bottom-up initiatives.

In the final chapter Stewart and White ask Reid's question once again: whose business values? They survey the utterances of the world's main religions on business conduct, finding some general exhortations to work hard and not cheat, attributing to the Chinese a predilection for eclectic assembly of religious beliefs and noting that few businessmen today are seen as deeply religious anyway. They then identify the spirit of mutuality as a common core to the earliest ethics both in the East and the West and the notion of a true gentleman as profoundly influencing early Western business practitioners. They end by pointing to recent evidence in the East as much as in the West that ethical concerns are being taken more seriously among both the government and civilian members of the business community.

One thing can be said for sure about all the writers in this book. None of them want to make stupidity a court martial offence. Drucker (1991) might infer from this that none of them are really business ethicists. As this preface began, so it finishes, with the reminder that studying business values is something different from promoting business ethics, but not *something completely different.*

REFERENCES

Bond, M.H. 1994. Chinese Values. In *The Handbook of Chinese Psychology*. Ed. Bond. Hong Kong: Oxford University Press.

Buchanan, A. 1993. The Morality of Inclusion. *Social Philosophy and Policy* 233-57.

De George, R.T. 1993. *Coping with Integrity in International Business*. Oxford, UK: Oxford University Press.

Devlin, Lord P. 1958. The Enforcement of Morals. Lecture to the British Academy, London.

Drucker, P. 1981. Ethical Chic. *The Public Interest* 63: 18-36. Reproduced in *Forbes* 160ff, September.

Dworkin, R. 1971. Lord Devlin and the Enforcement of Morals. *Yale Law Journal* 75: 986.

Evans, P. 1992. Management Development as Glue Technology. *Human Resource Planning* 15, 85-105.

Galtung, J. 1971. Gewalt, Frieden und Friedensforschung. In *Kritische Friedensforschung*. Ed. Senghass, 55ff. Frankfurt am Main: Suhrkamp.

Gattiker, U.E. and K. Willoughby. 1993. Technological Competence, Ethics and the Global Village: Cross National Comparisons for Organisation Research. In *Handbook of Organizational Behaviour*. Ed. Golembiewski, 457-85. New York: Marcel Dekker.

Hart, H.A.L. 1959. Immorality and Treason. *The Listener*, 30 July, 162-3.

Hoesle, V. 1991. *Philosophie der ökologischen Krise*. Munich: Beck'sche Reihe.

Jackall, R. 1988. *Moral Mazes: The World of Corporate Managers*. New York: Oxford University Press.

Lay, R. 1993. *Die Macht der Moral: Unternehmenserfolg durch ethisches Management*. Düsseldorf: Ekonomisch Taschenbuch Verlag.

Perry, L.T. and K.W. Sandholtz. 1988. A Liberating Form for Radical Product Innovation. In *Studies in Technological Innovation and Human Resources Vol 1: Managing Technological Development*. Ed. Gattiker and Larwood, 9-31. Berlin: de Gruyter.

Poole, T. 1994. Greasing the Dragon. *Independent on Sunday,* 3 April.

Ramphal, S. 1992. *Our Country The Planet: Forging a Partnership for Survival.* Washington DC: Island Press.

Rawls, J. 1993. The Law of Peoples. *Critical Inquiry* 20: 36-68.

Rokeach, M. 1973. *The Nature of Human Values.* New York: The Free Press.

Schwartz, S.H. 1992. Universals in the Content and Structure of Values: Theoretical Advances and Empirical Tests in 20 countries. In *Advances in Experimental Social Psychology.* Ed. Zanna, 25. Orlando: Academic Press.

Schwartz, S.H. 1994. Cultural dimensions of Values: Toward an Understanding of National Differences. In *Individualism and Collectivism: Theory, Method and Application.* Ed. Kam, Triandis, Kagitsibasi, Choi and Yoon. Newbury Park, CA: Sage.

Taka, T. 1993. Business Ethics: A Japanese View. In *Business Ethics: Japan and the Global Economy.* Ed. Dunfee and Nagayasu, 23-59.

UNCED United Nations Conference on Environment and Development. 1992. *The Global Partnership for Environment and Development: A Guide Agenda 21.* Geneva: UN.

1

THE ETHICS OF VALUES AND THE VALUE OF ETHICS: SHOULD WE BE STUDYING BUSINESS VALUES IN HONG KONG?

Sally Stewart

INTRODUCTION

This is, to the best of my knowledge, the first book on business values to have been produced in Hong Kong and it marks the setting-up of the new Centre for the Study of Business Values at the University of Hong Kong. The territory has until now lacked a centre concentrating solely on business values, rather than on more general ethical questions, although there are many elsewhere in the world. It might be asked why Hong Kong need its own; to which the simple answer is—because it is a unique place and its value system (like those of most cultures) has its own priorities, even while sharing much common ground with those in other societies. It may be that the findings of a research project in the physical sciences can be applied anywhere in the world but it is unlikely to be true of the results of a study on, for instance, the importance placed on providing for the next generation or on whether hiring a competitor's former employee mainly in order to get information on the rival is wrong.

There are probably four major reasons why only a few Hong Kong academics have so far written much on business values, and these almost certainly arise from the difficulties involved in:
- avoiding ethnocentricity;
- countering the accusation of preaching a particular set of values: the 'normative' objection;

- overcoming the arguments of those who believe that all that need concern those in the field of business (whether as teachers or practitioners) is obeying the law; and
- dealing with the sheer theoretical problems of such an abstract subject.

Let us take a brief look at these barriers.

ETHNOCENTRICITY

Is concern about business practices 'just another example of Western thinking that has no place in Asia' as *Asian Business* (1993) enquires? Southeast Asian leaders in countries such as Brunei whose state ideology is intended 'to filter out undue foreign cultural influences' (Hussainmiya 1994: 31), Thailand, and Malaysia are publicly committed to reinforcing the 'values of the region', as Thailand's deputy foreign minister put it at a conference where 'many speakers were highly critical of Western influence in the region' and Malaysia's Deputy Prime Minister spoke of 'our unique Asian heritage', defined by another Thai MP as the 'traditional Asian virtues of rationality, tolerance and moderation' (*Far Eastern Economic Review* 1994).

I would, however, argue that those virtues of rationality, tolerance and moderation are ones on which Britons, as well as Asians, have traditionally prided themselves and that, while it is essential in discussing business values to avoid the dangers of assuming that the beliefs of one society are necessarily relevant to another, there is, fortunately, solid evidence that there are in fact basic beliefs held in common by most, if not nearly all, communities. To take an extreme example, the Judaeo-Christian view that private killing of another human being is a sin and a crime is echoed in the Koran (1991: 70), and in the codes of all the great civilizations of the East.

Similarly, theft and lying under oath are condemned by all major societies and religions, probably because, like murder, such practices tend to lead to disorder in a community. The sanctity of the business contract, requiring trust and honesty, is another commonly held value that is particularly relevant in the present context and one which most business people would like to see advocated, as is the idea that employees owe a duty to their employers to do their best.

The 'Normative' Objection

This is the fear that those from one culture may attempt to impose their values on people in a different society and this is currently most controversial in areas such as workers' rights and environmental issues. The People's Republic of China and many other Asian nations are very sensitive to any apparent criticism from the West, as Dr Mahathir, Malaysia's Prime Minister, recently demonstrated by banning the award of government contracts to UK firms because of British press comments on alleged corruption in Malaysia.

It is, however, almost impossible to change the basic values of adults which are usually fixed by puberty (Hofstede 1991). Outward practices can be changed but inner beliefs are not really susceptible and are unlikely to be altered even at the tertiary educational level which, of course, raises many issues for academics and goes to the heart of the pedagogical argument. Geary and Sims (1994: 15) articulate the problem well when discussing the teaching of accounting students and make the important distinction between 'mastery of factual knowledge related to codes of ethics' and 'the ability to make careful and well-considered ethical judgements.'

Obeying the Law is Sufficient

The fundamental argument here is, that since maximizing profit is the central objective of business, managers should not be diverted from this aim by moral considerations. The unwritten laws of supply and demand, and the specific laws of a particular society, are all that have to be considered, since failure to create a profitable business may lead to bankruptcy and attendant misery for all the stakeholders, directly and indirectly involved, while success will create jobs and wealth and benefit society.

It can be argued, however, that this view ignores the fact that success in the long term is only likely to be achieved by paying attention to such issues as good employer-employee relations, mutually beneficial customer and supplier agreements, and, indeed, if cynicism is to be the basis for action, the public relations benefits of being a good corporate citizen. In short, enlightened self-interest justifies attention to something more than cost-effectiveness and immediate maximization of profit, as James Burke, CEO of Johnson & Johnson, showed by calculating that companies placing a strong emphasis on ethics 'grew at an average annual rate of 11.3%, while the corresponding rate for Dow Jones Industrial companies as a whole was just 6.2%' (*Asian Business* 1993).

The Intellectual and Theoretical Difficulties

This objection is, in one sense, irrefutable: agreement on what constitutes right and wrong seems no nearer after 2,500 years of furious debate. The uncertainties of moral philosophy are probably not susceptible to any final solution, except for one based on some type of religious faith. It is enough for our purposes to note that business people from all cultures share, as mentioned earlier, a wide measure of agreement about the concepts of right and wrong; truth and falsehood; honesty and cheating, etc. The fact that philosophers continue quite correctly to debate definitions does not prevent the ordinary person from taking these broad concepts into consideration in everyday life. Since Bertrand Russell (1954: 51-9) and Ludwig Wittgenstein (1921) were unable to agree on the fundamentals, there is little point in my joining in this particular debate here. I will simply say that I do not believe we have to do nothing just because we cannot lay claim to any certainty, any more than I believe we should not have any children because the world is such an uncertain place.

PHILOSOPHICAL NOTE

It may, however, be useful to outline briefly some of the main philosophical teachings—both Western and Chinese—which have affected the beliefs of Hong Kong people. Put at their simplest these can be grouped into the following categories:
- It is a general duty that good should be done and evil should be avoided (deontology);

- Actions should be designed to create the greatest good for the greatest number (utilitarianism);
- Definitions of good and evil cannot be established as universal absolutes (relativism, subjectivism);
- There are generally accepted definitions of right and wrong (objectivism).

Finally, there is a whole modern school based in the West which considers the entire topic is a matter of language and not a guide to conduct.

There is neither time nor necessity in this paper to delve deeply into the philosophical debate which has been raging since 500 B.C. and shows no sign of a final conclusion. But for those who wish to consider the theory further, there are libraries of books supporting, attacking, and criticising all these positions. Before, however, proceeding to the practical issues, it is worth taking a momentary look at the debate.

Deontology. This can be described as the Golden Rule, accepted around the world: 'Do unto others as you would have others do unto you.' Both Confucius and Christ agreed broadly on this and generations of English-speaking children had this unavoidable reciprocal element in moral or ethical claims personified for them in the kindly shape of Madame Doasyouwouldbedoneby in Charles Kingsley's *The Water Babies.*

Utilitarianism. While accepting that it is impossible to be certain of all the consequences of one's actions, its principle of the greatest good for the greatest number seems to be a practical universal objective, offering a sensible basis for decisions based on enlightened self-interest.

Relativism and subjectivism. This is the view that there are no universal absolute values: for example, the issue of cannibalism is not a matter of right or wrong but merely of personal taste.

Objectivism. The opposite position, objectivism, asserts that there *are* universally accepted moral imperatives, for example sadism (torturing people for enjoyment) is wrong, and doing one's best for one's children within the law is usually right.

It is often difficult to find direct references in any classical writings to business practice because the writers, whether in Asia or elsewhere, were concerned with politics and philosophy, not with the commercial world. As far as ethics is concerned, however, we are better placed: philosophers have sometimes found it convenient to talk of business in order to provide examples of ethical behaviour in everyday life.

Aristotle (1992: 207), for example, when discussing the question in general, puts the whole of everyday life, whether mechanical, business or wage-earning, into the category of 'things necessary' and defines business as 'being concerned with market purchase and retail selling'. He distinguishes the 'things necessary' from other forms of activity: the life of politics, philosophy, and enjoyment. But he goes on later to class lucrative business as a practical means of pursuing happiness—a 'good' (ibid.: 223). His view of human, indeed of all, affairs was to seek the middle path—not to be too greedy and not to be too stingy (ibid.: 335) and not to be spendthrift or reckless. Aristotle makes a point which seems relevant to Asian business customs and culture when he states: 'It is not natural for good men to go to Law.' And: 'Civic friendship looks at the agreement and to the thing but moral friendship at the intention' (ibid.: 425).

Probably the best known of the classic philosophers who was also a businessman, was Spinoza (1632–77), a grinder of optical lenses. Unfortunately for our purpose his philosophical work was concentrated on the mysteries of God and understanding, and he apparently wrote nothing on business or indeed everyday life. Kant, in his theory of ethics, was insistent that an act, to be moral, had to be carried out for moral motives, and gave little credit to the tradesman who charged a reasonable sum to all-comers, suggesting that the motive was a good reputation and it was not, therefore, a moral good (Kant 1873). But Kant may be in a minority: most people would give the businessman some credit for playing fair with the customer, even if self-interest was involved.

It is interesting to consider the similarities between Confucian and occidental values. Probably the most central character in the Confucian canon is *ren* (仁), an ideograph consisting of the character for a person (亻) and the number two (二). This character, which defies one precise agreed definition, is frequently translated as *love* (in the sense of benevolence) and is the description of the correct relationship between human beings. It coincides with Christ's injunction to 'love your neighbour as yourself', and Aristotle's view that *agape* (love, again as benevolence) is a fundamental ingredient in good human relations.

Needham (1970: 5) describes the Confucianists' doctrine as 'this worldly social mindedness'. Confucius was above all a teacher and transmitter, not an original philosopher, and he did not distinguish between ethics and politics. He used the word *dao* (the way) to mean the proper way of life, to produce a society where men co-operated, and assumed words like *good* and *virtue* had unequivocal meanings, unlike the Greek and later Western philosophers who were endlessly in contention on the definition of such terms. Confucius believed in the vital importance of education (Stewart 1994), holding that 'By nature men are nearly alike: by practice they get to be wide apart' (Confucius 1948: *Analects*, Book XVII, Chapter II).

Mencius, who lived 374–289 B.C., thought along the same lines as Confucius, holding that man's nature was basically good (Needham 1970: 17). This view was contested but the meaning of *good* was not defined by the disputants. The opposite view was expressed by Xunzi (ibid.: 19), who had a chapter headed: 'The nature of man is evil'. Xunzi's description of man is of a person naturally envious, rapacious, lustful, who likes praise, who 'possesses the desires of the eye and the ear': man must be trained to be good. A third view was provided in the Tang Dynasty when the Confucian Han Yü (762–824) took the line that men were divided into three classes: the superior who would be good in any circumstances, the middle who would be good or bad according to training, and the third irretrievably bad (ibid.: 21; He 1991).

It is generally thought that the Chinese military classics offer no help on ethical matters, but although, like Machiavelli, the military philosophers certainly recommended deception, they also stressed moderation and reciprocity in the spirit of the Confucian school. For example, Tai Kong (eleventh century B.C.), in the *Six Secret Teachings*, remarked to King Wen of the Zhou dynasty: 'Anyone who shares profit with all the people under Heaven will gain the world. Anyone who monopolizes its profits will lose the world' (Sawyer 1993: 40).

Remarkably, since there is no evidence of communication

between China and Greece at this early age, Aristotle and Xunzi came to extraordinarily similar conclusions about the nature of man's soul. The Appendix to this paper gives an indication of how closely Aristotle and Confucius seem to agree on what qualities go to make someone a virtuous person. As a final illustration of the point that East and West have many basic values in common, whatever their cultural differences, it is only necessary to look at the Ten Commandments which formed the basis of the Jewish, and later the Christian, codes, and to compare them with the doctrines of the Confucianists. Out of the Ten Commandments, four, which are concerned with rules for secular society independently of any theological concepts, require us: to honour our father and mother, not to kill, not to steal and not to bear false witness. Neither the Confucianists, the Legalists, nor any major school of Chinese philosophy, would disagree with the view that these are four very reasonable values in any society. The ancient Greeks would have supported them, as would Moslems or indeed Hindus. In short, on these, admittedly simple, fundamentals West, Middle East and East appear basically in agreement.

CATEGORIZING BUSINESS PEOPLE

It is perhaps time to look at how business people divide themselves on an ethical scale, and the following three main categories can be identified.

- The immoral and, indeed, illegal, cutting every corner, evading the law or breaking the law, if they think they can escape prosecution. Unfortunately there are many business people around the world in this category and the local court records show that Hong Kong does not lack them.
- The amoral, strictly legal but minimalist, obeying the letter of the law but unconcerned with the spirit of the law. Perhaps the majority belong to this category: fulfilling minimum requirements towards government, shareholders, employers, customers and suppliers without any attempt to take a view beyond immediate, short-term profit.

- The moral and forward thinking, looking beyond the minimum requirements of the law and the need for maximization of profit; not only to the spirit of the current legislation but also to the future, and societal requirements in the round.

It is the third type of manager who is most likely to introduce codes of practice and be interested in examining how to make them effective and, since they are the subject of current discussion in Hong Kong, some comments on them follow.

CODES OF PRACTICE

These can be set out variously as codes of ethics, working rules, mission statements, company philosophies, credos, etc. The main streams of thought concerning such codes can be described as:

- The opposition, who see codes as irrelevant or even positively harmful to business, since they distract management from its principal duty which is to maximize profit.
- The supporters, who see that business has, in addition to a duty to make a profit, other obligations to its staff, to its customers, to its suppliers and to society.

The dialogue between the two camps is seldom constructive: it is, as the French would say, un dialogue des sourds (a dialogue of the deaf), where each party's mind is made up in advance.

The risk is that the act of drawing up prescriptive (normative) codes of conduct may make people feel they are absolved from further considering moral issues: they may be content merely to obey the letter of the rules laid down. It seems probable, however, that this problem usually only arises if the organization concerned restricts its efforts to formulating and issuing a code, and can be overcome if the most senior managers are actively involved not only in establishing the code but also in regular discussions of its principles and practical applications. In short, I believe there is a place for codes of conduct not merely as guidelines for action but also as a means of education and stimulation of debate. Moreover, one great attraction of an institutionally-backed professional code is that it enables individuals to follow their consciences at reduced personal risk, although the person with moral courage will not require such a crutch.

Categorizing Codes of Conduct

The earliest known codes date from the beginning of the Industrial Revolution; they were paralleled by the attempts to legislate for minimum rights for workers which were greeted with howls of anguish from industrialists, who claimed that their businesses would be ruined. Some recent complaints in Beijing about the habits of foreign-invested enterprises (FIEs) are reminiscent of the problems of the nineteenth century: housing workers in fire traps and working them for 80 to 90 hours a week appear to be all too common practices.

In examining codes of conduct, three distinct types can usefully be distinguished:
- unwritten codes of values or norms that have evolved among a group of people as part of their group dynamics;
- a set of values set out by top management (all too often from a remote Head Office and not even in the local language);
- a set of values openly adopted and published, and arrived at after wide local examination of alternatives.

It is usually the case that organizations with high, agreed standards do not need codes of ethics, which are often only introduced after someone has cheated. As the past President of the Hong Kong Society of Accountants put it: 'Trust and honesty were always regarded as the most important code of human behaviour. Guided by these moral standards, qualified accountants of the older days actually behaved in the same way as what is required today' (Chow 1994). But it is also possible, of course, for a group to have a strict, unwritten code and still be deeply immoral, as in the case of the Mafia or a Triad society.

The second category seems typical, and such codes can often be criticized on the grounds that they are rooted in convenience and prudence, which are not a sufficient basis for a code since they are, by definition, temporary factors which will change with circumstances. The codes of many multinationals often have the great disadvantage of being seen as imposed from outside with insufficient account taken of local conditions.

The third category is more likely to receive general approval since, even if in the end it turns out to be much the same as the code in the second category, it has been based on a good process of thorough debate going beyond 'honesty is the *best* policy' to 'honesty is the *right* policy' and has been based on consultation with all members of the organization.

Donaldson (1989: 132) suggests that a code is sufficiently grounded if it rests on the principles of autonomy (people should be allowed to make up their own minds about morality); acceptance of pluralism (there are many different points of view) and the Golden Rule. A survey of British companies in the late 1980s found that, although many companies had codes of practice, these had, in many cases, been worked out not in consultation with those affected but imposed by top management.

Professional Codes of Practice

Hong Kong, like all sophisticated societies, has elaborate codes of conduct for lawyers, bankers, accountants, engineers, and so on. These have the same position in relation to decision and action as the laws of the land in that they do not teach morality, ethics or values: they lay down rules for conduct and, unless they are used in a positive manner as a basis for teaching principles, they will in daily practice be no more than guidelines for action.

CURRENT ISSUES IN HONG KONG

Among the obvious categories of ethical problems connected to business practice are employment and environmental issues; in Hong Kong both are the subject of legislation, as in other parts of the developed world, and offer rich fields for research on the ground into the values which Hong Kong business people hold in these areas. This is not the place to list all the relevant labour laws; it is enough to note that the duties of the employer and the duties and rights of the employees are set out in considerable detail (Williams 1990). The list of cases where employer and employee were unable to agree on whether the law (basically the Employment Ordinance 1968) applies to their case is equally long, and would be much longer were it not for the existence of labour tribunals, and the Labour Department's conciliatory role. There is little difficulty in gaining access to the cases but, as far as I can discover, this perhaps excessively emotive and sensitive subject has never been the subject of field research into the attitudes of either employer or employee. There would seem to be a rich quarry here for local research on such issues as industrial action, termination of employment, rewards for loyalty, health and safety, workman's compensation, etc. We know, for example, that Hong Kong has applied 31 international labour conventions without modification (Commissioner for Labour 1992), but we have no information on the views of Hong Kong business people on this wholesale application of international conventions unmodified to take account of Hong Kong's unique circumstances.

Protection of the environment is probably as controversial a topic as protection of workers. The Environmental Protection Unit was established by the Hong Kong government in 1977, and superseded by a weightier agency in 1981 and by the Environmental Protection Department (EPD) in 1986. We have recently been reminded that the views of the farmers of the New Territories do not coincide with those of the EPD when it comes to water pollution; similarly the new Hong Kong stadium has brought with it massive complaints of excessive noise. The case histories are numerous, but again no research seems to have been done at ground level to analyse the attitudes of the polluters and to discover their views on their own behaviour.

BUSINESS VALUES IN THE PEOPLE'S REPUBLIC OF CHINA (PRC)

The PRC is no exception to the global rule that business in all shapes and forms cannot be conducted without in some way confronting morality, ethics and values. The rapid growth since the beginning of the reform period of joint ventures, non-state enterprises, and private and individual firms has added new dimensions to an age-old problem (Stewart et al. 1992). Corruption and white collar crime are alleged to be flourishing mightily in parallel with economic development, the pollution is appalling, and in some of the new businesses which have been created with capital from Overseas Chinese there have been horrific stories of laxity, or even criminality. In March 1994, in an article on the setting up of unofficial trade unions a PRC author mentioned (BBC 1994a) workers' complaints that their factories did not observe safety laws, provide health care or proper ventilation, and imposed harsh discipline on the use of toilets. A shocking example surfaced when a Taiwanese factory owner in Fujian province was given a suspended two-year jail sentence for violating fire regulations: the fourth floor of the factory, designed and authorized as workshop space, had been used as a dormitory, and fifteen workers were badly injured in a fire caused deliberately by a discontented worker (*China Daily* 1994).

The Shenzhen labour laws appear to be easily flouted, perhaps because independent labour unions to protect workers' rights are illegal, and the official trade unions do not seem willing to be involved in fighting for workers' rights; in spite of this, 2,350 labour disputes apparently occurred in the first six months of 1993. Although a 44-hour week, to be implemented from March 1994, was announced in 'Procedures' issued by the Ministry of Labour and Ministry of Personnel, (BBC 1994b) and this decree has apparently been carried out in government enterprises, it does not seem to have had any significance for other firms. For instance, a factory worker in Shenzhen said that in her factory work started at 7:30 a.m. and continued with a 90-minute lunch break, and another for dinner, sometimes until 1:30 a.m.: pay for the overtime was about HK$1 per hour (under 15 US cents) (*Eastern Express* 1994).

Jiang Zemin, Secretary-General of the Communist Party, in a speech on 28 February 1994, spoke frankly about corruption, saying it 'has penetrated into broad sections of our society; in particular, it is corroding our Party and government organs, and the ranks of cadres. Criminal offences, including abusing powers for personal gains, participating in corrupt practices in violation of the law, and taking or demanding bribes, are widespread to an alarming degree (BBC 1994c).

THE FIELD FOR RESEARCH

When the subject of business values comes up, for example, we have not only such topics as those covered generally under the heading of that popular figure, the good corporate citizen, and what it means to behave positively and helpfully in society. We also have such complex issues as the ethics of collecting commercial intelligence by anything other than the most overt means: the morality of selling a product such as tear gas (toxic lachrymators) which can be used for crowd control and thus keep the peace, but in the process may cause more than momentary discomfort. Such a problem requires more than a general moral view: the definition of toxicity is by no means universally agreed and has caused great difficulty (Verwey 1977).

The existing literature and research on the subject of business ethics tends to be concerned with pedagogic theory and with analysis of the lessons to be learnt from major published cases, where business and society seem to have arrived at a confrontational situation in the context not merely of the legal framework of society, and its laws, regulations, and statutory bodies, but also of society's general perception of justice and injustice. Thus articles deal with the effects of the explosion of a chemical factory, the crash of an aeroplane, the sinking of an oil tanker, the collapse of a bank, a major white-collar crime, or a bitter strike, and these are clearly legitimate studies of what might be called macro-business ethics. There is, however, another dimension of the subject which seems hardly to have been investigated by academics from any discipline: the views of the individual directors, managers, staffs, customers, and suppliers, canvassed through the time-honoured methods of interview, on how they justify their own behaviour.

This is a huge subject and while universities and business schools teach, and students hopefully learn, there remains an almost untouched research field of what might be called micro-business value studies. It would seem that neither funds nor interest have been generated to a sufficient degree to pursue the micro, rather than the macro, scene. Hopefully the increased interest stimulated when Harvard Business School created its programme in Leadership, Ethics and Corporate Responsibility (Chiu and Wong 1994) will become more widespread, and the fact that this Conference has been given such wide support in Hong Kong and abroad gives grounds for optimism that there will be much more research and teaching in this area.

CONCLUSION

The subjects of morality, ethics, and values, whether in business or in society as a whole, are fraught with dangers, problems, and difficulties. It is vital, however, that the defeatists should not be allowed to command the battlefield: complicated as these topics may be, the issues are central to modern society whether developed or otherwise, and it is, therefore, important that the academic world contributes ideas and analysis, but equally essential that the end product should be related not only to scholarly disciplines but also to the decisions of practising businessmen.

I would like to conclude by suggesting that, instead of following Kipling (1912), who wrote in 1889 that: 'East is East, and West is West, and never the twain shall meet', we should accept the old Chinese proverb which says: 'All within the four seas are brothers' (Stewart 1958: 41), and build our study of business values in this region on that.

REFERENCES

Aristotle. 1992. *Eudemian Ethics.* (trans. H. Rackham). Cambridge, MA: Harvard University Press.

Asian Business. 1993. December: 24.

BBC. 1994a. *Monitoring Summary of World Broadcasts: Far East* FE/1944 G9: March 25.

BBC. 1994b. *Monitoring Summary of World Broadcasts: Far East* FE/1937 51/1: March 4.

BBC. 1994c. *Monitoring Summary of World Broadcasts: Far East* FE/1941 G/1: March 9.

China Daily. 1994. March 30: 3.

Chiu, E.K.C. and D.W.S. Wong. 1994. The Proper Role of Ethics in Accounting Education: Perspectives for Hong Kong and China. *Proceedings of the First South China International Business Symposium.* Macau (March): Vol. 1: 82-8.

Chow, F. 1994. Speech at the Dinner for December 1993 Graduates. *The Prospective Accountant* 2 (March/April): 24. Hong Kong Society of Accountants.

Commissioner for Labour. 1992. *Annual Report.* Hong Kong Government.

Confucius. 1948. *The Four Books.* (trans. James Legge). Shanghai: International Publication Society.

Donaldson, J. 1989. *Key Issues in Business Ethics.* San Diego, CA: Academic Press.

Eastern Express. 1994. April 11: 7.

Far Eastern Economic Review. 1994. February 10: 28.

Geary W.T. and R.R. Sims. 1994. Can Ethics be Learned? *Accounting Education* 3(1): 3-18.

He, Z. (ed.). 1991. *An Intellectual History of China.* Beijing: Foreign Languages Press.

Hofstede, G. 1991. *Cultures and Organisations: Software of the Mind.* London: McGraw Hill.

Hussainmiya, B.A. 1994. Philosophy for a Rich, Small State. *Far Eastern Economic Review.* February 10: 31.

Kant, I. 1873. *Theory of Ethics or Practical Philosophy.* (tr. Thomas Kingsmill Abbott). London: Longmans, Green, Reader & Dyer.

Kipling, R. 1912. The Ballad of East and West. *Collected Verse of Rudyard Kipling.* London: Hodder and Stoughton.

The Koran. 1991. (trans. N.J. Dawood). London: Penguin Books.

Needham J. 1970. *Science and Civilisation in China. Volume II.* Cambridge, UK: Cambridge University Press.

Russell, B. 1954. *Human Society in Ethics and Politics.* London: George Allen & Unwin.

Sawyer, R. 1993. *The Seven Military Classics of Ancient China.* Oxford, UK: Westview Press.

Stewart, B.T.W. 1958. *All Men's Wisdom.* Singapore: United Publishing House.

Stewart, S., M.T. Cheung and D.W.K. Yeung. 1992. The Latest Asian Newly Industrialised Economy (NIE) Emerges: The South China Booming Boomerang. *Columbia Journal of World Business* 27(2): 30-7.

Stewart, S. 1994. Integrating Chinese Traditional Values and New Approaches to Management Development in the People's Republic of China. *Proceedings of the First Regional Conference and Exhibition on Developing Managers in the Asia Pacific Region.* Hong Kong (May): 159-69.

Verwey, W. 1977. *Riot Control Agents and Herbicides in War.* Leiden: Sijthoff.

Williams, K. 1990. *An Introduction to Hong Kong Employment Law.* Hong Kong: Oxford University Press.

Wittgenstein, L. 1921. *Tractatus Logico Philosophic.* Oxford, UK: Blackwell.

APPENDIX

Some similarities between the Chinese and Western ethical views are shown below. The main difference between the two cultures would seem to be that, while the Confucians concentrated on the practical questions of how to teach and achieve virtue, the ancient Greeks were greatly concerned with *defining* virtue. It has been suggested that a distinction between the Chinese pragmatic approach and the Western more metaphysical questioning can still be found today.

Aristotle's View of Goodness

Aristotle (1992: 249) taught that: 'Moral goodness must be concerned with a middle state' and illustrated his view of the moral position by a table of 42 words including the following examples:

Excessive	The (Golden) Mean	Deficient
Shamelessness	Modesty	Diffidence
Rashness	Courage	Cowardice
Profiteering	Reasonable gain	Losing
Boastfulness	Sincerity	Self depreciation
Prodigality	Generosity	Meanness
Vanity	Greatness of spirit	Smallness of spirit
Rashness	Courage	Cowardice

He goes on to say the man who seeks gain from every source is a profiteer, he who seeks gain ... from few is a waster.

The Confucian Moral Vocabulary

At the centre of the Confucian ethic lay the ideal of the 'superior' person—*junzi*. The following list of a *junzi*'s attributes parallel Aristotle's list of virtues. It is, of course, impossible to produce precise translations of all these terms but the general sense seems clear. Confucius, like Aristotle, advocated the Golden Mean and also stressed 'reciprocity': do not to others what you do not want done to yourself (Confucius 1948: *Analects*, Book XV:23).

Superior Person	Mean Person
Loving	Anxious
Wise	Perplexed
Courageous	Fearful
Simple	Luxurious
Frugal	Extravagant
Virtuous	A seeker of comfort
In awe of Heavenly Laws	Ignorant of Heavenly Laws
Composed	Distressed
Careful & slow in speech	
Sincere & modest in speech but quick in action	} Reckless
Dignified without pride	Proud without dignity
Humble	Arrogant
A seeker after truth	Fearful of poverty
A follower of the middle path	Does not follow the middle path
Morally courageous	Physically aggressive
Respectful	Obsequious
Straightforward	Rude
Well-mannered	Uncouth
Kindly	Inhuman

2

ETHICAL VALUES AS PART OF THE CONCEPT OF BUSINESS ENTERPRISE

Robert E. Allinson

ABSTRACT

The orientation of this paper is that there is no special science of 'business ethics' any more than there is one of 'medical ethics' or 'legal ethics'. While there may be issues that arise in medicine or law that require special treatment, the ways of relating to such issues are derived from a basic ethical stance. Once one has evolved such an ethical stance and thus has incorporated a fundamental mode of relating to her or his fellow human beings, the 'how' to deal with various ethical 'issues' will follow as a natural consequence of one's ethical stance or modality. It would not be necessary, in the formation of one's fundamental ethical stance, to know if one were a utilitarian or a deontologist. It is doubtful whether Buddha knew what kind of ethics he was practising.

If one conceives of ethics as something extrinsic to various disciplines and attempts to first practise a discipline and then to apply ethics to modify the results of that discipline, it is entirely possible that conflicts will result between what is perceived of as the proper pursuit of that discipline and the ethical considerations. The argument of this paper is that it is more efficient (in addition to being more true) to take ethical considerations into account in the construction of the conceptual foundations of the discipline. While this is not new in medicine (consider the Hippocratic Oath that every new Doctor of Medicine is taught), it is, as is a well known irony, an infrequent phenomenon in law. It is equally rare in the business world. This paper is devoted to showing that business and ethics are not two different and competing fields of interest (thus requiring a discipline of business ethics to be grafted onto the study of business enterprise), but that ethical concerns are part and parcel of the very concept of a business enterprise.

INTRODUCTION

The orientation of this paper is that business ethics is not a separate subject from business administration. The danger of separating business from ethics is that one can easily justify unethical business practices by saying to oneself, or to others, 'this is business', as if business were a separate domain which wore an ethics-proof vest. Just as in the Mafia movies when before a contract is carried out, the contract killer says, 'nothing personal', so the businessman could always say, 'after all, this is business', or, 'business is business', which means that ethics is not considered. This attitude can be seen in such statements as, 'when I go home to my family, I will put on my ethical hat; now, I am wearing my business hat.' The emphasis in this paper thus differs from the emphasis one frequently finds in discussions of business ethics, which almost always focus on ethical considerations as being separate from and needing to be added onto business interests.[1]

If one were to attempt to start up a business and only later were to consider whether to apply ethics to modify the results of that discipline, it would be entirely possible that conflicts would result between what were perceived as the proper pursuit of that discipline and ethical considerations. The argument of this paper is that it is more efficient (in addition to being more true) to take ethical considerations into account in the construction of the conceptual foundations of the discipline. While this is not new in medicine, it has been an infrequent phenomenon in law as stated above. This is not the case with respect to the *current teaching* of law. An estimated 90% of law schools in the United States, for example, now require a course in professional ethics. No such course, to my knowledge, was taught twenty years ago. Almost every medical school in the United States today covers ethics in some manner.

The problem is that law, like business and unlike medicine, has been and still is perceived as a profession in which ethics is not considered a top priority (Dunfee 1987: 399). The general perception of the business world is one in which ethics is also not considered a top priority. It is an encouraging sign that business schools are including ethics as part of their curricula. Five hundred business schools now offer business ethics as part of their curricula. The most spectacular and celebrated example is that of John Schad, ex-chairman of the Securities and Exchange Commission, who pledged US$30 million to incorporate business ethics in the curriculum of the Harvard Business School (ibid.).

There are three fundamental ways in which ethics is involved in the concept of a business enterprise: first, in terms of the goal or goals of the business enterprise; secondly, in terms of the moral relationship that lies at the very basis of agreements and contracts; thirdly, in terms of the communicative infrastructure of the business organization.

ETHICS AS INVOLVED IN THE GOALS OF AN ORGANIZATION

No organization, even if it were interested in profitability as a prime goal, could avoid producing some kind of social benefit or avoid intending at least in some part to achieve some kind of goal which is other than purely making money. Even the examples of a mint that mints coins or a printer that prints paper notes to be used as currency are literally making money but they are also providing a service, that is, creating the means for everyone to have a medium of exchange, which is an incredible social benefit. Every business enterprise that involves providing a service or making a product must provide a service or make a product which is something other than the profit that is to be generated from the service or the product. Even the businessman who sets out simply to make a profit must have some idea as to how to go about doing this. 'Making a profit' does not give the businessperson starting up, any idea as to what to do or how to do it. The profit motive is a non user-friendly pole-star. The goal of simply 'making money' does not give one any direction as to how to start up, continue a business enterprise, or what kind of business enterprise to start up in the first place.

If something else were to be required in order to start up a business enterprise in addition to defining the essence or the goal of business as being 'the business of business is to make money', then there must be some other element which is part and parcel of business enterprise in addition to the profit margin. The directive to make profits is too empty: it does not define business. One must add something else, such as, to produce a product that is needed, or to provide a service that is needed. The notion of filling some kind of social need must be taken into account when one is beginning a business. What is really lacking here is a fuller definition of business enterprise than the ownership or use of capital investment or labour in order to generate revenue. A definition of business enterprise that includes the creation of social value or the fulfilment of social need is needed before one can really understand what is meant by the word 'business' in the first place.

One might require a definition of business such as the following: the ownership or use of capital investment, labour or land to produce a product, or to provide a service that fills some existent social need, or creates a new need to be filled or some social value in order to generate revenue for the owner or owners. For a non-profit business, that portion of the definition specifying that the revenue is to be generated for the profit of the owner or owners, may be omitted.

The very definition of business may require input from ethics in order to make sense of what it means to have a business in the first place. While no business ethics has, to my knowledge, considered the definition of business be part of the discipline of business ethics, it seems to me to be a most fundamental and important concern.[2] Whether one's real desire were to fill some social need or whether the social need were one which should be filled is another story. The point is, one cannot have a business enterprise in the first place unless one takes social needs into account.

Even the example of the stockbroker who claims to be one simply to make money could not be a stockbroker without serving some social need, which in this case might be to assist other people in making money from the money that they have already made, but which was only earning bank interest. He need not have this social need in mind as his main motivation, but he cannot help but serve this social need if he were to make his own profits. If it were to sound circular that the social need that is served is, in this case, also making money, one must keep in mind that in this case part of the money is being made for others, and thus social value is created for others. Thus, in the case of the stockbroker, even if his prime motive were to make a large profit for himself, he cannot avoid making money for others. He may lose money for others too but, in theory at least, he cannot make money without *some* others making money, for if all his transactions were to result in losses for his customers, he would find himself without a clientele. In addition, the directive to 'make money' is not sufficient to enable him to conduct his business. He must know what to do, how, in this case, to buy and sell stocks. Thus, his business enterprise cannot be simply defined as a means of making money.

Whether or not the provider of the service, or the manufacturer of the product, has in mind any social value to be gained from that service or product, the service or product must provide some social value. It may be argued that some services (such as prostitution), or some products (such as weapons), provide disvalue rather than value, but it would be difficult to provide an example of a good produced, or a service provided, that did not provide some social value. There may be debate as to whether the net effect of the product or service is a value or a disvalue to society, but this does not affect the point that every good produced, or every service provided, does not produce some social value, however minimal, or however counterbalanced it is by some social disvalue that is produced. What follows from this is that there is no such activity as a business venture that is totally divorced from producing some social value. It does not matter whether or not the social value is intended by the provider of the service or the manufacturer of the product.

ETHICS AS THE BASIS OF AGREEMENTS AND CONTRACTS

There is a second way in which ethics is already a part of business, which is at the basis of both the goals of business and the communicative infrastructure, and that is in terms of the moral relationship that lies at the very basis of agreements and contracts. The very idea of trade requires a moral relationship between at least two persons. One cannot conduct business without the trust required to keep agreements. It is impossible to eliminate the waiting time between the delivery of a product or service and the payment. Whichever comes first, there is always a time of trust. The relationship between buyer and seller requires morality. The moral relationship always underlies the communicative infrastructure between business partners and employer and employee relationships. Without an underlying moral relationship, business agreements between partners and contracts between employer and employee would not be possible.

SELF-CONSCIOUS ETHICS AS PART OF THE GOALS OF BUSINESS

If it were true that every business enterprise must produce some social value, and all business ventures require moral value as their daily cement, then to take the consideration of value as part of what is produced is a consideration which may be entertained at the very beginnings of a business enterprise. If one were to consider that ethics were relevant to business, then one could even take ethical considerations into account in large measure when one were contemplating the roles of business organizations. In 1984, Roger Smith, the CEO of General Motors, reportedly stated that the responsibility of CEOs and Boards of Directors needed to be expanded beyond the traditional concept of being responsible only to the shareholders of a company. Responsibility should be widened, according to Smith, to include the natural environment, the economic health of the entire country [this could be expanded beyond national boundaries], and the welfare of future generations (Cavanagh and McGovern 1988: 29). The notion that business is not there only to make a profit is, of course, not new to Smith. Henry Ford, the inventor of the Model T, also held the view that business has other concerns than the interests of its stockholders when he said: 'For a long time people believed that the only purpose of industry is to make a profit. They were wrong. Its purpose is to serve the general welfare' (Donaldson 1982: 62).

The stockbroker may concentrate on his own profits to a large degree and focus only as needs be on the profits of his clientele. But the fact that he cannot make money without making money for some others, and thus creating social value for some others, means that social value or ethics is not something which is inherently in conflict with his desire to make money. In fact, he cannot make money without making money for at least some others, so that he cannot help but produce social value, even if he were to have no interest in producing social value. Ethics in this case is his beneficiary even if he were to take little or no interest in being a friend to ethics.

One must bear in mind that for businesses to embrace ethics as their friend, it does not mean that businesses should give up the value of making profits. Values which are non-profit values can serve as a motivator at the same time that one is motivated by profit values. Ethics need not be seen as something antagonistic to the profit motive; it can exist alongside of the profit motive and even contribute to the profit motive. The separation of business and ethics is a part of a Western culture that considers that what is ethically good must belong to a non-body realm and that what is profitable cannot be ethical. For the Western mind, the notion that ethical and materialistic motivations can exist alongside of each other and even enhance each other is one which is a difficult notion to accept thoroughly.

What is being said is that the relation between business and ethics may be perceived as an internal relation, not as a relationship between two external realms. In the Protestant Ethic, if one were to earn a great deal of money, that would be a sign that one might have been favoured by the Deity. But in this case, ethics and business are still perceived as belonging to two separate realms. What is being maintained here is that ethics and business can co-exist in the same realm.

What is being said here is different from what Adam Smith was saying in his early formulations of the theory of wealth. For Smith, one only needed to think of one's private interest and the 'invisible hand' would take care of social welfare. While for Smith, ethics was built into business enterprise as a necessary side-effect of business enterprise, it did not require any self-conscious awareness, or added ethical action on the part of the entrepreneur. To quote Smith's famous passage:

> ... every individual ... intends only his own gain, and he is in this, as in many other cases, led by an invisible hand to promote an end which was no part of his intention ... By pursuing his own interest he frequently promotes that of the society more effectually than when he really intends to promote it (Smith 1937: 423).

While this can, of course, be disputed, it is interesting to note that for Smith there was not only no necessary conflict between the demands of business and the demands of morality; there was a necessary correlation. If one were to pursue one's self-interest, the interests of morality were necessarily served. Unlike Smith, one need not relegate ethical values to the status of a side-product which is created as an indirect effect of following one's own self-interest. Ethics need not be seen as something extrinsic to or antagonistic to the profit motive; it can exist alongside the profit motive and even contribute to the profit motive.

The modern day counterpart to Adam Smith is Milton Friedman, who has vigorously championed the idea that, 'there is one and only one social responsibility of business—to use its resources and engage in activities to increase its profits so long as it stays within the rules of the game, which is to say, engages in open and free competition without deception and fraud' (Friedman 1962: 133-6). Friedman actually separates ethics from business to a greater degree than does Smith, since Smith sees an ethical outcome as a necessary side-effect of pure business activity, while Friedman considers that possible unethical outcomes from business activities need to be redressed by government action and will not be taken care of by business pursuit alone. The difference between Smith and Friedman is that Friedman qualifies his wholesale endorsement of untrammelled business pursuit as best for society by stipulating that unethical business practices fall outside the range of legitimate business. In this respect, my position resembles Friedman's. However, it differs from Friedman's in that I argue that ethics can be an ally to business, whereas for Friedman it is an impediment and an antagonist. My position resembles Smith's in that business and ethics are not perceived as being in conflict. It differs from Smith's in that I argue that ethical concerns are part of business enterprise, whereas Smith sees them as necessary but gratuitous side-effects. It also differs from Smith's in that Smith thinks that the pursuit of business alone will invariably bring about the social good, whereas I argue that only some, and not necessarily the best, interests of society will be so served. My position, unlike both Smith's and Friedman's, takes the view that self-conscious ethics can be a part of the goals of the business organization.[3]

As a final argument concerning the merger of business and ethics, one might carefully consider the results of attending only to profits at the expense of ethical considerations. This is the old self-interest argument, or 'honesty is the best policy' argument. In *Global Disasters: Inquiries into Management Ethics* (Allinson 1993), the question is raised whether the cutting of corners to keep the budget down really proved to be a benefit to the space programme in the case of the *Challenger* disaster? In addition to the loss of the lives of the six astronauts and the one civilian passenger, the space shuttle itself represented a loss of US$3 billion. Did Pan Am's decision not to announce that Flight 103 was a possible bomb target (one assumes at least partially motivated by a desire not to appear vulnerable to such threats in general, and thus lose passengers, or lose passengers on this flight in particular) really pay off? Airlines, of course, can make their own decisions, and the public notification by Delta and Northwest of bomb threats may have helped these airlines, rather than hurt them, by having given them a business boost, since passenger confidence was thereby enhanced. If there were no public announcement of a bomb threat, passengers decided that the flight in question was safe as they trusted these airlines. The question is, where is Pan American Airlines today? The answer is that it has gone out of business.[4] It is not at all clear that even the hardest-nosed exponents of business at the expense of ethics are really right on their own behalf all of the time.

On the other hand, one can point to what one considers unethical corporations and the massive profits gained at the expense of ethics. It is not always the case that ethical corporations fare better profit-wise than unethical ones. The example of ethical mutual funds or unit trusts that normally do not perform as well as non-ethically designated mutual funds is sometimes cited as evidence that ethical corporations do not fare as well (Robin and Reidenbach 1989: 7). However, there is also evidence that some ethically designated mutual funds do perform better than non-ethically designated ones—while there are problems with the criteria.[5]

While honesty may sometimes be the best policy, it is not always so, at least in the short term. In the long term, it may be conjectured that ethics is an essential element for a long-lasting business enterprise. In their book *Business Ethics: Where Profits Meet Value Systems*, Robin and Reidenbach (1989: 161) argue that it is 'the conclusion of top executives from companies like Boeing ... Hewlett-Packard, Johnson & Johnson, McDonnell Douglas ... that, in the long run "Ethics Pays".' Robin and Reidenbach (1988: 9) quote from the summary section of a publication of the Business Roundtable entitled *Corporate Ethics: A Prime Business Asset*:

> ... many executives believe that a culture in which ethical concern permeates the whole organization is necessary to the self-interest of the company. This is required, they feel, if the company is to be able to maintain profitability and develop the necessary competitiveness for effective performance. In the view of the top executives represented in this study, there is no conflict between ethical practices and acceptable profits. Indeed, the first is a necessary precondition for the second. Sound values, purposes and practises are the basis for long-range achievement (ibid.: 161).

Ethics, of course, is not the only condition for business success. There are other ingredients which are vital to the profitability of a corporation which have nothing to do with ethical values.

ETHICS AND INFRASTRUCTURE

Up until now this inquiry has been limited to the examination of what a business enterprise is attempting to accomplish externally, or the outside goals of an organization. The inside of a business organization or its management structure can also be examined for ethical content. What is being claimed is that there is a fundamental congruence between the principles of sound managerial organization and fundamental ethical principles. It is surprising to discover that ethical considerations are already inherent in the basic rules of sound organization. Whether such ethical considerations are explicit is another matter; but ethical principles can be discovered to lie at the heart of the basic rules of how to manage organizations effectively. Most of the current business ethics literature (apart from Allinson 1993) does not come to grips with this issue, although Schlegelmilch and Houston (1989: 58), for example, discuss specific business codes.

THE WILL TO COMMUNICATE, AND INFORMAL AND FORMAL REPORTING CHANNELS

From the standpoint of management, one of the most pervasive and important factors is that of communication. The key concerns of management, such as leadership, motivation, organization, interpersonal interaction, problem solving and decision making, all involve communication. Unless one were to consider a one-person firm, the quality of communication is a very important factor in an internally well-managed organization. The quality of communication can in large measure be determined by what can be termed the desire or the will to communicate. First, one can examine the will to communicate from an ethical perspective in general; secondly, one can examine the will to communicate from the perspective of informal channels of communication; thirdly, one can examine the will to communicate from the perspective of formal reporting channels.

Ethics and the Will to Communicate

While there are many different perspectives one can take in forming one's ethical perspective, one perspective which cuts across most, if not all, ethical and religious perspectives can be defined as 'respect for persons'. If one were to take respect for persons to be one's most fundamental ethical value, then such a value would inform one's action towards others. As one's most fundamental value, there would be few instances, if any, in which one would be willing to violate one's respect for persons.

If the concept of respect for persons were analysed, it would be observable that one's attitude would remain the same whether the source of the attitude of respect for persons were the value that this attitude reflected what would be right, regardless of consequences (or deontological ethics), or the value that this attitude would conduce towards the greatest happiness for the greatest number of persons (utilitarian ethics). The selection of this principle of ethics thus cuts across the false dichotomy between deontology and utilitarianism and allows one to be ethical without worrying if one must first decide if deontology or utilitarianism were correct before one can choose to be ethical (see Appendix on p. 36). In addition, it is of interest that this principle appears to be both a cultural and a religious universal. One can trace this notion back to the Golden Rule both of the Judaeo-Christian and the Confucian heritage, which in its negative formulation in Confucius reads, 'Do not impose on others what you yourself do not desire' (Confucius 1979: 135). One can also find this most basic principle in early Buddhism. The classic philosophical source for the notion of treating persons with respect is Kant's Categorial Imperative which, in one of its three versions, reads, 'Act in such a way that you treat humanity, both in your person and in the person of all others, never merely as a means, but also always as an end' (Kant 1963: 47).[6]

This concept of respect can be expanded to include the natural environment and future generations if one views respect for persons to be too anthropocentric or present bound. For simplicity's sake, the expression respect for persons is employed, since despoiling the environment and upsetting the natural balance inevitably implies a disrespect for living persons and future generations.

When one is treating another as a person, one relates to that other not merely as an employee, but as a full human being. While this might translate into many different fundamental modes of relating to the other, such as with politeness, recognition of the other's human rights and human needs, in a day-to-day business context, the ultimate translation for according respect to another as a person is to communicate with that person, whether directly or indirectly, as an equal. In the Japanese management system, this is shown in non-verbal forms of communication such as giving lifetime employment to employees, which makes the employee feel as valued and safe as the employer, and following the *ringi* system of decision making, which makes the employee feel that his opinion matters just as much as the opinion of his employer.

This does not mean, of course, that there are no hierarchies of authority in a business context. But given those hierarchies, communication must be respectful. Respectful communication means both that one listens to the other, and that one talks to the other with an attitude that the other deserves to be both talked to and listened to. This might entail going out of one's way both to talk to the other, and to encourage the other to talk to one. Such an attitude springs from the fundamental ethical tenet that one's primary attitude towards others is one of respect.

Ethics and Informal Channels of Communication

The establishing of viable informal channels of communication is one extremely important method of ensuring that the will to communicate has some way of manifesting itself. It is not enough to possess the intention of respecting personhood; it is necessary to the concept of respecting persons to ensure that respect will be actualized. Otherwise, respect for persons will remain a hollow attitude which possesses no outlet and hence will not really constitute a genuine respectful relation to persons.

The setting-up of informal channels such as common rooms, tea rooms and coffee shops, which are genuinely frequented by all members of an organization, thus giving access to all members by all members, is a non-verbal communication that one really does possess an attitude of respect for persons. The legendary stories of such figures as Tom Watson, Sr. and Konosuke Matsushita walking the factory floors, and Akio Morita eating in the cafeteria with his blue-collar workers, are other examples of demonstrating that a genuine respect for persons does exist. IBM's open door policy is another example of an informal channel, which comes close to being a formal reporting channel, and thus cuts across the strict line of formality and informality. While all of these can be seen as integral aspects of good business policy, they can also be seen as emanating from a basic ethical attitude. Once again, there is no fundamental conflict between good business policy and ethical values.

Ethics and Formal Reporting Channels

Under the category of formal reporting channels, one can include the explicit responsibility for communicating clearly those sets of tasks which each level within the hierarchy is responsible for carrying out. Without the notion of a clear-cut set of responsibilities belonging to each member in a vertical chain, it is difficult to understand on what basis each member of a chain reports to another, except in terms of pure authority. Thus, every level must carry with it a clear-cut set of responsibilities, so that it is clear what must be reported upon, in addition to to whom one is responsible for reporting. If what an individual is responsible for, and to whom an individual is responsible, is not communicated to the individual, then that individual has not been treated respectfully. In addition to the matter of the possible neglect and/or conflict of responsibilities that might ensue, it is also not clear, from the reporting individual's standpoint, what matters that individual should report upon. It is also unclear to the individual who should receive the report what matters she or he should expect to receive reports upon, from which individuals. The absence of clear-cut and clearly communicated sets of responsibilities both to act upon, to report upon, and to receive reports about, undermines the process of communication both from the management standpoint and also undermines the importance of the communication process from an ethical standpoint. If there were clear-cut formal reporting lines of communication, without the accompanying designated content which is to be communicated, it would be difficult to understand on what basis each member of a chain were to report to another except in terms of pure authority.

Now, it could be said that the notion of clear-cut divisions of responsibility and reporting channels were simply elements of sound management policy. If there were an absence of knowing what one is responsible for, the notion of reporting channels leading to and from one's level in the hierarchy would be without efficacy. Likewise, if there were a clear-cut notion of what one is responsible for, without the presence of reporting channels, one would function as an isolate within an organization, and this can lead to management mistakes of great magnitude.[7] What is of interest to note here is that the presence of clearly defined roles of responsibility and formal reporting channels are not only the basis of organization in the first place: they are the consequences of a fundamental ethical orientation. The organization which functions without a clear-cut set of reporting channels functions disrespectfully, since it is not according individual persons any means for communication. An organization which does not set out both unique responsibilities for each level of power, and a clear line of reporting channels, treats all individuals within that organization with disrespect. Of course, the presence of the mechanisms would be but empty forms if they were not informed by a genuine spirit of the will to communicate. But the absence of such mechanisms is at the same time the trademark of an unethical organization, because no genuine means for communication are available and, therefore, there is no way in which respect for persons can be made manifest. While it is certainly not a new idea that clear-cut and clearly assigned roles of responsibility and reporting channels are the very basis of sound management policy, it is of interest to note that these very same mechanisms are a key ingredient in the formation of an ethical organization.

NOTES

1. Cf. Steiner (1972), Center for Business Ethics (1986), and Dunfee and Robertson (1988). There is a growing body of literature on the subject of business ethics. Extensive bibliographies are appended to two articles in particular:Bommer et al. (1987), and DeGeorge (1987).
2. The emphasis in this paper thus differs from the emphasis one frequently finds in works on business ethics which focus much more on ethical considerations being separate from and needing to be added onto business interests. Works which interpret business in this way are Steiner (1972), Center for Business Ethics (1986), and Dunfee and Robertson (1988). Of the different current writers on business ethics it may be that the work of Norman Bowie (1982) is most

similar to mine. While Bowie does not, to my knowledge, directly discuss the importance of considering ethical values when considering the very definition of business itself, he does show how ethics applies to certain business fundamentals, such as contracts.

3. For a view which considers Smith to be closer to ethics than Friedman but for different reasons than mine, cf. Donaldson (1982: 62-9).

4. According to the *Report of the President's Commission on Aviation Security and Terrorism* (1990: iii), 'Nine security bulletins that could have been relevant to the tragedy were issued between 1 June 1988 and 21 December 1988.' While the President's Commission states that one of these, the notorious Helsinki warning was 'later determined to be a hoax' (ibid.: 83), it apparently was considered credible enough at the time for the FAA Security Bulletin to report it on 7 December and for the State Department to redistribute it to its embassies worldwide on 9 December (ibid.: iii). What is perhaps more to the point is that whether a threat is considered credible or not, it could be argued that it is the potential passenger's right to know and make her or his own decision on the matter. Raymond R. Smith, of the US Moscow Embassy testified at the commission's staff interviews that: 'When I looked at this [the FAA bulletin on the Helsinki warning], and I thought about it, I said to myself, if I were planning to travel during this period of time, would I take this information into account? And the answer was yes. And the second question I asked myself is well, what right do I have to use this information and not to make it available to other people?' (ibid.: 84-5). FAA Administrator James Busey seems confused on the matter when he states that: 'I think the air traveller needs to know so he can make a responsible decision' (ibid.: 88). Nonetheless, 'our policy remains that we not go public' (ibid.: 95).

5. The first American 'ethical' fund was launched in 1971; the first British 'ethical' fund in 1984. More than US$800 million was invested in ethical funds in Britain as of 1994. One ethical fund has recorded average annual growth of 21.4% since its introduction in June 1984, compared with average annual growth rate of 15% for British funds generally. See *International Herald Tribune* (1994).

6. For a fuller discussion of the Golden Rule, cf. Allinson (1985), Nakamura (1988: 102), Kant (1904: 429) and Kant (1963: 47).

7. For a work that treats the connection between ethics and disasters in some detail, see Allinson (1993).

REFERENCES

Allinson, R.E. 1985. The Confucian Golden Rule: A Negative Formulation. *Journal of Chinese Philosophy* 12: 305-15.

Allinson, R.E. 1993. *Global Disasters: Inquiries into Management Ethics.* New York: Prentice-Hall.

Bommer, M., C. Gratto, J. Granvander and M. Tuttle. 1987. A Behavioural Model of Ethical and Unethical Decision Making. *Journal of Business Ethics* 6: 265-80.

Bowie, N.E. 1982. *Business Ethics.* Englewood Cliffs, NJ: Prentice-Hall.

Business Roundtable. 1988. *Corporate Ethics: A Prime Business Asset.* New York: The Business Roundtable.

Cavanagh, G.F. and A.F. McGovern. 1988. *Ethical Dilemmas In The Modern Corporation.* Englewood Cliffs, NJ: Prentice-Hall.

Center for Business Ethics. 1986. Are Corporations Institutionalising Ethics. *Journal of Business Ethics* 5: 85-91.

Confucius. 1979. *Analects.* (tr. D.C. Lau). London: Penguin.

DeGeorge, R.T. 1987. The Status of Business Ethics: Past and Future. *Journal of Business Ethics* 6: 201-11.

Donaldson, T. 1982. *Corporations and Morality.* Englewood Cliffs, NJ: Prentice-Hall.

Dunfee, T.W. 1987. The Case for Professional Norms of Business Ethics. *American Business Law Journal* 25.

Dunfee, T.W. and D.C. Robertson. 1988. Integrating Ethics into the Business School Curriculum. *Journal of Business Ethics* 7: 847-59.

Friedman, M. 1962. The Social Responsibility of Business is to Increase its Profits. (later title). In *Capitalism and Freedom,* 133-6. Chicago: University of Chicago Press.

International Herald Tribune. 1994. February 26-27: 19.

Kant, I. 1904. *Groundwork of the Metaphysic of Morals.* (tr. H.J. Paton). New York: Harper & Row.

Kant, I. 1963. *Critique of Practical Reason and Other Works on the Theory of Ethics.* Sixth Edition. (trans. T.K. Abbott). London: Longman.

Nakamura, H. 1988. The Significance of 'Harmony' in Buddhist Thought. In *Harmony and Strife: Contemporary Perspectives, East and West.* Ed. Allinson and Liu. Hong Kong: The Chinese University Press.

Plato. 1955. *The Republic.* (tr. H.D.P. Lee) Harmondsworth: Penguin.

Rand, A. 1957. *Atlas Shrugged.* New York: Random House.

Report of the President's Commission on Aviation Security and Terrorism. 1990. May 1. Washington, DC: GPO.

Robin, D.P. and R.E. Reidenbach. 1989. *Business Ethics: Where Profits Meet Value Systems.* Englewood Cliffs, NJ: Prentice-Hall.

Schlegelmilch, B.B. and J.E. Houston. 1989. Corporate Codes of Ethics in Large UK Companies. *Management Decision* 28 (7): 38-43.

Smith, A. 1937. *An Inquiry Into the Nature and Causes of the Wealth of Nations.* Ed. E. Cannan. New York: Modern Library.

Steiner, G.A. 1972. Social Policies for Business. *California Management Review* 15 (2, Winter): 17-24.

APPENDIX

As a brief breakdown of the different forms of ethics, deontological ethics may be defined as that version of ethics in which one embraces values from the standpoint of what one holds to be absolutely right or wrong, regardless of consequences. While the word originates from the Greek for duty, its use since refers more to the absoluteness of the choice. Sometimes, deontological ethics is also called formalist ethics to emphasize that one's values are held regardless of the context. Utilitarian ethics may be defined as that version of ethics in which one embraces or disengages from values from the standpoint of what social benefits or harms may be produced. Nowadays, consequentialism is a term used interchangeably with utilitarianism. Eudaemonistic ethics, not so common any more, may be defined as that version of ethics in which one embraces values from the standpoint of how an individual achieves his or her greatest self-actualization. Egoistic ethics is basically the pursuit of self-interest, and thus would not distinguish ethics from the typical picture of business as the pursuit of self-interest. As a result, such a definition of ethics adds nothing at all to the current conception of the non-ethical pursuit of business, and therefore adds no contrast for a fruitful discussion. Ayn Rand's philosophy is such a philosophy. Ayn Rand is like Adam Smith without the proviso that the greatest good for society will come about through the device of the invisible hand, or like Friedman without the proviso that the greatest good for society will come about through the survival of the fittest (Rand 1957). In other words, Rand seems to endorse self-interest without any regard for the public welfare. Hedonism (the pursuit of pleasure) is a species of egoism.

Religious ethics can, by and large, be perceived as a species of deontology, though the source of the deontology in this case may not be a matter of personal choice, but may come about through religious upbringing. For practical purposes, religious ethics may still be regarded as a variation of deontology. Virtue ethics, which is growing in popularity, extols the merits of character rather than specific acts, but is still either deontologically or eudaemonistically based. This paper, in the main, refers to the main forms of deontological ethics, utilitarian ethics and eudaemonistic ethics.

In some ways, the three main schools of ethics cannot be absolutely distinguished from each other. While utilitarianism might seem to be favoured by businessmen, one's absolute choice to be a utilitarian must be either a deontological one or an arbitrary one. Kant, who is perceived as the arch deontologist, tests his main ethical principle, the Categorical Imperative, in some of its formulations, by appealing to a consequentialist criterion. Plato's philosophy was certainly a blend of deontology, eudaemonism and utilitarianism. The entire deontologist versus utilitarian debate can be seen as a pseudo-conflict. Plato argued that one should be just, both because of the intrinsic goodness of justice (a form, it may be argued, of deontology) and because of the results that it brings (a form of utilitarianism). Plato adds an additional eudaemonistic component to the deontological–utilitarian or formalist–consequentialist mix by saying that when one values justice both for its own sake and for its results, one thereby derives one's truest happiness as well. In *The Republic*, Plato has Socrates say that justice must be placed in the highest class of things: '… as a thing which anyone who is to gain happiness must value both for itself and for its results' (Plato 1955: v. 358). Within the mixture, Plato takes the side that justice is to be valued more for its own sake than for its results (ibid.: v. 366), but this does not detract from his view that it is to be valued for both reasons, and that it can be valued for both is what places it among the highest class of things. The reliance upon the deontological-consequentialist mix with a slight built-in bias towards deontology offers a way out of dilemmas that confront both the pure deontologist and the pure consequentialist. For example, the classic critique of utilitarianism's 'greatest good for the greatest number' is that an injustice for a particular class could result such as the slavery of a minority. The built-in deontological portion rules out this version of consequentialism. On the other hand, if following the directive of producing the greatest good for the greatest number runs the risk of producing a mediocre society, then the deontological portion can act as a corrective. This was Plato's approach. While it may appear odd to classify Plato as a cross between a deontologist and a consequentialist, he does not think that one must make a choice between the Right and the Good. While it is traditional to describe Plato's ethic as a form of eudaemonism, such a label does not take sufficient account of his emphasis on the intrinsic value of justice. Most properly understood, valuing justice both for itself, and for its results, also brings about the greatest human fulfilment, so that Plato's ethics is actually a blend of all three types. While Plato's writings are not all consistent with each other on this point, in his key works, he did not see a conflict between the demands of happiness and the demands of morality. If one considers that Plato's vision of *The Republic* is for him the best and the happiest society, then the demands of deontology and utilitarianism can be seen to merge. If profit-making can be seen to represent a wider social interest, then it need not be intrinsically incompatible with an ethical orientation. That Plato saw it this way is clear from his division of society to include a capitalist class for whom making money is the prime value. The presence of this class is, for Plato, one of the ingredients in what he considers to be the best or most just society. It is an encouraging sign that some writers today are seeing that deontological or formalistic ethics and utilitarian or consequentialist ethics need not be seen as competing ethical viewpoints, but may be regarded as complementary perspectives. As a result, one can be a deontologist in some respects, a eudaemonist in others and a utilitarian in yet other respects. One's choice of ethics can be context-driven, that is, relative to the type of choice that one is making, without one becoming a relativist proper, that is, one whose ethics is wholly determined by the context or culture in which one finds oneself. While Plato's ethics was a blend of all three types, one would hardly class Plato as a relativist.

Within the limits of this paper, ethics is viewed from a utilitarian standpoint, when one refers to ethics as the social values which no business enterprise can escape from creating. This is still not an absolute utilitarianism, since it remains one's deontological choice that it is good to create social values. Ethics is viewed from both a deontological standpoint and a utilitarian standpoint when ethics is examined as a defining feature of the communicative infrastructure of a business organization.

It may be argued, from the standpoint of utilitarianism, that ethics may be a friend of business but, from the standpoint of deontology, that ethics can become the enemy of business whenever business violates certain absolute ethical principles. For example, if one were a drug dealer, then, while one would produce some social good (jobs), one would produce far greater social evil (drug addiction). From the standpoint of deontology, this is ethically wrong, even if some extremely minor social benefits were to be produced from the standpoint of the utilitarianism of the drug dealer and his employees. This business would also be considered ethically wrong from the standpoint of a wider utilitarianism, which takes not only the interests of this business into account, but the interests of the entire society. Thus, it would appear that from the standpoint of deontology and wider utilitarianism, ethics and business are enemies, not friends. The resolution to this sudden rift, that has arisen between what appeared to be good friends, is that, first of all, the thrust of this paper is to treat legitimate businesses, not illegal ones. Even illegal and unethical businesses have their own internal ethics, such as the code of the Mafia. It is important to remember that the ties between ethics and business are only being stressed in order to show the relationship between social values and business enterprises and not thereby to justify all business enterprises. Even the best of friends might have some fundamental differences and these differences can assist in forcing changes in both partners. While even the drug dealer produces some good, however minimal and outweighed by the harm he produces, his business activities are still value-related. It would be marvellous if one could put a stop to the drug business by adopting a eudaemonistic ethic and attempt to persuade dealers to understand that they can make money and realize their happiness in another way without producing such terrible social harm. But since drug dealers cannot normally be so convinced, that is why one requires legislation and a police force. Not every social problem can be corrected by an understanding of ethics, whether deontological, utilitarian, or eudameonistic ethics. Sometimes even friends part when the differences between them become too acute. It works the other way around as well. Ethical action can benefit from the profits made by legitimate businesses. Mother Theresa's work, while ethically sound, can only achieve success when supported by a strong monetary base. Mother Theresa is not interested therefore in alienating the business community. When I had the privilege of meeting Mother Theresa, I was struck by the smile which lit up her features when she received checks made out to her charity. The archetypical effective altruist did not see any conflict between her altruism and the means by which it was made possible.

Underlying the utilitarian-seeming approach taken to ethics presented here are fundamental deontological values such as not condoning murder, criminal businesses, mob violence, treachery, deceit, false representation, and other dishonest business practices. (To be fair to utilitarianism, the same values can be generated from a utilitarian base by thinking in terms of consequences, such as, if everyone were a murderer, then the greatest good for the greatest number would not be achieved, and so on, but this is a more roundabout method). The main point is that the data base from which one starts is the data base of legitimate business. By starting out with legitimate business as a data base, one builds in a deontology before setting out to examine the inherent connection between ethics and business enterprise from a utilitarian standpoint. One could also have an underlying eudaemonistic base, since part of what is being said here is that businesses can become more meaningful for their owners and workers as they become more ethically aware. The ethical business organization becomes a business community in which all members feel a sense of belonging.

While this is not designed as a paper on what is meant by ethics in a technical definition of business ethics, it would not be appropriate to say that only a utilitarian model is being advanced here, although it is the model of which it seems that the greatest use is made. With respect to the setting up of the definition of business, the built-in dimension of ethics appears to be utilitarian, but this choice of definition is itself deontologically driven. With respect to the ethical basis for agreements and contracts, the built-in dimension of ethics appears to be both deontological and utilitarian and even eudaemonistic, although primarily utilitarian. With respect to the choice of the ethical goals of a business, while it can be said that these goals are utilitarian (or eudaemonistically) based, the choice of such a utilitarian base remains deontological. With respect to the role that ethical values play in communicative infrastructure, it is clear that ethical values are chosen because of deontological, utilitarian and eudaemonistic considerations.

3

CODES OF ETHICS AND THE CIVIL SOCIETY: JOHN STUART MILL'S LEGACY IN THE 1990s

Anne Carver

MORALITY AND THE LAW

Wrestling with the limits of morality and the criminal law is not only the task of moral philosophers, it is also the task of the individual concerned with freedom of thought, expression, and action, such as the right to conduct private business transactions for commercial advantage, perhaps maximizing the profit and minimizing the risk within the confines of the criminal law. It is the concern of everyone in business to think about the areas of legitimate social control over the individual in society, and particularly to consider where the areas of legitimate social control affect the limits of business and the individual in the public and private sphere.

In 1859, John Stuart Mill asserted the profound principle of the individual's sovereignty over his or her body that still animates Western thinking on the limits of the criminal law and the protection of private morality. Gertrude Himmelfarb (1985: 49) has described *On Liberty* as 'the gospel of our time'. It survives in a secular age as the starting point on questions of law and morality and is repeated here because of its historic and current importance.

> The object of this essay is to assert one very simple principle, as entitled to govern absolutely the dealings of society with the individual in the way of compulsion and control, whether the means used be physical force in the form of legal penalties, or the moral coercion of public opinion. That principle is, that the sole end, for

which mankind are warranted, individually or collectively, in interfering with the liberty of action of any of their number, is self-protection. That the only purpose for which power can be rightfully exercised over any member of a civilized community, against his will, is to prevent harm to others. His own good, either physical or moral, is not a sufficient warrant. He cannot rightfully be compelled to do or forbear because it will be better for him to do so, because it will make him happier, because, in the opinions of others, to do so would be wise, or even right ... (Mill 1985: 68-9).

Nevertheless, in 1873 Sir James Fitzjames Stephen set out to discredit Mill's argument that the only criterion for coercing and punishing an individual is whether that individual's conduct is harmful to others. In *Liberty, Equality, Fraternity*, Stephen argues thus: 'To me the question whether liberty is a good or bad thing appears as irrational as the question whether fire is a good or a bad thing. It is both good and bad according to time, place, and circumstance' (cited in Wasserstrom 1971: 2).

Stephen therefore holds that the regulation of thought, discussion and morals is the concern of the public domain upon utilitarian principles; if the good outweighs the bad then compulsion by society towards that good cannot be bad. The argument is particularly relevant to the control and prevention of what the Victorians termed 'vice' and citizens of the late twentieth century might simply call sexual practices between consenting adults in private.

The argument between Mill's Libertarians and Stephen's Utilitarians is as difficult for us today as it was for the Victorians. The debate emerged 100 years later in the publication of the *Report of the Committee on Homosexual Offences and Prostitution* in 1957, the Wolfenden Report (Wolfenden Committee 1957). The Wolfenden Committee, under the Chairmanship of John Wolfenden, was established to consider the existing English laws concerning homosexuality and prostitution and to recommend changes, if thought necessary, to the existing criminal law in these respects. The Wolfenden Report recommended that homosexual behaviour in private between consenting adults should no longer be punishable under the law and that no change to the existing law (under which prostitution is not illegal) should be made. The Report focused upon the libertarian argument that the criminal law should have no dealings with private morality where no harm is done to others, but should concern itself with matters of public order, harm to others and public decency.

The argument of the libertarians must be among the most compelling principles proposed in a secular world: that is 'over himself, over his own body and mind the individual is sovereign' (Mill 1985: 68-9). Nevertheless, Lord Devlin felt the necessity of challenging Wolfenden's libertarian views the following year, in his lecture *The Enforcement of Morals*, when he insisted that it is impossible to talk sensibly of a public as opposed to a private morality in his public criticism of the report:

> I do not think that one can talk sensibly of a public and private morality any more than one can of a public or private highway. Morality is a sphere in which there is a public interest and a private interest often in conflict, and the problem is how to reconcile the two (Devlin 1965: 16).

Lord Devlin highlights the distinction or gap between morality and the law of the land:

> No man is worth much who regulates his conduct with the sole object of escaping punishment and every worthy society sets for its members standards which are above those of the law ... The destruction was well put in the judgement of African elders in a family dispute: 'We have power to make you divide the crops, for this is our law, and we will see that this is done. But we have not power to make you behave like an upright man' (ibid.: 43).[1]

Joining the debate, H.A.L. Hart, first quoted *The Times*' construal of Devlin's argument and then, chillingly, quoted a pertinent analogy as follows:

> When Sir Patrick's lecture was first delivered *The Times* greeted it with these words: 'There is a moving and welcome humility in the conception that society should not be asked to give its reason for refusing to tolerate what in its heart it feels intolerable.' This drew from a correspondent in Cambridge the retort: 'I am afraid that we are less humble than we used to be. We once burnt old women because, without giving our reasons we felt in our hearts that witchcraft was intolerable' (Hart 1959: 162-3).

The argument was taken up again in 1968 by Ronald Dworkin, who summarized the issue as being a debate on society's right to protect its own existence and on the majority's right to follow 'its own moral convictions in defending its social environment from change it opposes' (Dworkin 1968, in Wasserstrom 1971: 55). Dworkin comments thus 'what Lord Devlin thinks is at stake, when our public morality is challenged, is the very survival of society, and he believes that society is entitled to preserve itself without vouching for the morality that holds itself together' (ibid.: 56).

Dworkin argues, thus, that Devlin's position appears to be a moral position in the anthropological sense, that is to say that most ordinary people make judgements based on feelings rather than upon reason. Dworkin then asks whether we have to have a reason to make a belief a matter of moral conviction (ibid.: 65), and concludes that often people cannot give a reason for a particular moral position because they feel that their view is self-evident. At stake, however, underlying such a belief that a moral principle is self-evident, is a series of criteria that 'the ultimate grounds of immorality' (ibid.: 66) are limited to a small set of standards by which each of us judge an act to be immoral. Such a set of standards could be, for example, that the act involves a breach of an undertaking or duty or does harm to another or to oneself or is contrary to the law itself, or illegal. If the act does not have any of these features then the (so-called reasonable) person might well argue that to call an act immoral is arbitrary and therefore indefensible. The issue as summarized by Dworkin is therefore to identify and to define the small set of standards that unite the community in its shared moral principles (ibid.: 69), rather than to disagree with Lord Devlin's proposition of the moral consensus. Clearly, popular indignation, intolerance and disgust cannot remain the articulated criteria for a moral consensus in the world of libertarians where 'if all mankind minus one were of one opinion, mankind would be no more justified in silencing that one person than he, if he had the power, would be justified in silencing mankind' (Mill 1985: 76).

In identifying and defining Dworkin's small set of standards recognized as unconsciously or consciously shared by the community, there is a contrast to Immanuel Kant's categorical imperative of the rational agent who is capable of *directing his own behaviour by reason*. The fundamental test of the morality of a particular action is whether one's action should become a universal law of human nature. Thus the 'application of reason to action rather than God is the foundation of Kantian ethics' (Lyons 1984: 10). The attempt to articulate the 'universal law of nature' which applies reason to action therefore lies at the heart of our attempt to identify and define the small set of standards that test the morality of our actions. It is this specific task that refutes the otherwise compelling argument that 'the mores can make it right' (Summer 1907: 521). (The *Oxford English Dictionary* definition of 'mores' is: 'the acquired customs and moral assumptions which give cohesion to a community or social group'). For if we accept the argument that the mores can make it right then we must also accept that an act condemned by the mores makes it wrong and further an act not condemned by the mores makes it right. Stuart Hampshire (1989: 57) describes this argument as the 'fallacy of the false fixity', that is, to say that propositions such as slavery is a just institution, or that women should receive unequal pay for equal work, are embedded in our ways of life. Our own culture and education support a particular way of life and such propositions concerning slavery and unequal pay for women for example appear as an 'uncontrollable natural phenomenon' (ibid.: 57). He talks of the blindness of reasonable people whose way of life 'represents to them embedded and distinctive features of this life as unavoidable in general' (ibid.: 59).

Thus it may be that the accumulation of vast fortunes in industrial countries may be questioned by future generations who will ask, 'how can they have failed to see the injustice of allowing billionaires to multiply while the very same economy allowed abject poverty to persist uncorrected next door to preposterous luxury?' (ibid.: 59). The blindness of reasonable people, to use Hampshire's words, explains the existing social order's set of moral standards and the model of a social order on which their lives are built. How else can people identify themselves other than in terms of 'legitimate descent and of inherited status and role?' (ibid.: 60).

Thus, again in contrast to Kant's categorical imperative, Hampshire would appear to agree with Dworkin when he suggests it must be the case that 'a large shift in the non-rational, or imaginative presuppositions of a culture or community has to occur before such images of the self are open to challenge by practical reasoning about justice' (ibid.: 60). The contrast, therefore, is between the rational and the imaginative, highlighting Dworkin's focus on the difficulty of identifying the small set of standards that form the basis of a shared moral consensus.

MORALITY AND BUSINESS

In the current debate over business morality, Drucker (1981) argues that the term business ethics 'reeks of moral laxity' and more importantly denies the fundamental axiom that there is only one code of ethics 'for prince and pauper, for rich and poor, for the mighty and the meek alike. Ethics, in the Judaeo-Christian tradition, is the affirmation that all men and women are alike creatures— whether the creator be called God, Nature or Society' (ibid.: 44). For Drucker the paradox is that business ethics purports to find acts that are not immoral if done by ordinary people become immoral if done by business, thus contradicting the fundamental principle in the Western tradition of ethics that there is only one code, and it applies to all of us. One example Drucker gives is the Lockheed bribery scandal in which, during the early 1970s, Lockheed paid 'extortion money' to a Japanese airline to 'persuade' the Japanese to buy Lockheed's L-1011 passenger jets. In itself this example is a complex series of ethical dilemmas that could support an entire conference on the ethics of Lockheed's motives and the morality of its conduct, and does not appear to support Drucker's thesis.

The counterargument is that, far from finding a special set of rules for business, the topic of business ethics is introduced in order to subject business to the ordinary rules of ethics applicable to everyone in a community, that is to say the shared moral principles of a community. It is designed to try to direct moral goals in the apparently amoral sphere of business (Hoffman and Mills Moore 1982: 54, citing Friedman 1970) and its necessary predisposition to self-interest. Thus Hoffman and Moore identify the issues as being how, if at all, a business organization can be regarded as a moral agent; what the formation of a just economic foundation for business activity might be, what is the nature of corporations and what is the role of business in society? These questions provide a rational framework in which to examine specific problems in business such as 'hiring practices, just consumer relations, governmental regulation, the moral use of natural resources' (Hoffman and Mills Moore 1982: 55).

Business ethics, pace Drucker, seek to apply general moral principles to specific situations in business, and to identify the moral obligations of business towards society. The problem is further highlighted in discussions of international business and the moral foundation for multinational corporations as 'the most powerful organizations in existence' (Donaldson 1989: 6). There are two doctrines proposed by those concerned with the international dimension of business ethics: the notion of a social contract between business and society, and the doctrine of international rights. These doctrines lie at the heart of any discussions on the possibility of articulating a code of international business ethics. However, for the purposes of this paper, the argument focuses on the question of whether it is possible to separate the public morality from the private morality as suggested by the litertarians, since this paper is not concerned with international business norms.

MORALITY AND THE PROFESSIONS

In the search for a moral dimension to business and an attempt to articulate its moral foundation, an attractive example would *seem* to be offered by the professions and their established Codes of Conduct. As we shall see, however, there is a degree of high-minded moral lip service in evidence in the development and the function of these Codes. I shall take one example, the Code of Conduct for Solicitors in England and Wales, from personal knowledge and professional interest.

In one sense the term 'professional ethics' is an oxymoron if we accept Drucker's view that there is only one set of ethics for rich and poor, the prince and the pauper and the professionals.

However professional codes of ethics are an interesting halfway house of purely moral rules (in the case of solicitors or barristers in England, for example, the duty of confidentiality is a moral duty towards the client), of professional etiquette (for example, only a solicitor can 'brief' or instruct a barrister, and restrictions intended to benefit the group's economic interest (for example, it used to be the case in England and Wales that solicitors had a monopoly on conveyancing).

The English distinction between solicitors and barristers has a history that can be traced back to the thirteenth century, after the first centralized system of courts had been established, and when two groups of lawyers began to perform two different functions. 'The modern barrister and solicitor are remote descendants of the thirteenth-century pleader and attorney respectively' (Disney et al. 1989: 5). Towards the end of the thirteenth century, the two groups were given a monopoly to practise law and began to be regulated by the justices on behalf of the King. It seems that the pleaders were divided into the senior barristers, equivalent to today's Queen's Counsels, known as Serjeants at the apex of the legal profession (ibid.: 6), and the apprentices or juniors as they are sometimes called today. The apprentices were all members of the Inns of Court, four of which grew to immense importance in the fourteenth century and remain so today: the Temple, the Inner Temple, Gray's Inn and Lincoln's Inn.

By contrast to the pleaders, professional attorneys at the Court in Westminster were general practitioners 'giving legal advice, drawing legal documents and even managing the financial affairs of their clients' (ibid.: 9). Barristers could deal directly with clients and student apprentices often worked as attorneys before and after their call to the bar of their Inn, so that there was no clear demarcation of exclusivity until the second half of the sixteenth century in England. The mutual exclusivity of the two professions began to develop as the attorneys were refused admission to the four Inns of Court and became members of the 'Inns of Chancery', which continued to provide accommodation and social facilities for attorneys until the Victorians wound up the societies and sold off the Inns of Chancery.

One commentator has described the division as being one of

English class consciousness: 'In the fifteenth century the attorneys had often been housed in the Inns of Court where the barristers were organized but in the later sixteenth century the barristers ejected the attorneys. The barrister was a gentleman with the rank of esquire and he could not be expected to mix with a mere attorney' (Jackson, in Podmore 1980: 2).

How did solicitors raise themselves to a higher social status in society (although some would argue that barristers are still perceived as the senior branch of the profession in England today)? Podmore sees the side-effects of the Industrial Revolution as opening up a wide range of opportunities and new perspectives with 'the industrial and commercial developments of the eighteenth century' (ibid.: 3). Opportunities for the investment of client's money in business projects, land and property development and new legislation on 'turnpike trusts, canals and (later) railways' (ibid.: 3) were hugely profitable opportunities for the solicitors and their business flourished. Naturally, a growing number of unqualified and unscrupulous attorneys touted for custom and spoilt business for the professionals. The solution to the problem lay in the Attorneys and Solicitors Act of 1729, which laid down a basic training period, and a method of charging clients for professional services by individualized items of service, 'professional fees'. To ensure effective lobbying in Parliament of the interests of the profession, the Society of Gentleman Practisers in the Courts of Law and Equity was founded in 1739, the professional body of solicitors which laid down its Code of Conduct for members and set its own examinations for its articled clerks. Nevertheless solicitors were still, perhaps, 'little better than tradesmen' (ibid.: 4), while making themselves in some cases extremely rich. The masterstroke in changing their status appears to have been their emphasis on education and in 'the establishment of the profession as liberal' (ibid.: 5, citing Kirk 1976) although as late as 1846 a select committee of the House of Commons reported that 'the education of solicitors by apprenticeship still gave too little of what grounding in principles which was proper to gentlemen of a liberal profession' (ibid.: 5, citing Harding 1966).

How did solicitors elevate their status from that of tradesmen to liberal gentlemen? The tracking down of unqualified practitioners, and the pursuit of unethical or disreputable solicitors, appear to have been two major reasons for their success.

In 1888 The Solicitors Act gave the Incorporated Law Society the right to investigate complaints against solicitors and in 1919 legislation allowed the Disciplinary Committee to suspend a solicitor for misconduct or to strike his name off the roll, 'the ultimate step in the professionalization process' (Podmore 1980: 6). The crucial step, therefore, was to enhance the image of the profession by imposing its own examinations (the right was granted in 1877) and to discipline its members.

The interesting question for this paper is what makes people attempt to turn their occupations into a profession? (Hughes 1963, cited in Disney et al. 1989: 79). As we have seen, the answer may be to enable the particular group to improve their social status and economic position. The question of the role of a code of ethics for a professional group raises significant problems in any discussion of the professional body's solidarity and the maintenance of moral discipline. Codes of ethics are seen to be a way of ordering stability and social relations, and to avoid divisive conflict between the members.

A willingness to discipline members for misdemeanours also shows a serious intention to make the codes an *active* instrument for ethical practices, and is both a 'public' and a 'private' act.

> At the 'public' level it is a declaration that the profession is aware of its privileges and its duty—its duty, in particular, to merit public confidence in the proper use of its autonomy and 'dangerous knowledge'. In fact the idea of deserving the confidence of society is often explicitly mentioned as an important reason for promulgating ethical codes ... At the 'private' level, the individual professional, in joining the professional group or association, commits himself to the private, intra-professional morality and implicitly agrees to be bound by its authority or to risk its sanctions (Maley 1974: 393, cited in Disney et al. 1989: 82).[2]

Solicitors have access to clients' money, access to secrets, access to private gain from confidential information given to them by clients, and access to information about past and future criminal activity and intent. Above all, the Code of Conduct sets out to lay down guidelines about the solicitor's duty of confidentiality and the duty to avoid a conflict of interest at all times. There is an awareness of their own corruptibility, given the enormous access to secrets and consequent private gain. They therefore create a paradigm of intra-professional morality, an enclosed system of rules that binds only the members themselves. The rules themselves can change; for example, the prohibition against solicitors in England and Wales advertising has been relaxed by the Solicitors' Publicity Code of 1990 with amendments in 1992; or the prohibition on solicitors incorporating themselves as private limited liability companies, has been lifted by the Solicitors' Incorporated Practice Rules 1988 in conjunction with Section 9 of the Administration of Justice Act 1985. Solicitors can now conduct their business as companies, provided that the directors of the company are all solicitors.

This enclosed systematic world of rules, with punishment being the prerogative of the Disciplinary Committee, contrasts with the commercial world existing in a civil society. The business world seeks to minimize risk and maximize profit and obeys the 'law' as a member of a civil society recognizing the limits of a civil society in which business, morality, and the law have found an accommodation. The idea of a civil society is posited on the realm of social mutuality, 'on the legally free individual and on the community of free individuals ... A public realm, yet one constituted by private individuals' (Seligman 1992: 3). Seligman further describes civil society as 'most essentially that realm where the concrete person—that particular individual, subject to his or her own wants, caprices and physical necessities—seeks the attainment of these "selfish" aims. It is that arena where the "burgher" as private person seeks to fulfil his or her own interests' (ibid.: 5).

CONCLUSION

Is it therefore possible for business people to articulate a code of ethical conduct binding upon themselves and identifying the public and private spheres of morality that codes of ethics purport to enshrine? The English solicitors have created for and imposed upon themselves a code of additional rules, over and above the existing legal system, to preserve their reputation in the society in which they operate, for two major reasons. First, solicitors wanted to increase social and economic status. Second, they wished to maintain educational standards for admission to retain a monopoly on professional fees. The Code of Conduct itself seems almost irrelevant when examined in this context. The attempt to articulate professional codes can result in the high-minded lip-service of the English solicitors of the nineteenth century who succeeded in improving their social status from tradesmen to liberal gentlemen. Let us therefore be wary of drafting Codes of Conduct for business and seek instead to discover what small set of principles exists at the interstices of the commercial world and morality that can be universally agreed upon, lest we fall into Lord Devlin's trap of allowing indignation, intolerance and disgust to form the basis of the morality of the group in business and elsewhere.

NOTES

1. Lord Devlin was quoting Max Gluckman (1955: 172).
2. Maley analyses four professions: engineers, architects, doctors and lawyers.

REFERENCES

Devlin, Patrick, Lord. 1965. *The Enforcement of Morals.* London: Oxford University Press.

Disney, J., P. Redmond, J. Bastien, and S. Moss. 1989. *Lawyers.* Second edition. North Ryde, NSW: Law Book Co. Ltd.

Donaldson, T. 1989. *The Ethics of International Business.* Oxford, UK: Oxford University Press.

Drucker, P. 1981. Ethical Chic. In *Contemporary Moral Controversies in Business.* 1989. Ed. Iannone. Oxford, UK: Oxford University Press.

Dworkin, R. 1968. Lord Devlin and the Enforcement of Morals. *Yale Law Journal* 75: 986.

Friedman, M. 1970. The Social Responsibility of Business is to Increase its Profits. In *Capitalism and Freedom,* 133-6. Chicago: University of Chicago Press.

Gluckman, M. 1955. *The Judicial Process Among the Barotse of Northern Rhodesia*. Manchester, UK: Manchester University Press.

Hampshire, S. 1989. *Innocence and Experience*. London: Penguin.

Harding, A. 1966. *A Social History of English Law*. Harmondsworth: Penguin.

Hart, H.A.L. 1959. Immorality and Treason. *The Listener* (July 30): 162-3.

Himmelfarb, G. 1985. *Introduction to J.S. Mill's On Liberty*. London: Penguin.

Hoffman, W.M. and J. Mills Moore. 1982. What is Business Ethics? A Reply to P. Drucker. In *Contemporary Moral Controversies in Business*. Ed. Iannone. Oxford, UK: Oxford University Press.

Hughes, E.C. 1963. Professions. *Daedalus* (issue no. 4): 92.

Jackson, R.M. 1972. *The Machinery of Justice in England*. Sixth edition. Cambridge, UK: Cambridge University Press.

Kirk, H. 1976. *Portrait of a Profession*. London: Oyez Publishing.

Lyons, D. 1984. *Ethics and the Rule of Law*. Cambridge, UK: Cambridge University Press.

Maley, B. 1974. Professionalism and Professional Ethics. In *Social Changes in Australia*. Ed. Edgar. Sydney: Longman Cheshire Pty Ltd.

Mill, J.S. [1859] 1985. *On Liberty*. London: Penguin.

Podmore, D. 1980. *Solicitors and the Wider Community*. London: Heinemann.

Seligman, A. 1992. *The Idea of Civil Society*. New York: Free Press.

Summer, W.G. 1907. *Folkways*. Boston, MA: Girn & Co.

Wasserstrom, R.A. 1971. *Morality and the Law*. Belmont: Wadsworth.

Wolfenden Committee. 1957. *Report of the Committee on Homosexual Offences and Prostitution*. London: HMSO.

4

ETHICAL VALUES: A SOURCE OF CONFLICT— BUT WHOSE VALUES?

David M. Reid

INTRODUCTION

Much noise on the issue of ethics has been generated from the United States. It has become a hot topic in business schools (Andrews 1989; Hoffman 1989). Wright (1989) suggests that there are numerous factors that have led to the erosion of ethical values in the United States, foremost of which is the breakdown of the three major institutions that for 200 years shaped American values and the American way of life—the family, the church and the school system. Lapses of ethics in business, Wright avers, are the result of apparent conflicts of interest among a firm's various stakeholders. In many cases, short-term thinking has fostered unethical shortcuts that have led to trouble.

Unethical behaviour by domestic players in a foreign market can result in bad feelings and negative word of mouth reportage that is subsequently subsumed into the general mythology that pervades about a market. However, the issue of what is ethically correct is largely one that is culturally determined, and such issues usually become controversial when the values of either one of the parties are violated. Thus before ethical issues ethics can be considered the question must be raised: whose values are germane?

The purpose of this paper is to draw on data obtained from a study on foreign multinational corporations (MNCs) in Japan to illustrate the different ethical perspectives that may emerge on identical issues.

BACKGROUND

As an example, in Africa it is a tribal custom to give gifts to the chief. It is a way of showing respect as well as demonstrating an affinity with the culture. Yet, to an outsider it may look as if a rich person is being offered a favour in order to facilitate some business or administrative procedure—this may also be true. However, it may be extremely remiss to make accusations of corrupt behaviour without understanding the cultural context that pertains.

That this issue is culturally specific has been recognized and some comparative studies are reported in the literature (Beggs and Lane 1989; McDonald and Zepp 1988; Tsalikis and Nwachukwu 1988; Becker and Fritzsche 1987). This latter study involved a comparison of attitudes of French, German and US managers regarding ethical business philosophy and codes of ethics. The findings suggested that the French managers were generally idealistic and were more optimistic than the others regarding the effects of ethical codes. The Germans appeared to be relatively pessimistic regarding the codes' efficacy. US managers, whom the study termed realistic, disagreed most strongly with the statement, 'Let the buyer beware'. All groups generally agreed that good ethics made for good business.

Hall (1988), supporting the cultural perspective, in a study on international consulting, argued that to achieve success in work abroad, the consultant must study not only the political and economic conditions, but also the sociological details of the society concerned. Specific knowledge of a client's behaviour patterns will enable the consultant to create a climate conducive to optimal client development of resources. Moreover, consultants working in a foreign country should be sensitive to:

— societal foundations in the management structure;
— limitations on communications;
— reactions to physical attitudes and actions; and
— feelings regarding the separation of personal and business activities. Other important considerations are the basis for decision-making structures and the code of business ethics.

JAPAN

Here we draw on data obtained from a study on foreign MNCs in Japan to illustrate the different ethical perspectives that emerge on identical issues. In so doing we consider: gift giving, joint ventures and recruitment.

Gift Giving

Gift giving is a popular practice in Japan. There are traditionally two gifting seasons—*ochugen* in mid-summer, and *oseibo* at year end—when companies and individuals give to just about everyone with whom they are connected (Kilburn and Wilk 1988; Schofield 1988). Christmas has become a major business but is still considerably smaller than *oseibo*; however, major department stores report that it is growing in importance. Japan is now the second largest market for diamonds in the world. By successfully promoting the concept of engagement and wedding rings, and then broadening the idea to include other forms of jewellery, De Beers has introduced the notion that women should give diamond jewellery to the men they love—and vice versa—as a token of their feelings, especially at Christmas. Other Western gifting festivals have also been imported: the chocolate industry, for example, has virtually claimed ownership of St Valentine's Day.

Rolly Doll

One company that has been successful in building its concept around gift giving is Rolly Doll. The founder of this high-profile operation, Joseph Dunkle, described his philosophy as being based on segmentation and understanding the needs of a particular target group.

There is a tremendous market for cookies in Japan because of gift giving; 63% of Rolly Doll business is gift related. Whenever someone visits a friend's house, they will give a gift, and Dunkle believes food is the most appropriate choice: it is something the whole family can enjoy, and if it also has a story attached it will give people something to talk about at family gatherings.

Realizing this, Dunkle drew on his home state in the United

States: Pennsylvania Dutch County, the home of the Amish people. Since his Aunt Stella was Amish, he used some of her recipes, as well as those of his mother, and the rest he designed himself. Despite no previous experience in the bakery business, Joseph Dunkle developed twenty-seven different varieties of cookie. He attempted to appeal to the family unit, the grandmother, the grandfather, the son, the daughter, the mother. By providing a range from which they could choose, he was able to offer a diversity that would confound a large confectioner. Most bakers use one basic kind of dough to which nuts, fruit or some other ingredients are added; however, the Rolly Doll concept is that each cookie is home-made, different and made in small batches. On this basis, when developing the product, Dunkle was able to adjust the traditional recipes to accommodate Japanese tastes, changing the American soft texture to adapt to the Japanese preference for crispiness; thus he successfully Japanized his product.

Joseph Dunkle built his chain of cookies and cakes shops under the Aunt Stella's brand by being adept at spotting opportunities and building on personal strengths. He believed that the high level of literacy and intellectual curiosity of the Japanese could be utilized by building an Amish country theme around cookie shops. He exploits this curiosity on the cookies packaging by including information on the social history of the Amish people. At the same time he harnessed the widespread nostalgia for *furasato*—in other words the rustic birthplace existing deep in the Japanese imagination—to adventures in travel, and arranged group holidays to rural destinations, especially to Pennsylvania. Dunkle is still exploring the countless domestic and international possibilities for product development.

It would be easy to draw a cynical view that Japanese customs have been exploited by mercenary foreign marketers. An equally valid alternative view is that foreign marketers have built successful businesses around an innocent gift giving custom.

Joint Ventures (JVs)

The vast majority of foreign companies in Japan began operations via joint ventures (Kane 1981), but many quickly found out that they were difficult to manage, and as a result more companies are

attempting to go it alone. According to Berg et al. (1982), there are three primary reasons for the creation of joint ventures:
— the creation of greater market power by combining resources or generating economies of scale;
— the avoidance, reduction, or sharing of information;
— the acquisition or sharing of information.

Other reasons should be added to this list:
— to overcome cultural, political or legal impediments (Kent 1991);
— to meet host country requirements (Franko 1973; Harrigan 1987; UNCTC 1987);
— to manage rivalry in an industry by converting potential competitors into allies (Bernstein 1965; Boyle 1968; Fusfeld 1958; Hennart 1988; Mead 1973; Pfeffer and Nowak 1976).

JVs in Japan are usually structured around the foreign company bringing technological expertise or certain brands to the joint agreement, and the Japanese partner offering local market knowledge, connections and the general wherewithal to secure adequate distribution. Although JVs are political necessities in many Asian markets, in Japan this is no longer the case. Yet, in many cases, JVs have broken up because of difficulties that have been encountered in maintaining the relationship. Criticisms of the other party often involve charges of unethical behaviour.

Same bed different dreams? In many cases, JVs are tenuous marriages of large companies, often from distant lands, haphazardly joined for some single purpose. In many JVs, no one partner has absolute control, and this inevitably creates tensions. Moreover, the owners may disagree over matters of policy (if they can decide policy), and all too often the relationship is not based on mutual respect. According to executives interviewed, many JVs in Japan have failed simply because the foreign partner has abrogated its responsibility; either it has not written into the contract specific mechanisms by which it can provide serious input, or it assumes that whoever is the distributor or partner will take its interests to heart.

Many foreign companies have entered the Japanese market by way of JV arrangements with the *sogo shosha*, who are believed to offer both connections and entry points into what is often depicted as a complicated, inscrutable marketplace. However, interviewees suggested that this is an impression fostered by the *sogo shosha* to attract—thereafter limiting, rather than promoting—foreign brands' market penetration. To the Japanese partner this is a rational investment of resources. In its view there is no ethical conflict. Yet, when JVs are formed in Japan with global competitors from outside, foreign MNCs become perplexed when the JV company loses money. However, according to interviewees, the Japanese partner appears relatively unconcerned about its own share of the losses; because, apparently, JVs are used by the *kaisha* as devices to contain potential competitors. The Japanese believe that losing a few million dollars on a JV arrangement may be much more economical for the Japanese partner than having a major international company attacking their home market. It is merely a commercial judgement.

On the other side, the *nihonjinronists*[1] persuade the foreign partner that Japan is unlike any other market in the world, as if for some mysterious reason one need not pursue one's business interests to the full. However, if the Japanese partners do not behave as the foreign partner expects, this is usually because the Japanese side represents the interests of its total business holdings and these interests may conflict with the specific joint venture in question. As the President of Bristol-Myers Squibb, Mitchell Cybulski, explained:

> Providing he can do so without being dishonest, a Japanese partner will consider his wider business interests ahead of any joint venture, which may well mean some reduction in the JV's outcome. Even for the most senior of managers, working in a JV company means going to work every day to represent the interests of his own side of the partnership.

A typical scenario is that someone at corporate headquarters is given legal responsibility for the JV. That person may relocate to Japan or, even more unfortunately, remain at the home office. Meanwhile, the Japanese partner is carefully monitoring its own people in the JV, and will generally have a greater influence over those players. This results in a management imbalance, so it is inevitable that the arrangement comes under strain and one side seems to be far more committed than the other. A JV is by definition only successful when both parents have a vested interest in perpetuating the alliance.

According to most of the executives interviewed, JVs have become less popular as a mode of market entry—especially with those companies that have acquired Japanese market expertise and have the financial means to go it alone. Most of the foreign executives interviewed believe that a wholly owned presence is the best approach for the Japanese market. The majority see JVs as a transitory phase, often an unhappy one. Eric Weber, the former marketing manager of Friskies KK, Nestle, advises: 'Don't go into a JV. Don't ever JV in Japan if you've got a strong position world-wide. The JV partner has an interest in keeping you out; it never has the same orientation as you do or the same objectives.'

He argues that employees of the JV are in effect on secondment from the JV partner and have its interests at heart. The key employees in the JV are likely to return to the parent should it be disbanded; something to be considered when attempting to negotiate out of a JV arrangement.

Once the JV is established, it is essential to understand what recourse exists should problems arise. The financial implications should be considered, as must the legal position. If the Japanese partner is responsible for major functions such as distribution and manufacturing, what audit functions should the foreign partner have? How ought strategic direction be decided and through what process? Frequently, however, many of these fundamental matters were not well defined in the beginning, when the JV was established. Reports were received of the parties involved being highly enthusiastic about the opportunity, with the result that agreements ended up being rather loose and vague, and the partners then found themselves locked into rigid sets of unfavourable rules. These situations are further complicated by the fact that Japanese management remains more static than that of their Western, in particular US, counterparts.

Stultified Vision

In 1983, Heinz entered Japan's frozen foods market by way of its frozen foods subsidiary, Ore-Ida, and a JV with Mitsubishi. From a US perspective, the arrangement initially seemed very promising; however, when it failed to widen its distribution base an ethical question was raised: was Mitsubishi failing to carry out its side of the agreement? Investigations revealed that the JV was not actively pushing Ore-Ida's products to fast-food outlets because it already had exclusive access to its own—not insignificant—Mitsubishi businesses (Mitsubishi owns one of the largest wholesale grocery companies in Japan), but had no vested interest in systematically selling product to outlets owned by its competitors.

The way the issue was tackled by Heinz was to perform a marketing audit that showed that 80% of Japanese households had toaster ovens. The subsequent evaluation suggested that an opportunity existed for Ore-Ida to differentiate its product by implementing a branding strategy, since the Japanese competitors treated the product—frozen French fries—merely as a commodity.

In pursuing its strategy, Heinz was limited by its distribution arrangement because it was tied to a team willing only to make a fraction of the potential distribution coverage available to the Ore-Ida brand. When challenged, the JV partner appeared uncomfortable and unenthusiastic about making efforts beyond the Mitsubishi network. The Ore-Ida team conducted an attitude study of the retail sector and was thus able to demonstrate to Mitsubishi that opportunities existed far beyond its own network. Mitsubishi's reluctance was based on recalcitrance rather than a lack of ethics. The JV partner finally agreed to an extension of its distribution coverage for the brand.

However, many other interviewees indicated that the major trading companies ran tightly controlled operations and did not want to be pestered about possible changes by their partners. Some interviewees used the above examples to argue that Japan remains characteristically different from other markets in their collective experience. However, what they miss is that the *sogo shosha* usually share interests in competitive fields and, to put their quandary into Western terms, if Campbell's Foods approached Heinz in the United States and asked it to distribute its soup products, would it not be naive to expect 100% dedication? It appears that a number of foreign MNCs have learned this lesson rather late in the day, and have perhaps overreacted by claiming that their Japanese business partners were dishonest, whereas from the Japanese point of view, a JV appears to be a perfectly intelligent arrangement to keep competitors at bay. From the MNC side, expectations can be much too high, since the MNC typically commits very little, other than money, to the JV relationships it forms.

As greater experience is obtained in international management issues, US businesses are now being exhorted to carry their ethical baggage with them. For example, as US corporations prepared to enter into joint ventures with former Soviet states, many viewed the development warily. Guidelines were proposed to direct US companies in their relationship with these states. US firms were encouraged to promote reform on human rights, arms control, and diplomatic issues (Skelly 1988), and a campaign was promoted to use the Slepak Principles, which discourage commercial transactions that serve the military and discourage using forced labour or discriminating against workers because of political or religious views or ethnic background. The Slepak Foundation had seven members of the House of Representatives and seven Senators on its advisory board. However, businesses have shown little interest in the principles. James H. Giffen, director of the US–USSR Trade and Economic Council, considers the principles unacceptable. The Slepak faction, according to Skelly, insists that its goal is not to block joint ventures but to inform businesses of the political risks. A Senate resolution called on the President to instruct his department heads to begin talks with allied nations about the security dangers of untied lending to the former Soviet bloc.

Recruitment Experiences

In the following example the foreign company was considered by an indigenous Japanese company to be an unethical aggressor. The foreign company imported an American perspective with which all of its actions were totally justified.

Ore-Ida's Recruitment Experience

Heinz Ore-Ida management sought the advice of McKinsey and Co. to assist the company in the recruitment of a sales manager. The company was advised to find someone who understood consumer products and could speak English; he would be required to communicate well with the home office and expatriate management. As a result, Heinz went to three of the largest head-hunting operations in Japan then and briefed them accordingly. Heinz was uncomfortable with the available choices. The majority of the applicants had experience with one or more foreign companies, but these encounters had been failures, and even if the applicant spoke good English it was unlikely that he or she had any knowledge of the frozen food industry—a necessary criterion. Eventually, Heinz decided to change the job specification and asked one of the recruiters to locate a frozen food specialist, regardless of whether he could speak English. In the event, a candidate with twenty-three years' experience in the business was identified in a fishing company that was in decline and who, quite by chance, also had a background in the frozen food industry. Once hired, he was able to raid his previous company and recruit five or six of the most talented young people. In this way, Ore-Ida acquired a virtually ready-made sale force, but also the less welcome reputation of being a corporate raider.

Subsequently, the managing director of the fishing company called the managing director of Heinz Ore-Ida and requested an interview. The meeting that ensued crystallized some of the key cultural differences between US (Western) and Japanese management. The Heinz Ore-Ida version is:

I went to talk to him. He was perplexed and said, 'What are you doing?' I said, 'I do not understand.' And he said, 'Why are you taking all my people? I have spent years training these people, I have built them into qualified managers and you just come in and take them away.' I said, 'Well you know I have a problem. I have got to build a business and I have to build it fast in order to get the returns my company needs to justify the expense of setting up this business. If I come in here and hire all the young people and spend ten years having them go through the learning process, what good is that going to do me? I am not going to be around here to justify my own existence.'

He could not understand how I could come and steal his people, even if his business was in decline and his company was paying on the 30th percentile of the food industry at the time. I obtained good people and I gave them a chance to run a branded business with a big marketing budget. These guys, who had been frustrated for so long, all of a sudden had an opportunity to have some independence and freedom.

That was 1984, and now there is an awful lot more personnel movement. Young people are finding out that with the [Japanese] seniority system working the way it has in the past, bringing a group of people in from the same university class at the same time, doesn't give them [the students] anything really responsible to do until about fifteen years after they have joined the company. They let the stars rise to the top. That's a tough system; people do not want to wait that long. Within fifteen months from the time that we launched our business, we had a 38% share in the product category. Furthermore, we were driving the category at double digit annual growth.

CONCLUSION

We have examined three issues: gift giving, joint ventures and recruitment. Each of these gave rise to ethical debate depending upon the cultural perspective of the critics. Yet in each case there were two sides to the ethical equation, which highlights the problem that often only one side is assessed.

Much energy is being expended—in particular by the US government—in exhorting Japan to be more like the West. However, it is too easy to be partisan, based upon one's own cultural perspectives. In any situation where business ethics is a matter for concern, it can be more efficacious to view the issue through a different cultural lens from one's own.

NOTE

1. Dale (1986: 14) characterized *nihonjinron* (talking about Japan) as 'the commercialized expression of Japanese nationalism ... it gathers within its ample embrace writings of high seriousness imbued with deep, often specious, erudition, all the facile dicta of interpretative journalism.'

REFERENCES

Andrews, K.R. 1989. Ethics in Practice. *Harvard Business Review* 67: 99-104.

Becker, H. and D.J. Fritzsche. 1987. Business Ethics: A Cross-Cultural Comparison of Managers' Attitudes. *Journal of Business Ethics* 6: 289-95.

Beggs, J.M. and M.S. Lane. 1989. Corporate Goal Structures and Business Students: A Comparative Study of Values. *Journal of Business Ethics* 8: 471-8.

Berg, S.V., J. Duncan and P. Friedman. 1982. *Joint Venture Strategies and Corporate Innovation.* Cambridge, MA: Oelgeschlager, Gunn and Hain.

Bernstein, L. 1965. Joint Ventures in the Light of Recent Antitrust Developments. *Antitrust Bulletin* 10: 25-9.

Boyle, S. 1968. An Estimation of the Number and Size Distribution of Domestic Joint Subsidiaries. *Antitrust Law and Economic Review* (Spring): 81-92.

Dale, P.N. 1986. *The Myth of Japanese Uniqueness.* London: Croom Helm.

Franko, L.G. 1973. *Joint International Business Ventures in Developing Countries.* Geneva: Centre d'Etudes Industrielles.

Fusfeld, D.R. 1958. Joint Subsidiaries in the Iron and Steel Industry. *American Economic Review* 48: 578-87.

Hall, R.D. 1988. Intricacies of People Problems Abroad. *Journal of Management Consulting* 4: 23-31.

Harrigan, K.R. 1987. Joint Ventures: A Mechanism for Creating Strategic Change. In *The Management of Strategic Change.* Ed. Pettigrew. London: Blackwell: 195-230.

Hennart, J.F. 1988. A Transactions Costs Theory of Equity Joint Ventures. *Strategic Management Journal* 9: 361-74.

Hoffman, W.M. 1989. The Cost of a Corporate Conscience. *Business and Society Review* 69 (Spring): 46-7.

Kane, R. 1981. A Ritzy Joint Venture That Works. *The Journal of the ACCJ* (November).

Kent, D.H. 1991. Joint Ventures vs Non-joint Ventures: An Empirical Investigation. *Strategic Management Journal* 12: 387-93.

Kilburn, D. and R. Wilk. 1988. Japan Makes it Personal. *Winds* (August): 40-5.

McDonald, G.M. and R.A. Zepp. 1988. Ethical Perceptions of Hong Kong Chinese Business Managers. *Journal of Business*

Ethics 7: 835-45.

Mead, W.J. 1973. *Joint Ventures—Anti-competitive and Pro-competitive Effects.* Testimony before the United States Senate Committee on Insular Affairs, Special Subcommittee on Integrated Oil Operations, Market Performance in the Petroleum Industry. United States Senate (abstract).

Pfeffer, J. and P. Nowak. 1976. Joint Ventures and Interorganisational Interdependence. *Administrative Science Quarterly* 21: 398-418.

Schofield, M.J. 1988. What Does the Consumer Want? *Look Japan* 33: 21-4.

Skelly, J. 1988. A Code of Conduct for the American Partners. *Across the Board* 25: 37-8.

Tsalikis, J. and O. Nwachukwu. 1988. Cross-Cultural Business Ethics: Ethical Beliefs Difference Between Blacks and Whites. *Journal of Business Ethics* 7: 745-54.

United Nations Centre on Transnational Corporations (UNCTC). 1987. *Arrangements Between Joint Venture Partners in Developing Countries.* UNCTC Advisory Studies Series B. New York: UN.

Wright, J.W. 1989. What is the Status on Ethics in American Business? *Bottomline* 6: 11-4.

5

THE RELEVANCE OF EQUITY VALUES IN EASTERN CULTURES

David A. Ralston, Lee P. Stepina, Yu Kai-Cheng, Paul A. Fadil and Robert H. Terpstra

INTRODUCTION

Over two decades ago, Hofstede (1980a) asked the question, 'Do American theories apply abroad?' Many researchers have approached this issue by testing straightforward translations of American instruments to determine whether the same theoretical relationships hold in India, Britain, Hong Kong or wherever. Conclusions range from support for the 'universality' of Western theories to results which suggest that they are not valid elsewhere. The latter papers invariably conclude with admonitions for Westerners to change their parochial ways.

Meanwhile, American companies go overseas and continue to use 'home-logic' to run their overseas operations. In some sense, academics are to blame for this state of affairs through the ethnocentric education we provide in our business schools and through our failure to modify our theories to provide useful guides to managers operating in non-American and especially non-Western cultures. We have, on one hand, done an excellent job of describing cultural differences. On the other hand, we also can find abundant literature on the failure of Western theories, developed primarily in America, to apply outside the United States. Yet, we have failed adequately to develop and test theories which bring together culture and management research. In short, we have answered Hofstede's first question on applicability of our theories but have failed to explain how our theories can be modified and broadened to provide effective tools for international managers. One of the most critical skills that managers can possess is their ability to motivate their subordinates. While intrinsic factors can be powerful motivators, a manager only has limited power to help a subordinate achieve intrinsic satisfaction. Thus, the central motivational factor under a manager's control is the allocation of extrinsic rewards. Rewards normally are designed to motivate performance and reduce turnover and absenteeism. However, should the reward allocation be perceived as unfair or inappropriate, the opposite may result. Since individuals in organizations typically work in groups, or at least in the presence of other employees, the value of the reward allocation system is judged in terms of its overall acceptability to all.

The consequences of reward allocation have been studied mainly in light of equity theory, which has been in the mainstream of the reward allocation research since Adams' initial work in 1963 (Adams 1963, 1965; Adams and Freedman 1976; Walster et al. 1978). However, the majority of the research on equity has been conducted in the West. Not until the last decade did cross-cultural research begin to investigate whether equity theory is culturally universal, culturally specific or applicable in some modified form (Mahler et al. 1981; Bond et al. 1982; Bond and Wang 1983).

The purpose of this paper is to investigate the cross-cultural validity of equity theory by focusing on the equity–equality dichotomy in Western and Eastern cultures. Based on this examination, the authors will derive a more global, pervasive interpretation of equity theory which incorporates culture into its construct. This view illustrates how cultural values affect the perception of important equity variables, and, in turn, have an impact on how individuals evaluate and react. This paper is an attempt not only to identify and evaluate the impact of cultural variables on equity theory, but to provide a more realistic representation of the model, thus leading to a more applicable and practical framework.

THE TRADITIONAL BASES OF REWARD ALLOCATION

Three bases of reward allocation have been identified (Deutsch 1975). Equity has been the most frequently studied of the three. Using equity, rewards are allocated to individuals according to their performance or 'inputs'. Individuals compare the exchange they receive to that received by a significant other to determine fairness. Thus, as one's performance increases, the rewards must also increase for that situation to be viewed as equitable, *ceteris paribus* (Walster et al. 1978).

Equality is a second means of reward allocation. According to the equality philosophy, all individuals are rewarded equally, without regard to their performance or inputs (ibid.). An example of this is sales commissions being distributed equally among all members of a sales team that have worked together to secure a contract.

The third base of reward allocation is need. In this instance, rewards are allocated to all individuals according to their level of need. In other words, the greater the need, the higher the reward (Elliott and Meeker 1984). For example, a company that pays married men with families more than single employees is employing a need-based reward allocation philosophy. Since the focus of reward systems in the West has been upon equity, the emphasis of our research has been upon equity theory. Thus, we shall use this philosophy as the starting point for our investigation of reward allocation preferences in the Eastern culture.

PREMISES OF EQUITY THEORY

The underlying premise of equity theory is that individuals should be rewarded in proportion to what they produce. As such, equity theory is a social and interpersonal comparison concept. To operationalize this concept, individuals compare their outcome–input ratio with that of a referent person or group, as illustrated in Figure 1. If there is equity, then the individual will be satisfied. If there is inequity, then the individual will find the situation stressful and be motivated to reduce this inequity.

$$\frac{\text{OUTCOME/person}}{\text{INPUT/person}} = \frac{\text{OUTCOME/comparison other}}{\text{INPUT/comparison other}}$$

Figure 1   Equity Theory Equation

The two types of inequity that are experienced are overequity and underequity. In overequity situations, individuals perceive themselves as being treated better than those with whom they are comparing themselves. The converse is true in the underequity situation (Lawler 1968 a, b). Research has shown that the ability to tolerate an inequitable situation is better in the case of overequity than in the case of underequity.

The research findings on equity theory have primarily been obtained by sampling individuals in Western cultures. However, are the cultural norms in the Eastern culture consistent with the Western view of equity theory? Since the tenets of reward allocation are based on the assumption that equity is perceived as the fairest norm, can these consequences be valid if other bases, such as equality, are perceived as more fair? Based on these questions, it becomes essential to study thoroughly which aspects of Eastern culture affect reward allocations. We begin by briefly identifying relevant tenets of Eastern values, and then compare and contrast these principles with Western values.

EASTERN CULTURAL VALUES

Traditional Chinese values, specifically convictions of Confucianism, are important to consider in this regard because they provide the foundation of Eastern cultural values. Besides Chinese societies such as mainland China, Hong Kong and Taiwan, traditional Confucian values also affect Japan, Korea, the Southeast Asian countries of Singapore, Malaysia, and Vietnam, and overseas Chinese around the world.

Many Chinese cultural values are largely formed and created from interpersonal relationships, and can be traced to the Confucian value of relational orientation (Kindel 1983; Yau 1987). Regarding reward allocation, the following aspects of Chinese values should be considered.

Respect for Authority

Confucius' Five Cardinal Relations, which include relationship between friends, teach Chinese that they have an obligation to treat friends in a truly friendly way.

Interdependence

The Chinese value doing favours. Favours are regarded as social investment, inasmuch as reciprocity for these favours is highly expected. As the following Chinese proverb notes: If you honour me a linear foot, I should in turn honour you ten feet. Besides, the Chinese emphasize social consciousness, mutual dependence, harmony and development of a social-self rather than a private-self. That is, their focus is upon their role in their group(s).

Group Orientation

It is Chinese to sacrifice oneself for the benefit of the group (Hsu 1970). However, the Chinese are only group-oriented toward the social units or in-groups in which relationships have been developed, most notably the extended family. As such, they are more motivated toward achieving the goal of this group than their own personal goals. However, they also can be quite suspicious and cold towards those not a part of the in-group with whom relationships have not been established (Hsu 1970).

This group orientation is tied to the idea of face. *Mianzi* is one type of face as classified by Hu (1944). It stands for the kind of prestige that is emphasized (that is, developing a reputation by getting ahead in life). Though the Chinese are always under a strong constraint to maintain their *mianzi*, they also endeavour to avoid causing others to lose *mianzi* since the Chinese are group-oriented towards their respective in-group. From the teachings of Confucius comes the desire to live in harmony and avoid social embarrassment and conflict.

There is evidence that the majority of the traditional Chinese cultural values are still held in modern days. Yang (1979) revealed that while there was a change in the hierarchy of the value system, the majority of the traditional Chinese values are still held. Yang (1981) later showed that the Chinese are still highly socially oriented, though the more modernized individuals do tend to be somewhat less so.

A COMPARISON OF EASTERN AND WESTERN VALUES

A sharp contrast can be found between Chinese and Western values. In a seminal study, Hofstede (1980b) surveyed over 100,000 IBM workers, located in forty countries, in an empirical search for value dimensions over which countries vary. Through a factor analytical treatment of country value measures, Hofstede derived four cultural dimensions related to basic anthropological and societal issues.

The first dimension was labelled Power Distance. This was defined as the 'extent to which less powerful members of institutions and organizations accept that power is distributed unequally' (Hofstede 1980b: 45). The second dimension was classified as Uncertainty Avoidance. This was defined as the 'extent to which people feel threatened by ambiguous situations, and have created beliefs and institutions to avoid these' (ibid.: 45). The third dimension was labelled Individualism versus Collectivism. On one end of this bipolar continuum, Individualism was defined as the 'extent to which people look only after themselves and their family'; whereas, on the other hand, Collectivism was defined as 'a situation in which people belong to in-groups or collectivities which are supposed to look after them in exchange for their loyalty' (ibid.: 45). The final dimension was labelled Masculinity–Femininity. Masculinity was defined as a 'situation in which the dominant values in society are money, success, and things'; while Femininity was defined as 'a situation in which the dominant values are caring for others and the quality of life' (ibid.: 46).

Collectivism and Individualism

From these derived values, the individualism–collectivism dimension clearly contrasts the differences between Eastern and Western cultures. This specific dimension has been employed numerous times when applying Western theories to Eastern cultures and a perusal of the literature indicates that it is particularly relevant to a discussion of reward allocation. Research continues to support the divergence of Eastern and Western values, especially along this dimension.

Countries or areas of Chinese origin (Hong Kong, Singapore and Taiwan) were on the collectivistic end of the scale in Hofstede's study. In the Eastern culture, only Japanese respondent scores were near the middle of the continuum. China was not included in the Hofstede study. The United States had the highest score on individualism in the Hofstede (1980b) study. The scores of the above countries are shown in Table 1.

Table 1   Selected Individualism/Collectivism Scores from Hofstede's Research

Country	Individualism Score	Rank
USA	91	1
Japan	46	22
Hong Kong	25	37
Singapore	20	40
Taiwan	17	44

Source: Hofstede and Bond (1988).

Implications

The most straightforward implication that can be drawn from the above discussion is that a collectivist Eastern society will prefer equality-based reward allocations. Further support is provided by Swap and Rubin (1983), who found that subjects with higher scores on their interpersonal orientation scale used the equality norm to a greater extent, and the subjects who had lower scores were more likely to use the equity norm. Thus, collectivist cultures, where interpersonal sensitivity is high, and harmony, solidarity and cohesion are more favourably valued, should prefer equality to equity. To further understand this dichotomy, we now focus our attention upon the reward allocation in Eastern cultures.

REWARD ALLOCATION PREFERENCES IN EASTERN COUNTRIES

A literature review identified several studies on reward allocation that involved Eastern countries. Chu and Yang's (1969) study used only Taiwanese Chinese subjects, and as such was not cross-cultural. However, their findings were the first to show that when the Chinese subjects' input was low, they preferred equity, and when their input was high, they preferred equality.

Research on the cross-cultural effects of reward allocation preferences of individuals in Eastern countries began during the last decade. Leung and Bond (1982) and Bond et al. (1982) found that Hong Kong Chinese subjects used the equality norm more than did American subjects in allocations to in-group members. Leung and Bond (1984) suggested that when the subject's input was high or the recipient was an in-group member, Chinese subjects followed the equality norm more than did American subjects. However, Chinese subjects followed the equity norm more closely than did American subjects when the subject's input was low or when the recipient was an out-group member.

Mahler et al. (1981) found that the Japanese perceived equality as being a more fair reward system than did their American counterparts. When compared with Australians, the Japanese consistently favoured an equal distribution over an equitable distribution of rewards as being fairer of two alternatives (Mann et al. 1985; Kashima et al. 1988). However, Kashima's study also investigated the basis of need and found that the age of the worker was a more important determinant of fairness judgements for Japanese than for Australians, and that the debt of a worker was a more important determinant for Australians than for Japanese. Leung and Park (1986) found that Koreans, in comparison with Americans, evaluated equality more favourably and equity less favourably. Kim et al. (1990) also found that US subjects, being more individualistic, preferred equity more, whereas Korean subjects, who were less individualistic, preferred equity less. However, all subjects supported a universal reward allocation pattern that the approximated the equity norm.

Apart from these studies, which focused on Eastern cultures

with Confucian values, two other studies with Asian subjects found somewhat different results. First, Marin (1984) revealed that for both Indonesians and Americans, an equitable allocation was also perceived as fairer than one based on equality. They chose the equity norm more than the equality norm. However, there is no indication that Indonesians are collectivistic. Second, Berman et al. (1985) showed that both American and Indian subjects chose to distribute on the basis of equity in positive resources conditions, but on the basis of need in negative resources conditions. Both cultures favoured equity over need in time of abundance, but they refused to worsen the plight of the needy by equitably distributing in times of scarcity. This similar preference could be attributed to the fact that Indians tend to be individualistic. In Hofstede's (1980b) study, the Indian individualism index was 56, which may be compared to the scores of the Chinese cultures and the United States in Table 1.

IMPLICATIONS

Based on the literature reviewed above, equity, as described in Western research, has been inappropriately applied to Eastern cultures. Due to their relative positions on the Individualism– Collectivism continuum, members of Eastern cultures prefer rewards to be allocated equally to individuals based on membership in the group, while members of Western cultures prefer an equitable distribution of rewards based on the performance of the individual. Although this dichotomy may be a parsimonious explanation of reward distribution in Eastern versus Western cultures, its simplicity limits its applicability and, in many situations, renders it ineffective.

The equity–equality dichotomy has two major limitations. First, even though Eastern cultures tend to be collectivistic and reward equally within the group, reward allocation at the group level has been relatively ignored. Hsu's (1970) description of differential treatment of in-group versus out-group members supports the notion that while equality may be an acceptable form of reward allocation among group members, as different groups compete for scarce resources, equality may have its limits, at least in Chinese society.

This limitation suggests that the collectivist-equality, individualist-equity classification may fail to fully describe the complexity of the relationship between culture and reward allocation. Second, although the dimension of individuality–collectivism can be easily incorporated in the above framework, the equity–equality dichotomy does not and cannot include other important cultural values (masculinity–femininity, power distance and uncertainty avoidance) into its framework. These limitations raise serious questions about the accuracy of this dichotomy, as well as its subsequent application beyond a very limited scope.

REFORMULATION

The question now becomes, can the equity–equality categorization be synthesized and reformulated into a pervasive framework so it can effectively include other cultural values into its paradigm? In other words, at a certain level, can equality be viewed as a special case of the equity formulation and, if so, will this new interpretation be able to go beyond the individualism–collectivism dimension? In order to utilize culture as an important variable in this new theoretical structure, we must examine how cultural values impact each individual component of reward allocation. The authors argue that value differences between Eastern and Western cultures will impact the choice and perceived value of inputs, outcomes, referent other, and responses to inequity. Although the present paper focuses only on the former two aspects of equity theory, responses to inequity and choice of referent other are equally fertile grounds for future research.

Since equity evaluations are built on the comparison of one's input and outcome ratio relative to a comparison other's, the choices of each component of the model are totally up to the individual. For example, one person may view age as an input while another may not perceive age to be important at all. How one determines these inputs or assigns value to them is culturally based. Furthermore, some factors can be assigned as either inputs or outcomes (Weick 1969). Challenging work, for instance, could be viewed as an input by a worker who sees it as requiring greater effort and, thus, justifying higher outcomes. On the other hand, another worker may view challenging work as a positive outcome which occurs as a result of his or her high level of inputs. It can be argued that both of the above mechanisms are at work in Eastern equity conceptions.

EASTERN VERSUS WESTERN CULTURES

The key to understanding Eastern perceptions of equity are the concepts of group membership and collectivism. While Western research has limited its list of inputs to factors such as effort, experience, and education, the Chinese have a somewhat different list of input factors or may attach different weights to mutually agreed upon inputs. Foremost on their Chinese list of inputs is group membership. Group membership influences the formulation of equity perceptions by directly leading to entitlement to a certain set of group-based outcomes.

Group membership does, however, make some demands on input requirements on the individual in order to maintain their share of outcomes. Possible inputs include effort, loyalty, support, respect and adherence to group norms. Clearly, the nature of the group will determine the input requirements. Family groups may require no more than adherence to the head of the family, while voluntary groups such as social groups and work groups may have more complex input requirements.

On the outcome side of the equation, Eastern concerns may also be broader. Besides rewards such as pay and other material factors, Eastern conceptions of appropriate outcomes most certainly focus on group-based rewards such as acceptance and harmony. Harmony with other members of the group is a trade-off for higher material returns suggested by Western equity formulations.

The above explanation is consistent with Leung and Bond's (1984) findings on differences between allocation rules for in-groups versus out-group members. When evaluating the fairness of a comparison-other who is outside the group, the role group Input/ Outcomes factors identified previously does not come into play. The out-group comparison person does not bring group membership to the individuals' list of relevant inputs nor is the outsider entitled to the outcomes associated with group membership. Thus, relations between the individual and the outsider can be explained using the traditional Adams equity formulation.

However, when the comparison person is a member of the same group as the individual, the group's inputs and rewards become part of the equation that balances equal group membership with equal reward allocation. Since the limits of group inputs and outcomes extends only as far as the membership of the group, a relevant concern becomes perceptions of group membership. In other words, to access the relationship accurately, it is now necessary to know the importance of specific groups to the individual.

The relevance of group membership will vary based on culture. More traditional rural cultures would emphasize familial groups, while urban cosmopolitan cultures would focus more on work and social groups. Thus, rural Chinese from farming backgrounds would use family comparisons, while urban Chinese and Japanese would emphasize work group or organization-based comparisons. The level from which rewards are being allocated serves as a focusing mechanisms for these comparisons.

BEYOND COLLECTIVISM–INDIVIDUALISM

Although the above discussion has focused on equity formulations in collectivist cultures, collectivism is but one cultural dimension that can affect equity equations. In the following section, broader conceptions of possible inputs and outcomes are applied to several of Hofstede's cultural dimensions.

Masculinity–Femininity

Prior to the women's rights movements of the 1960s and 1970s, many US managers devalued the inputs of women to the job and subsequently paid female-dominated jobs less. Hofstede's masculinity–femininity scale, which more accurately reflects perceptions of women's role in society, presents an index of these beliefs in various countries. A highly masculine society like Japan would tend to view maleness as an input and to evaluate male–female salary differences for the same work as fair. In this type of society, masculine values such as assertiveness, aggressiveness and materialism may be viewed as valued inputs to obtain desired outcomes. These outcomes may include money, power, or an upwardly mobile career path. A highly feminine society may view need, positive relationships, or family time as potential inputs, while regarding quality of life as a positive outcome. In other words, in a feminine society, an individual may perceive a quality of life increase if he increases the time spent with his family.

Power Distance

Similarly, societies with high power distances (Singapore, Hong Kong), where differences in social classes are accepted, might view membership in a ruling elite as an appropriate input to the much higher outcome achieved relative to the peasant class. Another example of this is the 'caste' system in India. Consistent with the group membership concepts discussed above, place in hierarchy and, at its extreme, birth into a royal family, entitle certain individuals to more rewards with no problems of inequity. However, when cultural changes undermine the legitimacy of such hierarchies, violent equity restoration programmes may occur. So, in high power distance countries, social class or the position held in an organization can be seen as input which may necessitate higher outcomes. In countries with a low power distance, the ability of a subordinate to interact on an equal level with his supervisors, through suggesting ideas or even socializing outside the organization, may often lead to higher outcomes.

Uncertainty Avoidance

Societies that have a high level of uncertainty avoidance will tend to view the long-term stability of a situation as a desirable outcome. Examples of pleasant outcomes in a society that promotes stability include a steady job, comfortable salary, long-term employment, written job requirements, promotion by tenure, etc. A potential input that would facilitate these outcomes is to do only what is explicitly required by the job and nothing more. Since extra effort does not automatically lead to reward, high uncertainty avoidance individuals only partake in organizational activities that they believe will lead to tangible rewards. Also, since these cultures find it difficult to deal with ambiguity, promotion (outcome) of individuals is exercised by employing 'concrete' inputs: age, tenure, obvious performance achievements, etc.

Low uncertainty avoidance societies will be more achievement-oriented and less apt to stay in unpleasant situations for long periods of time. Some possible inputs may include hard work, risk taking, and abstract goals, because they are used to dealing with ambiguity. Desirable outcomes may include challenging work, autonomy, power and materialistic acquisitions. Organizations in these societies promote their workers based on such abstract illustrations of superior performance as effort, some evidence of ability, or interpersonal skills.

CONCLUSION

It has been argued that the prescription of equity–equality as the standard for evaluating the fairness of exchanges in Western and Eastern societies fails to consider the cultural biases built into equity theory as applied in Western societies. By expanding possible inputs and outcomes to include culturally based requirements and rewards, it is possible to apply equity theory to non-Western cultures. However, empirical tests of cultural value effects on all components of the theory are needed before the ability of equity theory to explain motivation and behaviour validly can be determined.

The framework presented in this paper is an attempt to fill a small part of a huge gap in cross-cultural research. This gap concerns the ability to relate differences in cultural variables to major organizational issues. The proposed interpretation of the equity–equality dichotomy provides a mechanism by which cultural values play a vital role in the development of this construct. The strong theoretical foundation of equity theory, fortified through years of Western research, combined with this cross-cultural reformulation, should widen the scope of its application, thus making it a more practical and useful theory.

REFERENCES

Adams, J.S. 1963. Toward an Understanding of Inequity. *Journal of Abnormal & Social Psychology* 67: 422-36.

Adams, J.S. 1965. Inequity in Social Exchange. In *Advances in Experimental Social Psychology* 2. Ed. Berkowitz. New York: Academic Press.

Adams, J.S. and S. Freedman. 1976. Equity Theory Revisited: Comments and Annotated Bibliography. In *Advances in Experimental Social Psychology* 9: 43-90. Ed. Berkowitz. New York: Academic Press.

Berman, J.J., V. Murphy-Berman and P. Singh. 1985. Cross-cultural Similarities and Differences in Perception of Fairness. *Journal of Cross-Cultural Psychology* 16 (1): 55-67.

Bond, M.H., K. Leung and K.C. Wan. 1982. How does Cultural Collectivism Operate? The Impact of Task and Maintenance Contributions on Reward Distribution. *Journal of Cross-Cultural Psychology* 13: 186-200.

Bond, M.H. and S.H. Wang. 1983. Aggressive Behavior in Chinese Society: The Problem of Maintaining Order and Harmony. In *Global Perspectives on Aggression*. Ed. Goldstein and Segall. New York: Pergamon.

Chu, J.L. and K.S. Yang. 1969. The Effects of Relative Performance and Individual Modernity on Distributive Behavior among Chinese College Students. *Bulletin of the Institute of Ethnology of Academia Sinica* 41: 79-95 (In Chinese).

Deutsch, M. 1975. Equity, Equality, and Need: What Determines Which Value will be Used as the Basis of Distributive Justice? *Journal of Social Issues* 31: 137-49.

Elliott, G.C. and B.F. Meeker. 1984. Modifiers of the Equity Effect: Group Outcome and Causes for Individual Performance. *Journal of Personality and Social Psychology* 64: 586-97.

Hofstede, G. 1980a. Motivation, Leadership, and Organisation: Do American Theories Apply Abroad? *Organisational Dynamics* 9: 42-63.

Hofstede, G. 1980b. *Culture's Consequences: International Differences in Work-related Values*. Beverly Hills, CA: Sage.

Hofstede, G. and M.H. Bond. 1988. The Confucius Connection:

From Cultural Roots to Economic Growth. *Organisational Dynamics* 16 (4): 4-21.

Hsu, F.L.K. 1970. *Americans and Chinese: Passage to Differences.* Honolulu: The University Press of Hawaii.

Hu, H.C. 1944. The Chinese Concept of Face. *American Anthropologist* 46 (January-March): 45-64.

Kashima, Y., M. Siegal, K. Tanaka and H. Isaka. 1988. Universalism in Lay Conceptions of Distributive Justice: A Cross-cultural Examination. *International Journal of Psychology* 23: 51-64.

Kim, K.I., H.J. Park and N. Suzuki. 1990. Reward Allocations in the United States, Japan, and Korea: A Comparison of Individualistic and Collectivistic Cultures. *Academy of Management Journal* 33 (1): 188-98.

Kindel, T.I. 1983. A Partial Theory of Chinese Consumer Behavior: Marketing Strategy Implications. *Hong Kong Journal of Business Management* 1: 97-110.

Lawler, E.E. 1968a. Effects of Hourly Overpayment on Productivity and Work Quality. *Journal of Personality and Social Psychology* 10: 306-14.

Lawler, E.E. 1968b. Equity Theory as a Predictor of Productivity and Work Quality. *Psychological Bulletin* 70: 596-610.

Leung, K. and M.H. Bond. 1982. How Chinese and Americans Reward Task-related Contributions: A Preliminary Study. *Psychologia* 25: 32-9.

Leung, K. and M.H. Bond. 1984. The Impact of Cultural Collectivism on Reward Allocation. *Journal of Personality and Social Psychology* 47: 793-804.

Leung, K. and H.J. Park. 1986. Effects of Interactional Goal on Choice Allocation Rule: Cross-national Study. *Organisational Behavior and Human Decision Process* 37: 111-20.

Mahler, I., L. Greenberg and H. Hayashi. 1981. A Comparative Study of Rules of Justice, Japanese versus American. *Psychologia* 24: 1-8.

Mann, L., M. Radford and C. Kanagawa. 1985. Cross-cultural Differences in Children's Use of Decision Rules: A Comparison between Japan and Australia. *Journal of Personality and Social Psychology* 49 (6): 1557-64.

Marin, G. 1984. The Preference for Equity when Judging the

Attractiveness and Fairness of an Allocator: The Role of Familiarity and Culture. *Journal of Personality and Social Psychology* 125 (5): 543-9.

Swap, W.C. and J.Z. Rubin. 1983. Measurement of Interpersonal Orientation. *Journal of Personality and Social Psychology* 44: 208-19.

Walster, E., G.W. Walster and E. Berscheid. 1978. *Equity, Theory and Research.* Boston: Allyn & Bacon.

Weick, K.E. 1969. *The Social Psychology of Organizing.* Reading, MA: Addison-Wesley.

Yang, K.S. 1979. Research on Chinese National Character in Modern Psychology. In *Modernisation and Change of Value.* Ed. Chung et al. Taipei: Thought and Word Association.

Yang, K.S. 1981. Social Orientation and Individual Modernity among Chinese Students in Taiwan. *Journal of Social Psychology* 113: 159-70.

Yau, H.M. 1987. *Chinese Cultural Values and Marketing Implications.* Unpublished manuscript.

6

AN OUTSIDER'S VIEW OF THE EAST ASIAN MIRACLE: LESSONS AND QUESTIONS

Georges Enderle

INTRODUCTION

A miracle is something extraordinary and transcends our usual understanding of the world and how it works. We are struck that the miracle occurs against our expectations. According to our 'normal' experience of the world, we consider the miracle exceptional. By putting it into the category of 'non-classifiables', we maintain and do not question our traditional mental classification scheme. Thus we cannot learn anything from miracles and questions about them hardly ever find answers, if they are asked at all; otherwise, miracles would lose their enigmatic character and no longer qualify as such.

By contrast, when miracles stimulate reflection on our preconceived notions of the 'normal', there is an opportunity to learn some lessons, which, in turn, provoke new questions. That is what I will attempt to do, from the perspective of an outsider, in discussing the East Asian miracle. Although I have some knowledge about recent developments in East Asia and have travelled quite extensively in Japan, I consider myself an 'outsider', albeit one who is very familiar with Europe, has a strong interest in 'Third World' countries, and now lives in the United States. In other words, I would like to explore 'new territory' and ask what it means for the understanding of international business ethics.

HIGH PERFORMANCE OF EIGHT ASIAN ECONOMIES

In its Policy Research Report, *The East Asian Miracle*, the World Bank (1993a: 2) identifies eight High-Performing Asian Economies (HPAEs) which share some economic characteristics that set them apart from most other developing countries. These HPAEs are Japan (124 million people[1]); the four 'Tigers': Hong Kong (6 million), the Republic of Korea (44 million), Singapore (3 million), Taiwan (21 million); and the three newly industrializing economies (NIEs) of Southeast Asia: Indonesia (184 million), Malaysia (19 million), and Thailand (58 million), making a total population of approximately 459 million.[2]

I would like to draw attention to three features of the East Asian Miracle: the unusual combination of high growth with declining income inequality, the effective fight against poverty, and the export push strategies that may be interpreted as a pro-active orientation towards international business. These features are of particular interest from the European and North American perspective because they contrast, at least to some extent, with the current situation in these parts of the world: low and essentially 'jobless' growth (that is, even when output increases, increase in employment lags way behind; see UNDP 1993: 34ff.), increased inequality and poverty, and high expectations about export strategies for solving domestic problems. Of course, these features would have to be analysed in a broader context: first in the economic one (by studies such as those of the World Bank), and also in the political and cultural one (some questions of which I will discuss in the third part of this paper).

Rapid Growth with Equity

Although the eight HPAEs are highly diverse in natural resources, population, culture, and economic policy, they have in common rapid, sustained growth between 1960 and 1990, in itself unusual among developing countries, combined with highly equal income distribution. Figure 1 shows their high GDP growth per capita percentage and their low income inequality, measured by the ratio of the income shares of the richest 20% and the poorest 20% of the population. The World Bank Report says:

Figure 1 Income Inequality and Growth of GDP, 1965-89

GPD growth per capita (%)

Note: Income inequality is measured by the ratio of the income shares of the richest 20% and the poorest 20% of the population.
Source: World Bank (1993:31).

When the East Asian economies are divided by speed of growth, the distribution of income is substantially more equal in the fast growers ... For the eight HPAEs, rapid growth and declining inequality have been shared virtues ... The developing HPAEs clearly outperform other middle-income economies in that they have both lower levels of inequality and higher levels of growth. Moreover, ... improvements in income distribution generally coincided with periods of rapid growth (World Bank 1992: 30; see also 72-4).

This combination of rapid growth and decreasing inequality is an extraordinary fact and deserves to be called a 'miracle'. It runs counter to the widely held economic theory that economic growth

Table 1   Changes in Selected Indicators of Poverty

Economy	Year	Percentage of population below the poverty line			Number of poor (millions)		
		First Year	Last year	Change	First year	Last year	Percent change
HPAEs							
Indonesia	1972–82	58	17	-41	67.9	30.0	-56
Malaysia[a]	1973–87	37	14	-23	4.1	2.2	-46
Singapore	1972–82	31	10	-21	0.7	0.2	-71
Thailand[a,b]	1962–86	59	26	-30	16.7	13.6	-18
Others							
Brazil[a,b]	1960–80	50	21	-29	36.1	25.4	29.6
Colombia	1971–88	41	25	-16	8.9	7.5	-15.7
Costa Rica[a]	1971–86	45	24	-19	0.8	0.6	-25
Cote d'Ivoire	1985–86	30	31	1	3.1	3.3	6.4
India	1972–83	54	43	-9	311.4	315.0	1
Morocco	1970–84	43	34	-9	6.6	7.4	12
Pakistan	1962–84	54	23	-31	26.5	21.3	-19
Sri Lanka[a]	1963–82	37	27	-10	3.9	4.1	5

Note: This table uses economy-specific poverty lines. Official or commonly used poverty lines have been used when available. In other cases the poverty line has been set at 30% of mean income or expenditure. The range of poverty lines, expressed in terms of expenditure per household member and in terms of purchasing power parity (ppp) dollars, is approximately $300–$700 a year in 1985 except for Costa Rica ($960), Malaysia ($1,420) and Singapore ($860). Unless otherwise indicated, the table is based on expenditure per household member.
a.   Measures for these entries use income rather than expenditure.
b.   Measures for these entries are by household rather than by household member.
Source: World Bank (1993:33).

be necessarily linked with increasing inequality.[3] Rather, the East Asian economies prove the contrary is possible. Moreover, these astonishing examples show that lower income groups do not have to wait for the 'trickle-down' effects of economic growth from the top of the income distribution.

Substantial Poverty Reduction

Related to this observation, although not identical with it, is the fact that a substantial reduction of poverty has taken place in the HPAEs (see Table 1; also Johansen 1993). For the years to come, the World Bank estimates that poverty in these countries will further decrease, significantly more in relative and absolute terms than in Sub-Saharan and Latin American countries (see Table 2).

Table 2   Poverty in the Developing World, 1985–2000

Region	Percentage of population below the poverty line			Number of poor (millions)		
	1985	1990	2000	1985	1990	2000
All developing countries	30.5	29.7	24.1	1,051	1,133	1,107
South Asia	51.8	49.0	36.9	532	562	511
East Asia	13.2	11.3	4.2	182	169	73
Sub Saharan Africa	47.6	47.8	49.7	184	216	304
Middle East and North Africa	30.6	33.1	30.6	60	73	89
Eastern Europe[a]	7.1	7.1	5.8	5	5	4
Latin America and the Caribbean	22.4	25.5	24.9	87	108	126

Note: The poverty line used here — $370 annual income per capita in 1985 purchasing power parity dollars — is based on estimates of poverty lines from a number of countries low average incomes. In 1990 prices, the poverty line would be approximately $420 annual income per capita.
The estimates for 1985 have been updated from those in World Development Report 1990 to incorporate new data and to ensure comparability across years.

a.   Does not include the former USSR.
Source: World Bank (1992:30).

Export Push Strategies

As the World Bank Report (1992) states, export promotion has played a crucial role in the East Asian miracle. The governments of the HPAEs have been fostering a supportive macroeconomic climate by easing the liberalization of restraints on trade and by facilitating realistic and, in some cases, undervalued exchange rates. They also have been providing suitable microeconomic incentives, which significantly differ according to these economies:

> All (except Hong Kong) began with a period of import substitution, and a strong bias against exports. But each moved to establish a pro-export regime more quickly than other developing economies. First Japan, in the 1950s and early 1960s, and then the Four Tigers, in the late 1960s, shifted trade policies to encourage manufactured exports. In Japan, Korea and Taiwan, governments established a pro-export incentive structure that coexisted with moderate but highly variable protection of the domestic market. A wide variety of instruments was used, including export credits, duty-free imports for exporters and their suppliers, export targets, and tax incentives. In the Southeast Asian NIEs the export push came later, in the early 1980s, and the instruments were different. Reductions in import protection were more generalized and were accompanied by export credit and supporting institutions. In these economies export development has relied less on highly selective interventions and more on broadly based market incentives and direct foreign investment (World Bank 1992: 12).

Table 3 provides a survey of the evolution of export push policies in all seven developing HPAEs.

To describe the East Asian economies' success, the World Bank Report (1992) discusses a number of factors: dynamic agricultural sectors, rapid growth of exports, rapid demographic transitions, high investment and savings rates, the creation of human capital, and rapid productivity growth. It develops a functional approach to understanding growth in these HPAEs. According to Johansen, the factors behind the poverty reduction are increased public provision of basic services, targeted interventions by governments, and broad-based economic growth (Johansen 1993: xv).

This positive picture of high performance is confirmed and enhanced by the Human Development Report, published annually

Table 3 ... Trade Regimes

Indonesia	Rep. of Korea	Malaysia	Taiwan	Thailand
			Land reform and reconstruction, 1949-52	Natural resource-based exports, 1950-70
	War and construction 1950-60		Import-substituting industrialization, 1953-57	
		Market-led development, 1950-70	Export promotion, 1958-72	
Nationalism and guided development, 1948-66	Tilting toward exports–industrial takeoff, 1961-73			
Outward-oriented new-order government, 1967-73		Export promotion and import substitution, 1971-85		Favouring import substitution, 1971-80
	Selective intervention through heavy and chemical industries drive, 1973-79		Industrial consolidation and export growth, 1973-80	
Oil and commodity boom, 1974-81				
	Functional incentives and liberalization, 1980-90		High technology and modernization, 1981-present	Reform and export incentives, 1980-present
Adjustment to external shocks, 1982-85		Adjustment and liberalization, 1986-90		
Deregulation and outward orientation, 1986-present	Financial sector liberalization, 1990-present			

Source: World Bank (1993:124).

since 1990 by the United Nations Development Programme (UNDP). It defines human development in more broader terms than purely the economic ones:

> Human development is a process of enlarging people's choices. In principle, these choices can be infinite and change over time. But at all levels of development, the three essential ones are for people to lead a long and healthy life, to acquire knowledge and to have access to resources needed for a decent standard of life. If these choices are not available, many other opportunities remain inaccessible (UNDP 1993: 10).

On the basis of this definition, the Human Development Index (HDI) captures three crucial dimensions of human development: longevity; educational attainment; and access to resources, which are measured, respectively, by life expectancy, literacy, and income.

Applied to the HPAEs, the index shows that they bypass a great number of developing countries. Not only do they belong to the high and medium human development group (in the ranges of 0.800 and above, and 0.500 to 0.799) but due to the above average level of life expectancy and literacy, they also fare better than in terms of GNP per capita ranking (except Singapore; UNDP 1993: 128; 135f.). All these countries made significant progress from 1970 to 1990 and rank in the first quarter of all 105 listed countries; South Korea, Malaysia, Indonesia and Thailand excel in particular (UNDP 1993: 103; see Table 4).

Table 4

HDI ranking 1990 (total 173 countries)		Diff. to GNP ranking	Changing HDI 1970-1990 (total 105 countries)
1.	Japan	0.983	2	0.130 (rank 22)
24.	Hong Kong	0.913	0	0.151 (rank 16)
33.	South Korea	0.872	4	0.283 (rank 2)
43.	Singapore	0.849	-17	0.119 (rank 27)
57.	Malaysia	0.790	9	0.252 (rank 6)
74.	Thailand	0.715	15	0.180 (rank 10)
92.	Philippines	0.603	22	061 (rank 64)
101.	China	0.566	41	n.a.
108.	Indonesia	0.515	14	0.199 (rank 9)
115.	Vietnam	0.472	41	n.a.
141.	Lao PDR	0.246	20	n.a.
148.	Cambodia	0.186	20	n.a.

NB: Taiwan not available because it lacks national status.

LESSONS TO LEARN

Of course, this brief overview of three outstanding features of the East Asian miracle is anything but complete and leaves a great deal of intriguing questions unanswered. In addition to searching for economic and political explanations, it seems equally important to ask about the ethical underpinning of such an economic success. When provoked by the high performance of other economies and companies, we might be more willing to question our own assumptions, including the ethical ones, and be more open to learn a few lessons from economic successes. The attitude to learn from others does not imply, of course, to give up our critical thinking and to assume that what comes from others is always superior. However, it involves the conviction that, being aware of our own incompleteness, it is better to learn from others than to criticize, or even blame, them. If this attitude were more widely held, Europeans would have a more productive relationship with the United States and Americans would benefit more from the Japanese challenge.

The lessons I suggest can be drawn from the following proposition I would like to advance and argue for: the ethical underpinning of the East Asian miracle is a morality of inclusion that is incorporated into the understanding of the economy, the relationship between government and private business, and the conception of the company.

Morality of Inclusion

By 'morality of inclusion' I mean the morality which basically encompasses all human beings in a given economy (or state), no matter if they are young or old, capable or not to actively participate in economic life. As Allan Buchanan (1993: 233) states, the chief question about the morality of inclusion is this:

> What general obligations, if any, do we have, either as individuals or collectively, to endeavour to include others in our states or our economies (when they would find it beneficial to be included)? (By 'general' obligations I mean to exclude special obligations arising from past joint activity as well as those arising from promises, contracts, or agreements.)

It is easier to determine what inclusion is *not* than to describe what it *is*. The morality of inclusion is not based on self-interested reciprocity (as Buchanan argues correctly) but rather on some characteristics that are not negotiable by individuals; for instance, what we may think of as being human, having basic rights, being a citizen or national, belonging to the same ethnic or religious group, etc. While Buchanan founds his approach on subject-centred theories of justice, I would leave it open and question if the morality of inclusion necessarily has to rely on this (rather Western) type of theory. However, I maintain his description that

> our duties of justice are *owed* to others in virtue of *their* (nonstrategic) characteristics. Moreover, a proper appreciation of these characteristics entails the conviction *that the beings who have them are not to be treated in certain ways*, not simply that *I* am not to treat them in those ways (Buchanan 1993: 241).

This relationship to others involves that we, either as individuals or collectively as a society, are obligated not only to refrain from violating what we are owed to them, but also to contribute to institutional arrangements for ensuring this relationship.

It appears to me that all eight economies under discussion are underpinned by such a morality of inclusion (see note 17). Basically the national bonds seem to be constitutive and prevailing over ethnic or religious bonds. To some extent, this can probably be explained by the build-up of newly independent nations after 1945 or, in the case of Japan, by the economic reconstruction of the country. However, there must be more than such a historical explanation because this argument can be made for numerous non-East Asian countries as well. The morality of inclusion we find in East Asia assigns a decent place to each member of the nation and, at least in principle, does not exclude any group. It is not identical with the Western understanding of democracy and human rights (although they may also have some influence) but rather is rooted in Confucian morality.

The morality of inclusion does not mean that these countries apply open immigration policies. Most prefer to balance labour and capital by exporting capital rather than by importing unskilled labour (ILO 1992: 48-53). In contrast to other developed countries,

Japan has not relied on legal foreign workers to overcome labour shortages (although it must be mentioned that there is now a growing number of illegal foreign workers). It has instead exported many of its labour-intensive processes and increased the productivity of those industries it kept at home. The Republic of Korea has absolutely prohibited unskilled overseas migrants. Hong Kong and Taiwan have applied a relatively open approach, whereas Singapore, with substantial numbers of 'guest workers', has very carefully controlled immigration. For the years to come, immigration policies will become even more restrictive. As the World Labour Report 1992 says, 'all the NIEs are looking for a change of direction. They see the next phase of their development as a move to higher technology and higher productivity—and are nervous that allowing more migrants in would delay this' (ILO 1992: 52).

Compared to the European and North American scenes, the rather restrictive immigration policies of the HPAEs are striking and may express a certain prudence. They certainly help ease social pressure stemming from a high percentage of immigrants, which tend to erode the morality of inclusion. Thus, for the sake of this goal of national coherence, the HPAEs have apparently opted for relatively impermeable borders to unskilled workers. While promoting free movement of goods, services, and capital across the borders, there has been, by and large, no free movement of labour— in contrast to the 'four freedoms' within the Single European Market.[4] One may ask whether the lack of freedom of labour among countries is the price for attaining the morality of inclusion within countries. My answer is not a straightforward yes or no; I do believe that there is a relation between them but certainly not a simple trade-off. The morality of inclusion appears to depend more on the country's capacity to integrate new members, that is, on its dynamic force, than on the degree of openness of its borders.

The Economy as an Interconnected Process of Production and Distribution

The morality of inclusion as the ethical underpinning of the East Asian Miracle is incorporated, first, into the understanding of the economy. Although this is seldom explicitly stated, I think it is fair to say on account of the performance of the HPAEs that these economies are outstanding in two basic characteristics: first, production as well as distribution are considered equally important and mutually related dimensions of the economy; and secondly, this interconnected process brings about rapid growth and declining inequality. Both features are astonishing and intriguing, and provoke a reconsideration of our 'normal' understanding of growth.

The distribution of economic resources, political power, manageable knowledge, etc., has always been a cause of both open struggles and covert conflicts, often motivated by claims for (more) 'distributive justice'. It is obvious that these fights and claims go beyond the economic domain, but they are included in it as well. Therefore, to understand their relevance from the perspective of business ethics, it is crucial that the role distributional issues play within the economy and economics is firmly established. The underlying conception of the East Asian Miracle with its features mentioned above clearly contrasts with two other conceptions. According to the one, the economy and businesses are essentially (only) production processes while distribution processes have to be dealt with in the political domain, by politics, politicians, political parties, etc. Consequently, distributional issues in business and economy do not belong to the field of business ethics but of political ethics. (For this view see, for instance, Barry 1989 and Rich 1984/ 1990.)

The second, distinct, and widespread view holds that while distribution is an economic problem, it is subordinated to production and only relevant as the distribution of outcome. As J.B. Clark (1847-1938) introduced his article on 'Ethics of Distribution' in the (old) *Palgrave's Dictionary of Political Economy*, 'The primary fact of economics is the production of wealth. The division of the product among those who create it is secondary in logical order and, in a sense, in importance' (Clark 1987: 867). In other words, first the cake must be baked, before it can be distributed. In consequence, distributive justice is limited to the outcome of the production process. When, however, both production and distribution are considered equally important and mutually related dimensions of the economy, then distributional issues pervade all economic activities, including factor endowments and processes and outcomes as well. Distribution is not only an 'explicandum' (that is, what has to be explained by other factors), it is also an 'explicans' (that is, what explains other economic variables).

Applied to the HPAEs, this understanding of the economy requires an explanation of not only declining income inequalities by rapid growth but also, conversely, rapid growth by low income inequalities. Universal education, equitable land holding and land reform, numerous small and medium-size enterprises, successful targeting of low-income households for housing, and co-operative trade unions, are important factors for relatively low income inequalities, which, in turn, are crucial for growth with equity.[5] In the labour markets, slower growth of supply and more rapid growth of demand have caused a more rapid rate of increase of wages than in other developing regions, which has been helping to reduce poverty. These experiences confirm the view that creating jobs is the route to reduce poverty.[6]

Furthermore, as the World Bank Report makes clear, a major factor for this economic success was 'an explicit commitment to shared growth' (World Bank 1992: 157). To a larger extent than in other countries, the HPAEs' leadership adopted specific institutional mechanisms tailored to these goals, and these arrangements worked with regard to both the whole economy and the substantial reduction of poverty as well. In line with the report, the principle of shared growth can be interpreted as an answer to the basic challenge for those leaders. They 'hoped that rapid, widely shared improvements in economic welfare would bring legitimacy'. Although I do not disregard this argument, it seems to me quite insufficient. Leaders in all countries need and look for legitimacy, but they may gain and maintain it in spite of extreme inequalities of economic welfare. Rather, I suggest that the principle of shared growth is ultimately based on the morality of inclusion that is a 'cultural fact' in the HPAEs and has to be respected if its leaders want legitimacy.

To better understand this crucial point, we may compare it with Adam Smith's view. In *The Wealth of Nations* (Smith 1869) he highlights the productive dimension of the economy, the importance of work (including 'liberal', that is, generous wages), the division of labour theory and the natural price model, but, in my judgement, he does it at the expense of the distributive dimension (to which afterwards the labour movement has responded in many ways). Also, in *The Theory of Moral Sentiments* (Smith 1853), that provides the ethical underpinning of business and economic life, his view clearly differs from the morality of inclusion. On the one hand, under Stoic influences, his philosophy is cosmopolitan; on the other hand, unlike Buchanan, he did not develop a subject-centred theory of justice on which a morality of inclusion could be founded.[7]

A Government-led Relationship Between Government and Private Business

The morality of inclusion in the HPAEs has also deeply influenced the relationship between government and private business. During decades and without the burden of huge military expenditures[8] and foreign policy ambitions, these countries have persistently been pursuing the clearly defined national goal to build up the economy along the principle of shared growth. This dominant goal-orientation was not a matter of course but often grew out of fierce, domestic conflicts (of which usually little is known of in the United States and Europe). As a case in point, I recall the situation of Japan in 1960. After violent struggles about the military treaty with the United States and deep conflicts between management and labour, culminating in the murder of the socialist leader Asanuma, a strong consensus came up, supported by government and the people as well, 'to heal the nation by economic development'.

Because the national goal was unambiguously stated and inclusive with regard to the whole population, it was critical that the means to achieve this goal be flexible, chosen in a pragmatic way, and be changed if they no longer served the goal. This relates not only to policy issues but, first and foremost, to the roles of government,[9] markets, and businesses in general. An antagonistic relationship between government and private business (as it is still the case, to a large extent, in the United States) is a serious hindrance to the build-up of a national economy, and a simple juxtaposition between both does not take advantage of the potential synergetic effects resulting from such co-operation. Markets have to be used if they help achieve rapid growth with equity (the World Bank Report (1992) mentions labour markets and international markets: 261-73; 292-316). If they do not, they must be assisted (for instance, financial markets; see World Bank 1992: 273-92).

To me as a Western observer, this pragmatism and flexibility is rather surprising. In the West we tend to overemphasize the importance of instrumental rationality and to lose sight of the common goals we want to achieve. Formulated in Max Weber's (1947) terms, we tend to exaggerate the relevance of 'Zweckrationalität' at the expense of 'Wertrationalität'. As a result, we risk becoming dogmatic and, worse, take the means as goals. Government is good or bad for its own sake, not as far as it helps attain common goals; likewise, markets are praiseworthy or reprehensible by themselves, not as efficient or inefficient instruments for higher purposes. Ironically, the overemphasis of instrumental rationality in the West undermines its instrumentality, whereas the clear goal-orientation in the HPAEs improves its instrumental rationality.

According to the World Bank Report, the HPAEs' pragmatism and flexibility have been able to carefully combine the 'fundamentals' on the one hand and 'selective interventions' on the other hand.[10] They also combined co-operative behaviour—including the sharing of information among firms and between the private and public sectors, coordination of investment plans, and promotion of interdependent investments—with competition by firms to meet well-defined economic performance criteria (World Bank 1992: 93). They used coordination when markets were incomplete or missing, and established competition when co-ordination became collusion among firms, as they sought to raise prices, led to managerial slack or a more general loss of efficiency, and encouraged firms to seek favors from government. A good example of this skilful management in experimentation and adaptation are the export push strategies. They were major factors that led to the creation of jobs and an increase in productivity simultaneously. They offered high economic gain, whether they resulted from either an open economy with strong economic fundamentals or from a combination of strong fundamentals with prudently chosen interventions. Thus the Report concludes: 'Of all the interventions we surveyed, those to promote exports were the most readily compatible with a wide diversity of economic circumstances' and are a major lesson that other developing economies can learn from the East Asian miracle. However, the authors concede that they have not discovered fully why the governments of these economies have been more willing and better able than others to experiment and adapt. I would suggest that the answer is found in the ethical underpinning of these economies in the morality of inclusion incorporated in their national goals of shared growth.

A Group-oriented Conception of the Company

A third implication of the morality of inclusion concerns the conception(s) of the company in the HPAEs. In this regard, my reflections are intuitive ideas and speculations, which need to be tested by your knowledge and judgement, rather than propositions based on reports by international organizations. By the way, it is interesting to note that the publications quoted so far by the World Bank, UNDP, and ILO almost never address issues of corporate strategies and behaviour (with a few exceptions in the ILO Reports), in spite of their crucial importance in understanding the East Asian miracle.

To talk of the conception of the East Asian company is admittedly a strong simplification that is far away from the complex picture reality paints. But sometimes it is helpful to look at it from a certain distance in order to perceive some essential characteristics (as is the case with the geometric figures and animals in Nazca, Peru, which can only be seen from a distant point of view). Moreover, it seems to be reasonable to assume that the economy of a particular country or region shapes the understanding of its companies which, in turn, has an impact on the country or region as well. An interesting example for this relationship is *Kaisha: The Japanese Corporation* (Abegglen and Stalk 1985).

The morality of inclusion suggests that not only at the societal but also at the corporate level, there is a stronger sense of community in the HPAE companies than in the average Western, individualistic company. The group normative environment, which characterizes the Japanese company (see Taka 1993), may exist, to various degrees, in the other HPAEs as well. Against the backdrop of the build-up of national economies and labour shortages, workers are not considered and treated solely as means to achieve immediate financial performance and returns to shareholders. Rather than being costs to be cut (in order to make the company more efficient), they are assets to invest and become more productive. Exposed to international competition by export push strategies, management was willing (and sometimes forced) to experiment with and adapt to new circumstances. Faced with falling demand and increased energy costs in the 1980s, management created jobs and improved real incomes to a much greater extent than in other developing countries. As the World Labour Report 1992 says, the actions of individual enterprises have been just as significant as those of government: 'Employers responded with a variety of measures, including shedding outmoded technology, reorganizing production, retrenching some labour and increasing training. A study in Indonesia, the Philippines, Malaysia and Singapore asked employers the kind of measures they were taking. Their responses ... indicate the priority which employers gave to technological development' (ILO 1992: 41). The way these changes were introduced seems to resemble more a Japanese as opposed to a Western style. 'Western managers place priority on innovation, Japanese managers and workers put emphasis on *Kaizen* (continuous improvement of products, ways to work and decision-making processes). While innovation can be done intermittently only by a mere handful of elites in a society, *Kaizen* can be carried on continuously by almost every person' (Taka 1993: 30).

This emphasis on continuously improving the workers' productivity along with the group-orientation suggests that the company is not simply understood as a 'productive animal' or production function. Rather, as at the level of the economy as a whole, its distributional dimension is equally important and interconnected with its productive dimension. It would be interesting to investigate the wage structures of the HPAE companies and to compare them with American and European ones.

Corporate ethics presupposes that the company has some discretion to choose among different options regarding its goals, strategies, and relations with various stakeholders. In other words, market 'mechanisms' and regulations by law and government do not fully determine the range of corporate conduct but leave some freedom. Thus it is up to the individual company to use its freedom in an ethically responsible way.

What this could mean is hard for me to say because it depends not only on how big the space of discretion is, but also on what ethical standards, always influenced by the cultural environment, should be applied. Given these circumstances, I nevertheless attempt to advance some suggestions. The first is that rapidly growing economies involve more discretionary spaces for companies than stagnant or shrinking economies. This is the case not only because legal regulation tends to lag behind social and economic development but also, more basically, because an expanding economy can evolve in various directions and create different conditions for tomorrow's social and economic life. Therefore, business and corporate ethics, fundamentally, have an anticipatory and preventative, and not solely a reparational, role to play.

More specifically speaking, in most HPAEs, the labour markets are significantly less regulated in terms of basic ILO Conventions than in many other countries in Europe, America and Africa (ILO 1993: 86-7). Consequently, the HPAEs' companies have more discretionary spaces in this regard than others, given the prevailing morality of inclusion and the reserved attitude of governments. Therefore, important questions of corporate ethics relate to workers and employees: What does it mean to treat them humanely? To do so is a fundamental requirement stated in the declaration *Toward a Global Ethic* (Council 1993), supported by numerous leaders of the world's religions. Should workers be treated equally, regardless of their gender, religion, and national as well as ethnic origin? The ethical demand for equal treatment is rooted both in the Japanese transcendental logic that 'everybody has an equal microcosm' (Taka 1993: 51) and the subject-centred understanding of human rights. It would be an extraordinary lesson—a kind of miracle, too—to see that corporate ethics, without many regulations, provides a higher level of humane treatment of workers than with regulations.

A third set of questions relates to the fact that a growing number of companies operate outside the HPAEs, by establishing subsidiaries and doing business with subcontractors mainly in the garments, footwear, and woodworking industries (see ILO 1992: 41). Here again is raised the twofold question about the spaces of freedom available to the companies and the ethical standards these companies should adopt, but this time the question involves an international context, an even more complicated area.

CHALLENGING QUESTIONS IN THE REGIONALIZATION AND GLOBALIZATION PROCESSES

Having presented some basic features of the East Asian miracle and attempted to learn several lessons from it, I now turn to the questions, already touched upon in the previous paragraph, which seem to me particularly challenging in the processes of regionalization and globalization. They obviously concern the HPAEs but go far beyond them and are equally important from the perspectives of other parts of the world: developing countries, the former Soviet Union, Europe and North America. By and large, my inquiry follows the line developed above. I shall ask a few questions about the ethical underpinning of regionalization and globalization, the understanding of the economies, the relations between government and private businesses, and the conceptions of regional and global companies.

Searching for a Morality of Good Neighbourhood but Not at the Expense of Third Parties

While the processes of economic regionalization and globalization are advancing at a rapid pace, their moral foundation is lagging far behind. In the post-Cold War era, fortunately, the world is no longer divided into 'friend and foe' and devoted to negative-sum activities. However, this situation does not diminish the need for vigilance since military confrontation has often been replaced by economic contests (Thurow 1992: 23).[11] At best there exists a *modus vivendi*[12] regarding certain international regimes (see Preston and Windsor 1992), but one not founded on the firm common ethical ground that is needed for fair and stable international relations.

Nevertheless, the current regionalization and globalization processes put each society under additional pressures to reflect about, and take a more explicit stand with regard to, other societies. In John Rawls' words: 'Every society must have a conception of how it is related to other societies and of how it is to conduct itself toward them' (Rawls 1993b: 38). Such a conception tackles the normative dimension of how these relations ought to be shaped and how the society ought to conduct itself. It also includes basic positive features of the current situation specified by regionalization as well as globalization.

Therefore, it is crucial to distinguish between the two kinds of processes. Regionalization differs from globalization insofar as the former includes closer geographical, geopolitical, and cultural linkages, as well as more economic exchanges in terms of cross-national trade and transfers of production factors, management systems, technology, and monetary assets.[13] At least in principle, yet often not in reality, globalization (of economies and companies as well) does not recognize any boundaries, whereas regionalization takes place within, albeit somewhat fuzzy, borderlines. Both processes do not exist completely independent of one another but are interconnected to some extent.

Given this brief characterization, the question about the ethical underpinning of regionalization and globalization is to find and implement both a morality of good neighbourhood and a global ethic which are not only distinct but compatible and desirably reinforce each other. This purpose may also be called 'a morality of good neighborhood but not at the expense of third parties', emphasising the first part of the twofold problem that is widely neglected in discussions on international ethics and globalization, and following an ascendent methodology that starts from small unities and progresses to ever more comprehensive ones.[14]

My first point is that while the morality of inclusion is fundamental for each HPAE, it is a necessary presupposition for, but does not seem to suffice as the ethical underpinning of, the regionalization process. Admittedly the domestic morality cannot be totally separated from moral issues with neighbouring countries. A morality of exclusion that prevents parts of the population from participating fully in economic and societal life has a discriminatory impact on foreign relations as well. By contrast, a morality of inclusion may bring about a sense of equal treatment at the regional level. In spite of their differences, neighbours across national borders also share numerous common features, due to historical experiences, often enhanced by ethnic or religious bonds and provoked by environmental challenges. Such interconnections involve potential benefits as well as risks for both sides and make it difficult, if not impossible, to separate one country's interests from those of its neighbors. As history tells us, it may happen, yet not necessarily, that a sense of reciprocity evolves among neighbours based on a morality of inclusion. What is good for natives is also good for neighbours who live and travel in this country because the former want to be treated equally when they, in turn, are in the neighboring countries.

Nonetheless, the morality of inclusion is basically a domestic conception and does not suffice to qualify the relations with neighbouring societies. Therefore, there is a need for a morality of good neighbourhood that must be opted for in a more or less explicit way.[15] Thus, secondly, what does 'good neighbourhood' mean? My tentative answer largely draws on Rawls's article 'The Law of Peoples'[16] and is intended to serve as a 'grid of questions' that certainly is somewhat biased by the Western viewpoint and needs input and response from the East Asian perspective.

With regard to free and democratic peoples, Rawls (1993b: 46) says the principles of justice

> ... will include certain familiar principles long recognised as belonging to the law of peoples, among them the following:
> 1.   Peoples (as organized by their governments) are free and independent, and their freedom and independence is to be respected by other peoples.
> 2.   Peoples are equal and parties to their own agreements.
> 3.   Peoples have the right of self-defence but no right to war.
> 4.   Peoples are to observe a duty to nonintervention.
> 5.   Peoples are to observe treaties and undertakings.
> 6.   Peoples are to observe certain specified restrictions on the conduct of war (assumed to be in self-defence).
> 7.   Peoples are to honour human rights.

These principles require much explanation and interpretation; for example, the sixth and seventh are superfluous in a society of well-ordered democratic peoples because these principles are already included in their own conception of justice. In addition, the charter of their association would have to include other principles for forming and regulating federations (associations) of peoples, standards of fairness for trade and other co-operative arrangements, certain provisions for mutual assistance among peoples in times of famine and drought, and provisions for ensuring that in all reasonably developed liberal societies a people's basic needs are met (ibid.: 47).

It seems to me that this list of principles between free and democratic peoples could only partially be applied to the HPAEs basically for two reasons. First, most of the HPAEs do not fit into the conception of 'free and democratic peoples'; and second, some of them are developing countries, that is, burdened by 'unfavourable conditions' in terms of material and technological resources, human capital, and know-how. This explains why Rawls' extension of liberal ideas of justice to 'hierarchical societies' becomes interesting for a region where different types of societies exist and, in some cases, unfavourable conditions hold. The shared law of peoples would include both types of societies, liberal as well as hierarchical, provided they are 'well-ordered' (ibid.: 35-40). While Rawls extensively discusses the meaning of a 'well-ordered' liberal society in *A Theory of Justice* (1971) and *Political Liberalism* (1993a), he briefly describes three requirements for a well-ordered hierarchical regime as follows (Rawls 1993b: 50-6):

1.   The hierarchical regime is peaceful and gains its legitimate aims through diplomacy, trade, and other ways of peace. Its religious doctrine, assumed to be comprehensive and influential in government policy, is not expansionist in the sense that it fully respects the civic order and integrity of other societies. If it seeks wider influence, it does so in ways compatible with the independence of, and the liberties within, other societies.

2.   The hierarchical regime imposes moral duties and obligations on all persons within its territory. It is guided by a conception of justice that takes, impartially, into account what is seen not unreasonably as the fundamental interests of all members of society. Judges and other officials who administer the legal order sincerely

and not unreasonably believe that the law is indeed guided by such a common good conception of justice.[17] The political institutions of such a society constitute a reasonable consultation hierarchy.

3. The hierarchical regime respects basic human rights. The conception of the common good of justice secures for all persons, at least, certain minimum rights to: means of subsistence and security (the right to life), to liberty (freedom from slavery, serfdom and forced occupation), and (personal) property; as well as to formal equality as expressed by the rules of natural justice (for example, that similar cases be treated similarly).

According to Rawls, these three requirements hold for a well-ordered hierarchical society, which is an 'ideal theory'. However, the conditions of our world, with its great injustices and widespread social evils, are highly non-ideal. Therefore, we need a non-ideal theory which presupposes that ideal theory and asks how this goal might be achieved, or at least worked toward, generally in gradual steps. These questions are questions of transition: to start from where a society is, then to seek effective ways permitted by the law of peoples to move the society some distance towards the goal defined by the law of peoples.

Hence, applied to the HPAEs, both dimensions of the regionalization process are indispensable: the normative orientation and the positive (economic) analysis. Regionalization can flourish, in the long run, only if it is economically sound and grounded on the mutual understanding and recognition of the peoples and governments in the region. Like at the national level, it is shortsighted to believe that 'pure' economic progress, if possible at all, automatically brings about better moral relations among economies. Rather, there are good reasons to assume that several factors which have proved beneficial within each HPAE might cause tensions and conflicts at the regional level. When the build-up of an economy has advanced far beyond its young age, this national goal becomes more complicated and loses its unifying force for co-operation among various, often rivalling, actors. The strong leadership by government that has characterised its relationship with private business up to this point, tends to weaken because many companies, by reaching out beyond national borders, depend less on government, and increasing numbers of citizens want to play a more active role in society. Still, the export push strategies may remain crucially important for the HPAEs in terms of growth with equity and poverty reduction, as well as offer a wide range of opportunities in broader regional and global markets. However, the further pursuit of these strategies will significantly intensify competition at the regional and global levels. As a result, the HPAEs will face similar challenges as economies in other parts of the world which depend on export promotion to create jobs.

A List of Questions About the Morality of Good Neighbourhood

Given these (and many more) critical issues in the regionalization process of the HPAEs, I now attempt, with the help of Rawls' conceptual framework, to set up a list of questions which relate to the morality of good neighborhood. It basically includes two parts: the external relations between peoples and the (internal) treatment of persons within each people.[18] Both parts are indispensable and interrelated. Without consideration of persons, relations between peoples lack their bases while the exclusive focus on persons denies the peoples the sovereignty to constitute their own orders. Thus the morality of good neighbourhood includes the following questions:

Part I: Regarding the relations between peoples

1. *Mutual respect of freedom and independence.* Is each people (as organized by their government) in the region free and independent, and does it respect the freedom and independence of its neighbours?
2. *Equality of partners.* Are the peoples recognized as basically equal partners in their agreements of neighbourhood, in spite of their differences in size, economic development, political power, cultural, ethnic, and religious foundation?
3. *Non-aggressive self-defence.* Does each people refrain from intervening into neighbours' affairs and pursue peaceful, non-expansionist foreign relations while being empowered to defend itself? When disputes and conflicts arise, how do the parties involved settle them (perhaps with the help of other parties)?

4. *Compliance with treaties and undertakings.* How much is each partner committed to fulfil the obligations of such agreements? Under what conditions is it allowed to withdraw or break them?

Part II: Regarding the treatment of persons

1. *Subsistence and security.* Does each person have the means to a decent livelihood, and is he or she secure against substantial and recurrent threats?
2. *Freedom from slavery, serfdom, and forced occupation.* Is every person, women and children as well as men, free from these forms of treatment which take away their minimum liberty to choose how they wish to lead their own lives?
3. *(Personal) property.* Is each person allowed to have (personal) property that enlarges his or her freedom to act?
4. *Formal equality of treatment.* Is each person equally treated by the rules of natural justice, not exposed to systematically arbitrary judgement?

This description of the morality of good neighbourhood is certainly incomplete. For instance, it does not explicitly address the environmental responsibility. Furthermore, we would have to ask what moral, philosophical, and religious resources are needed to develop and maintain such a morality of good neighbourhood. Being aware of this incomplete outline, I leave it as it is for the time being and attempt to relate it to the regional economy as a whole, the relationships between government and business, and the conception of the regional companies.

Ethical Implications for the Regionalization Process

The morality of good neighbourhood intends to provide the ethical underpinning of the regionalization process and, therefore, is exposed to two sets of forces. On the one hand, along with this process, it must go beyond well-tried national experiences, and, on the other hand, it has to face the challenges of globalization. Although these forces encompass many more aspects than the economic ones (all of which must be tackled by such a morality), I now concentrate on the economic side of the 'problematique' which displays a particularly strong drive in the HPAEs as compared to other regions of the world. This focus may also shed light on how the HPAEs endeavor to cope with the trend of 'economization'.[19]

In my view, the implications of the ethical underpinning described above relate, at least, to the six following issues:

1. What does the morality of good neighbourhood imply for shaping the market morality in this region? Can the approach to combine competition and coordination that has been so successful in each HPAE be transferred and applied to the regional level as well? What modifications, if any, would be necessary to ensure similar success?

2. How can the balance between the productive and the distributive dimension of economic development be maintained at the regional level? Is rapid growth with equity still achievable? In spite of the increasingly fierce international competition, can the process of creating jobs and reducing poverty be continued or even enhanced? (To be sure, this is a pressing question for Europe that shows a bad record in terms of job creation and poverty reduction and attempts to counter-balance the high income inequalities among countries and areas by the political provision of the 'cohesion fund'.)

3. After the strong focus on 'producer economics' (Thurow 1992: 113-51), including high rates of human capital formation, savings, and investment (World Bank 1992: 191-242) all of which are characteristic of young and thriving economies, the emphasis now is shifting towards more consumption and leisure in each HPAE to a different extent. What ethical challenges are involved in this process? Is the morality of good neighbourhood sufficiently firm to hold its ground in the view of this shift?

4. So far environmental problems have not been mentioned, although they are of paramount importance and must be taken seriously by any kind of morality at the personal, corporate, national, regional, and global levels. Is the regionalization process in East Asia moving towards 'sustainable growth', defined by the World Commission on Environment and Development (1987) as 'meeting the needs of the present without compromising the ability of future generations to meet their

own needs?' Or do nature and future generations have to carry the burden of destruction inflicted by nonsustainable growth?

5. To the extent that the 'economization' of the region is progressing, what are the safeguards built in the ethical underpinning that retain and reduce this process?

6. Finally, like in other parts of the world, the question arises whether, and to what extent, the regionalization process occurs at the expense of third parties outside the region, above all in developing countries. It goes without saying that the regional perspective is to be completed by the global perspective, both from the positive and normative viewpoint (which opens a wide field to further discussions).

A Changing Relationship Between Government and Business

To date, in all HPAEs, the governments have played a strong leadership role in the build-up of the national economies. But now the situation seems to be changing for internal as well as external reasons, which I briefly discussed above. As Stopford, Strange and Henley (1991) argue, a new, 'triangular' diplomacy is needed in competing for world market shares. No longer do governments merely negotiate among themselves. They now must also negotiate with foreign firms,and multinationals themselves are increasingly having to become more statesmanlike (as they seek corporate alliances) to negotiate with other companies. As a result, the interaction of all three dimensions calls for new skills in management and government. Moreover, this triad of relationships tends to weaken the hitherto dominant role of individual governments. It may also lead to more co-operative relations among less unequal partners within each country because they have to cope with the same international challenges. However, on the basis of the morality of good neighbourhood outlined above, the increasingly fierce international competition raises crucial ethical questions:

1. What does the principle of 'non-aggressive self-defence' involve in terms of trade and foreign investment? What ethical responsibilities do the governments and the companies have to both avoid economic wars and to build up 'peace economies'?

2. What treaties and undertakings should they set up and

implement in order to pursue this peace goal in economic and business terms?

3. Regarding the treatment of persons, what is the most efficient way of co-operation between government and business to overcome, in Rawls' words, the 'unfavourable conditions' (poverty) and ensure, at least, subsistence and security to each member of the society? What ethical responsibilities do the governments and the companies have to create jobs, improve working conditions, and provide for welfare benefits.

Is There an 'East Asian Company'?

My questions regarding the corporate level of analysis cover a wide range of issues which, to some extent, have been addressed, implicitly or explicitly, in the paragraphs about the ethical implications for the regionalization process and the government-business relationship. Given the limited space, I now would like to ask a few additional questions, although I know that this topic requires more, extensive treatment.

In the discussion about the high performance of East Asian companies, three factors seemed to me particularly important for their success: (1) the view that workers are assets to invest and become more productive (rather than costs to be cut); (2) the group normative environment; and (3) the attitude of continously improving products, ways to work, and decision-making processes. Hence the following questions:

1. Exposed to the strong regionalization process, how are these factors going to be affected? Will the high priority that workers have so far enjoyed be diminished, possibly under the pressures of international financial markets?

2. Is the group-orientation with different forms in the HPAEs changing as the companies increasingly go regional and global and hire foreign workers? Is the sense of inclusion diminishing while, in other parts of the world, a more inclusive approach is advocated in which the company includes all its relationships in its definitions and measures of success?[20]

3. Is the continuous improvement of products, ways to work, and decision making processes sufficiently expeditious so that

it can keep pace with the revolutionary technological changes at the turn of the century?

4. What does the morality of good neighbourhood involve for corporate conduct? As guests in a neighbouring countries, should the companies display higher ethical behaviour than the domestic ones? What would that mean? Are specific ethical guidelines for operating in the East Asian region advisable or even needed?

NOTES

1. See World Bank (1993b) (figures of 1992) for seven countries; see World Resources Institute (1994) for Taiwan.

2. The enlarged European Union has a population of 378 million, now including also Finland, Sweden, Austria and Norway, whose entrance negotiations are accomplished but still have to be ratified by the respective countries. The North American Free Trade Agreement with Canada, Mexico and the United States includes 368 million people (1992 figures in World Bank 1993b).

3. Sometimes one refers to the 'Kuznets curve' that expresses this inverse relationship. In fact, Kuznets investigated the relations between growth and income distribution in numerous studies but did not claim that such a link be necessary (see Kuznets 1955, 1959, 1966).

4. The German sociologist Hans-Joachim Hoffmann-Novotny sharply criticizes the prevailing free-market ideology because it defends, or at least admits, the contradiction between freedom of goods, services and capital on the one hand and no freedom of labour on the other hand (Hoffmann-Novotny 1993).

5. Although these factors are explicitly discussed in the World Bank Report (1992: 160-7), they are not explicitly stated in the 'Functional Approach to Growth' (87-90; also 11, 79) which mentions the distributional issue only with regard to outcome, not inputs and processes.

6. 'Employment is central. If there is one point on which everybody agrees, it is that the route to reduce poverty is through creating jobs' (*The Courier* 1994: 53).

7. See my criticism of Adam Smith with regard to poverty in Enderle (1994).

8. Except the Republic of Korea. From 1977 to 1988, its military

spending as a percentage of combined spending on education and health has, however, declined from circa 200% to circa 100% (UNDP 1993: 9).

9. I deliberately speak essentially of governmental goals and strategies, disclaiming the question regarding the forms of government. A strong and persistent goal-orientation is not necessarily linked with authoritarian leadership and (benevolent) dictatorship.

10. 'Fundamentals' are defined as those policies that encourage macroeconomic stability, high investment in human capital, stable and secure financial systems, limited price distortions, and openness to foreign technology. 'Selective interventions' include mild financial repression (that is, keeping interest rates positive but low), directed credit, selective industrial promotion, and trade policies that push nontraditional exports. Those interventions that attempt to guide resource allocation to succeed must—as a guideline—address failures in the working of markets (World Bank 1992: 10ff.).

11. I believe it remains true what Harry Hawkins of the United States said in a 1944 speech: 'Trade conflicts breeds noncooperation, suspicion, bitterness. Nations which are economic enemies are not likely to remain political friends for long' (quoted in Jackson 1992: 10).

12. Rawls uses this term in *Political Liberalism* (1993a: 145-50). *The Macmillan Contemporary Dictionary* (1979) defines 'modus vivendi' as 'temporary agreement between contending parties pending a final settlement of matters in debate'.

13. This tentative definition does not include regional political arrangements (as it is the case in the European Union), although I believe that in the long run they will be advisable, in one form or another, since what happens in the economic domain cannot be entirely separated from the political domain.

14. In numerous publications there seems to exist only the alternative of either 'local' (national) or 'global' without recognising the importance of the regional level (for instance, Stopford et al. 1991, esp. 24-9 and 66-9). Against this trend of underestimating regionalization, see Johnson (1991).

15. This is a crucial reason for the following question addressed by Gerald O. Barney to the religious leaders gathered at the Parliament of World's Religions in 1993 in Chicago: 'What are the traditional teachings—and the range of other opinions—within your faith tradition concerning a proper relationship with those who differ in race or gender (conditions one cannot change), or culture, politics or faith?' (Barney 1993: 78-9).

16. Rawls does not use the term 'good neighbourhood' but does, in fact, apply a stepwise approach. First, he asks for the principles of justices between free and democratic peoples, then he extends his approach to 'hierarchical societies', and finally he raises the question about the relationship with the remaining societies of the earth (dictatorships, etc.).

17. This second requirement includes most features of the morality of inclusion discussed above yet not the feature of 'a decent place for everybody' that is included in the third requirement.

18. In the Universal Declaration of Human Rights as well as in numerous other documents, the standards of treating persons are usually expressed in terms of moral and, sometimes, legal rights. Although the philosophy and language of rights has mainly developed in Western culture, it does not necessarily follow from this fact that the core meaning of rights be unsuitable for a morality of good neighbourhood and global ethic, nor should it be rejected as a form of Western cultural imperialism. In my view, it is possible and recommendable to distinguish between the contents and the justification of moral rights. The contents may be formulated in different languages while basically keeping the same meaning; for instance, in terms of basic capabilities (see Sen 1992). By contrast, the justification of these contents may differ according to cultural and religious backgrounds.

19. 'Economization' of the society means that economic thinking and acting are penetrating and dominating more and more domains: large investments, research and development, mass media, politics, education, culture, and the family, for example. Only what counts economically and yields profit is relevant. This trend might be seen as a major, but not the most important, reason for the need of business ethics. Challenges like 'sustainable development' which require not only a re-active but a pro-active approach certainly are even more crucial (see Enderle 1993: 136).

20. See the Interim Report *Tomorrow's Company: The Role of Business in a Changing World* (RSA 1994). It criticizes the conventional wisdom in the UK 'to define the purpose of business in terms that stress the importance of immediate financial performance and returns to shareholder, and treat other participants merely as means to this end.'

REFERENCES

Abegglen, J.C. and G. Stalk, Jr. 1985. *Kaisha: The Japanese Corporation.* New York: Basic Books.

Barney, G.O. 1993. *Global 2000 Revisited. What shall we do? The Critical Issues of the 21st Century.* Arlington, VA: Millenium Institute.

Barry, B. 1989. *Theories of Justice. A Treatise on Social Justice, Volume I.* Berkeley, CA: University of California.

Buchanan, A. 1993. The Morality of Inclusion. *Social Philosophy and Policy* 10 (2): 233-57.

Clark, J.B. 1987. Ethics of Distribution. In *The New Palgrave: A Dictionary of Economics*, 867-9. Ed. Eatwell, Milgate and Newman. London: Macmillan.

Council for a Parliament of World's Religions. 1993. *Towards a Global Ethic (An Initial Declaration).* Chicago: Council for a Parliament of the World's Religions.

The Courier: Africa-Caribbean-Pacific-European Union. 1994. Interview with the head of the Labour Institutions and Economic Development Programme at the ILO's International Institute for Labour Studies in Geneva: 50-3.

Enderle, G. 1993. What is Business Ethics? In *Business Ethics: Japan and the Global Economy.* Ed. Dunfee and Nagayasu. Dordrecht/Boston/London: Kluwer Academic Publishers: 133-50.

Enderle, G. 1994. *Business Ethics as a Goal-Rights-System.* Manuscript.

Hoffmann-Novotny, H-J. 1993. Migration. In *Lexicon der Wirtschaftsethik.* Ed. Enderle, Homann, Honecker, Kerber and Steinmann. Freiburg/Basel/Vienna: Herder: 705-17.

International Labour Office (ILO). 1992. *World Labour Report 1992.* Geneva: International Labour Office.

International Labour Office (ILO). 1993. *World Labour Report 1993.* Geneva: International Labour Office.

Jackson, J.H. 1992. *The World Trading System. Law and Policy of International Economic Relations.* Cambridge, MA: MIT Press.

Johanson, F. 1993. *Poverty Reduction in East Asia. The Silent Revolution.* World Bank Discussion Paper 203. Washington, D.C.: World Bank.

Johnson, H.J. 1991. *Dispelling the Myth of Globalisation. The Case for Regionalisation.* New York: Praeger.

Kuznets, S. 1955. Economic Growth and Income Distribution. *American Economic Review* 45 (1): 1-28.

Kuznets, S. 1959. *Six Lectures on Economic Growth.* Glencoe, IL: Free Press.

Kuznets, S. 1966. *Modern Economic Growth.* New Haven, CT: Yale University Press.

Preston, L.E. and D. Windsor. 1992. *The Rules of the Game in the Global Economy: Policy Regimes for International Business.* Dordrecht, Boston, London: Kluwer Academic Publishers.

Rawls, J. 1971. *A Theory of Justice.* Cambridge, MA: Harvard University Press.

Rawls, J. 1993a. *Political Liberalism.* New York: Columbia University Press.

Rawls, J. 1993b. The Law of Peoples. *Critical Inquiry* 20: 36-68.

Rich, A. 1984/1990. *Wirtschaftsethik.* Band I/II. Gütersloh: Mohn.

Royal Society of Arts (RSA). 1994. *Tomorrow's Company: The Role of Business in a Changing World.* London: RSA.

Sen, A. 1992. *Inequality Reexamined.* Cambridge, MA: Harvard University Press.

Smith, A. 1869. *An Inquiry into the Nature and Causes of the Wealth of Nations.* Oxford, UK: Clarendon Press.

Smith, A. 1853. *Theory of Moral Sentiments.* London: Bohn.

Stopford, J.M., S. Strange and J.S. Henley. 1991. *Rival States, Rival Firms. Competition for World Market Shares.* Cambridge, UK: Cambridge University Press.

Taka, T. 1993. Business Ethics: A Japanese View. In *Business Ethics: Japan and the Global Economy.* Ed. Dunfee and Nagayasu. Dordrecht/Boston/London: Kluwer Academic Publishers: 23-59.

Thurow, L. 1992. *Head to Head. The Coming Economic Battle among Japan, Europe, and America.* New York: Morrow and Company.

United Nations Development Programme (UNDP). 1993. *Human Development Report 1993.* New York: Oxford University Press.

Weber, M. 1947. *The Theory of Social and Economic Organization.* (tr. A.M. Henderson and T. Parsons). London: Edinburgh.

World Bank. 1992. *World Development Report 1992. Development and Environment.* New York: Oxford University Press.

World Bank. 1993a. *The East Asian Miracle. Economic Growth and Public Policy.* New York: Oxford University Press.

World Bank. 1993b. *The World Bank Atlas 1994.* Washington, D.C.: World Bank.

World Commission on Environment and Development. 1987. *Our Common Future.* New York: Oxford University Press.

World Resources Institute. 1994. *The 1994 Information Please Environmental Almanac.* Boston, MA: Houghton Mifflin.

7

FEUDALISM, ETHICS AND POSTMODERN COMPANY LIFE

Gabriel Donleavy

INTRODUCTION

Between the fall of Constantinople in 1452 and the fall of the Soviet Union in 1990, the world economy was moved forward by colonialism, mercantilism and capitalism—all being variations of a basic law of survival of the fittest. From the late fifteenth-century voyages of discovery to the late twentieth-century *Voyager* missions, the age of Modernity was characterized in the West by the cult of the individual: individual enterprise, individual heroism, and individual freedoms. This essentially cultural manifestation was uplifted into a system of philosophy by the invention of economics during the peak period of Modernity, the European Enlightenment of the eighteenth century. Classical economics glorified the individual just as neo-classical architecture glorified the pillar; both openly acknowledging their debt to the individualism of ancient Athens. Economics had its invisible hand; architecture had its golden mean, and masonry had its meaningful handshake. After the Enlightenment, individualism was apt to inflate into cults of personality, beginning with Napoleon, progressing through Lincoln, and peaking with Hollywood and the European dictators of the mid twentieth century. Great business empires like Ford were, and still are, associated with great entrepreneurial individuals. Faceless bureaucracy became the antagonist of individual enterprise in the rhetoric of capitalism while remaining its behind-the-scenes friendly fixer in the continuing reality of mercantilism, especially in France,

Japan and Singapore. As much within the business community as on the political left, the greatest term of abuse, the term of ultimate condemnation, was feudalism. It conjured up a picture of reactionary serfdom, warlordism, lawlessness and superstitious poverty. Capitalism, in particular, was portrayed as the emancipator and greatly preferable successor to feudalism. This paper considers the possibility that enterprise culture is rediscovering the essential features of that long-despised social arrangement.

THE ORIGINAL FEUDALISM SUMMARIZED

The original feudalism slowly arose in Europe after the barbarian dismemberment of the Roman empire when Germanic tribes overran Europe. Vassalage, the principal relationship in feudalism, meant holding estates in return for service, usually military service. The fief was land plus peasants to work it; land on which the vassal was immune from law, so was ruler of it in all respects. To become a vassal a man had to appear before his lord of the manor (his 'demesne' lord), put his hands inside the lord's by way of homage and swear faith against all men to his lord by way of fealty. An edict of Charlemagne in the ninth century justified desertion by a vassal if his lord failed to protect him when able to do so, when the lord ravished his wife, when the lord attacked him with drawn sword, when the lord plotted against his life, or the lord sought to reduce him to servitude. A faithless lord (or vassal) was thus a felon. Fiefs were eventually hereditary but the successor had to swear fealty for his title to be secure. Vassalage was always personal and was mostly restricted to fighting men. Similarly only one possessed of a *cheval* (horse) could display chivalry in its initial meaning. Noble boys started as pages, at around fourteen became squires, then graduated by means of the 'accolade' to knighthood at around twenty-one. The accolade was often accompanied by the formula *sois preux* (one who displays prowess), a combination of skill and bravery and loyalty to lord and his own plighted troth (Stephenson 1942). The troth was the origin both of the modern word 'truth' and the medieval idea of faithfulness to one's word (Way 1986). It was a quite central idea in feudal Europe that a promise was unbreakable.

THE OFFICE AS A FIEF

Vassalage was, in some senses, the medieval equivalent of employment. The vassal employee paid homage to his lord in a ritual act promising aid and obedience in exchange for protection, succour and the fief itself, which came to be conveyed in a ritual called investiture, immediately following the homage. The vassal held his fief only so long as he served his lord, and could be ejected on failure to do so. Since homage and fealty obligations were personal, the lord of a lord (the suzerain) was owed nothing by the vassals of the intermediate lord (the demesne lord) (Ganshof 1952: 88).

A fief was granted against an obligation to serve, often in a specialized way with skilled military, managerial, or clerical labour. In this it was unlike the villein tenement (or serfdom) which was granted in return for unskilled labour obligations usually associated with work in the fields.

Serfs could be sold by their lord to other lords, together with their holdings (Hyams 1980: 6-14). Serfs were not allowed to alienate their own land without the permission of the lord of their manor (Hyams 1980: 43).

The distinction between serfdom and vassalage compares to the modern distinction between wages and salaries. Eventually a detailed covenant elaborated the ceremony of homage and investiture. The serf was a free man with recourse to the assize courts *except* in relation to his lord whose word and court were unappealable. In modern parlance, the serf could not take the boss to court for mistreatment short of murder. The serf was thus more like the modern unlawfully employed and exploited illegal immigrant labour than like the more usual kind of wage earning worker. The free vassal was more like the modern office worker with the office being remarkably similar to a fief. Like a fief, an office is a piece of real estate to which duties of service attach. Like a fief, an office can be removed from the occupier on demand by the boss, with no recourse whatever by the tenant to the courts. In this respect, medieval tenants were better off, as they had available the writ of novel disseisin at the assizes where their claim to have been wrongfully dispossessed by the demesne lord would be heard. The lord would usually argue that dispossession was imposed for failure to perform the services implicit or explicit in the fief. The courts would decide on the evidence, and evidence was even more crucial then than now. The modern employee has the possibility of bringing an action for wrongful dismissal altogether but not for wrongful dispossession of an office. There is no right in any law to occupy specific office space as an employee, but it is natural and observable that occupation thereof is in the gift of the boss of the manor and that his disposition judgements will reflect a combination of seniority, function and the extent to which the vassal is in favour. It is almost universally observed that personal status in a firm is associated with office size and comfort; and this association is the essence of fiefdom.

STATE AS CHURCH: FIRM AS MANOR

A crucial element in the transformation of the Roman system into the wholly different medieval feudal system was the influence of the new religion of Christianity, which at first undermined the old order and later provided the spirit and shaped the institutional forms of the new order (Heilbroner 1976: 94-5).

As for the importance of the Church and religion in feudalism, this should be understood as essentially a means of bringing order and peace to a society of warriors (Foss 1975). Around 989, a council of bishops at Charroux began to impose the Church's limit on violence, anathematizing anyone who stole from churches or peasants or struck an unarmed cleric. The synod of Le Puy in 990 extended the Church's protection to merchants, their mills and vines. This was the beginning of the *Pax Dei* (Peace of God) which by 1041 extended to forbidding fighting on holy days. On 27 November 1095 Pope Urban II bitterly condemned the depredations of the gangster knights throughout Europe and promised them eternal damnation unless they threw the Turks out of Jerusalem. By the mid thirteenth century the ceremony of conferring knighthood exhorted the knight to defend widows and orphans against the cruelty of heretics and infidels. Thus had the Church transformed a simple rite of passage into a sacrament and general pillage into a crusade. The quick success of the First Crusade in capturing Jerusalem in July 1099 seemed to confirm the divine blessing on Western knighthood. The Templars, constituted in 1128, were the extreme example of the union of arms and cross, approved explicitly by no less a figure than St Bernard who, in *De laudibus novae militiae*, said Templars committed not homicide but 'malicide'.

These days, private battles mean business battles and battlefields mean markets. Raids mean hostile takeovers and white knights mean white knights.

A novel entitled *Black Easter* by James Blish draws to its conclusion with Satan having replaced God and finding that he has to do the job of running the universe in very much the same way as God had done (Blish 1968). The decline of the Church in the West has been paralleled by a rise in state responsibility for regulation of the relationship between people and corporations involving criteria of equity, contractual freedom, good faith and honesty. This emerging role of the state received an important boost in mid-century with the New Deal, with Keynesianism, and with the phenomenon of Nazism and Stalinism persuading a large number of people that the state was very much a moral force for good or evil, with secular ideology filling the gap left by ecclesiastical theology (but not doing so adequately). Since the Second World War, the dominant world conflict of economic ideologies resembled the post-medieval conflict between Catholicism and Protestantism; but as the Cold War waned and finally faded away, so the tensions between the West and Islam grew more pronounced in an ironic echo of the medieval Crusades. At the same time, human rights became a more central political concern in much of the world. Indeed, it is arguable that as the 'peace of God' was to the Church 900 years ago, so human rights are now both to much of the modern Church and to the secular successors of the Church's authority in the West. The chief behaviour-modifying instrument of such authority is the law. When the law has to deal with the managerial behaviour of the modern company, it is as reluctant to interfere with business decisions as the old royal courts (especially the assizes) were to interfere with what they might have characterized as proper manorial decisions.

The duties of directors in company law critically focus on the notion of acting in good faith in the interests of the company. In the leading case on the matter in the Commonwealth, an important perspective was expressed by Lord Greene in *Re Smith and Fawcett Ltd ([1942] Ch 304 CA)* thus; 'They [the directors] must exercise their discretion bona fide in what they consider—not what a court may consider—to be in the interests of the company.' Nonetheless the courts limit the directors' discretion by the test of the interest of shareholders generally, which tends to mean maximising profits within a reasonable period (for example, *Parke v Daily News [1962] Ch 927).* When a director uses the company to benefit third parties, the courts will punish this as a breach of the duty of loyalty even though the company is unharmed by it (*Regal (Hastings) Ltd v Gulliver [1967] 2 AC 134).* As regards the standard of care required of directors, the courts take the view that those who appoint the board must bear the consequences of their foolishness (*Re City Equitable Fire Insurance Ltd [1925] 1 Ch 407).* A recent American judgement was that directors were distinguishable from trustees in that directors were appointed to take and manage risks and that imposition of liability for mistakes would hamper that role (*Dynamics Corp of America v CTS Corp [1986] 794 F 2d 250/256).* In contested takeovers the directors are obliged to accept the highest offer, and here the courts will review ordinary business judgement, per L.J. Lawton in *Heron International Ltd v Lord Grade [1983] BCLC 244(CA).* In the United States this is known as the Revlon principle after the objective test of care—whether the highest offer was recommended or not—in *Revlon Inc v Macandrews and Forbes Holdings Inc.* However, in England, J. Hoffmann in *Re Welfab Engineers Ltd (1990) BCC 600,* held that it was not a breach of directors' duty to accept other than the highest of three very closely similar offers in order to secure the workforce's future employment. The law steers clear then, of interfering with business judgements of directors so long as they act in the interests of their company, and this will usually be presumed. Thus the board of a company is like a medieval chief vassal who has *de facto* immunity from interference by the law on his own manor, so long as he is a faithful vassal. A whole literature of scholarship, that of agency theory, has grown up to examine the economic pressures on the board–shareholders relationship that might make the board act in something less than the shareholders' best interests. However, the law does not require directors to act in the shareholders' *best* interests other than in takeover situations: only that they do not try and benefit outsiders at the expense of the company—a much less onerous burden. Stock options, lavish treatment of leading non-executive shareholders, and the maintenance of dividend levels are among the several mechanisms commonly observed to build mutual confidence between boards and shareholders. These things exemplify the creation of trust by institutional mechanisms; and it is to the creation of trust that we turn next.

TRUST CREATION

The notion of trust is central to all economic exchange. Implicit within exchange is a set of common expectations that define appropriate and inappropriate behaviours. These common expectations exist prior to contracting; they provide the necessary background conditions that allow individuals to come together and barter or contract (Neu 1991). Zucker (1986) identifies three different modes of trust production, as follows:

1. Process based, where trust is built on experience of transacting between the parties which builds reputation that goes outside the parties themselves;
2. Characteristic based, where trust is evoked by membership of a class, club, race, profession, school, family, clan or just appearance;
3. Institution based, where trust is tied to formal structures such as contracts, professional certification, use of neutral intermediaries and subjection to effective regulatory structures.

Zucker argues that in the American industrial revolution of the nineteenth century, process-based trust was disrupted by high rates of corporate birth and death, rapid increase in human population, diversity of cultures of origin arising from massive immigration, and by industrialization itself. Institution-based trust became necessary once there was significant social or geographic distance between transacting groups, and the bureaucratic form of organization is argued to be one of the most important of such mechanisms. Zucker posits that institutional mechanisms insure organizations against inability to rely on process-based trust.

> Managers insure the workers against shirking, unions and other employee organizations insure wage earners against owner opportunism, stock markets insure investors against fraud and misrepresentation, professionalization is designed to insure that the training is adequate to the task, regulations insure the parties to a transaction that is regulated against the use of a different set of rules. This kind of 'insurance' forms the basis of transactions when trust needs to be recreated (Zucker 1986: 101).

Thus, the process of industrialization involves a process of replacing process based trust by institution based trust. This applies *a fortiori* to export-led development and to the process of trade globalization, since these things involve dealing with strangers in foreign countries. What is left unsaid here is the possibility that, as process-based mechanisms shrink and institutional-based mechanisms expand, character-based trust may expand temporarily to fill the gap between the other two mechanisms. This might help explain the rapid rise of racism in newly marketizing East Europe, Russia and China. When you no longer rely on old Party friends and cannot yet believe that contracts guarantee performance, it must be tempting to put some minimum degree of trust in racial kinship.

An influential analysis of the economic reforms in China since 1978 highlights the important role played by culture and level of development in shaping transactional structures. One of the ways in which bureaucracy has failed there is in giving way to fiefs so that the distribution of impacted, uncodified information is skewed in favour of a very few opportunistic players (Boisot and Child 1988). They define 'fief' as 'small numbers, hierarchically organized through face-to-face and power relationships that often have to be charismatically legitimated—by such means as the laying on of hands, initiation rites, commendation ceremonies and the like' (ibid.: 508). Like their idea of a bureaucracy, a fief is hierarchically co-ordinated; but a fief differs from a bureaucracy in being materially more concerned that its members share values and beliefs, in the personal rather than impersonal nature of relationships, and by the lack of codification of information. They see the fief as the least efficient way of diffusing or codifying information. They are using the word 'fief' almost as a synonym for the word 'clique', rather than in a way that compares with the medieval fief. The fief as they see it has 'a warm, "involved" rationality of vaguely defined ethical principles applied particularistically' (ibid.: 522). They say China's mishandling of decentralization and delegation issues in its modernization has created new fiefs, and perhaps reinforced old ones in some places, in that country. If we allow that fiefs as cliques in China often facilitate the acquisition of private power, intermixed with public office and occupation of buildings both commercial and residential, then we have made an important link between Boisot-Child fiefs and traditional fiefs. The very important implication of that is, that marketization of command economies involves a significant and possibly inevitable dose of neo-feudalism. If that is to be true of China, it is pertinent to ask whether it was or is true of its neighbour, Japan.

NEO-FEUDAL CHARACTERISTICS OF JAPANESE BUSINESS

The best known techniques of Japanese management are just-in-time inventory control, total quality control and quality circles, lifetime employment expectations, singing the company song at morning rallies, and respect for seniority. All these characteristics are trust-producing mechanisms that combine some institutional characteristics with some process-based ones. They are essential features of Japanese as opposed to Western capitalism.

A recent series of experiments showed that Japanese managers see a work team as an environment in which information is shared in pursuit of improved performance, while Americans used groups to share responsibilities and reduce risks (Sullivan 1992).

In Kaoru Ishikawa's book *What is Total Quality Control?* (1985) he states that the basic teachings of Christianity appear to say that man is by nature evil and that this teaching has cast a shadow over the Western nations' management philosophy. It suggests that people cannot be trusted (Stewart 1992).

Some of the distinctive features of Japanese capitalism may reflect an unbroken feudal tradition in some respects at least. In contrast to the view that, in Japan, capitalism destroyed feudalism and undermined the rule of the elite during the Tokugawa period, commercial wealth was the salvation of the lord and his retainers, since samurai and merchants retained economic primacy and developed innovative institutions, which increased their own profits while providing financial services which sheltered tenant residents from the most severe market dislocations (Johnson 1983).

Even in the present, scandals in Japan have less severe consequences for their perpetrators than in the West. The recent Recruit scandal, involving Japan's four largest securities brokers, has exposed a system in which politicians, bureaucrats, big business and sometimes even gangsters, co-operate to keep the country's economic engine primed. When the Japanese stock market crashed in 1990, Nomura Securities and its three main competitors covered the losses of their best clients and reported the payments as tax-deductible entertainment expenses. The payments broke few laws and shocked few Japanese, but the tax evasion attempts incurred the wrath of the powerful Finance Ministry, whose tax officials began talking publicly about widespread corruption. Nonetheless, the case of Yoshihisa Tabuchi, former president of Nomura Securities, exemplifies how Japan's disgraced business and political leaders can bounce back. Tabuchi resigned from Nomura after acknowledging that the company secretly compensated big clients for stock market losses. News reports charged that Nomura had financed some business enterprises with the Japanese mob. Tabuchi is not out of a job, however; he is now Nomura's new vice-chairman (Rapoport 1991). This extra legal act of nurture could be viewed as an incident of modern vassalage. To put it another way, in order for us to say to you, 'we look after our people', first you have to become one of our people.

A sense of mutual obligation and public weal even extends to the Yakuza. Japan's biggest Yakuza crime syndicate has issued its own code of conduct. The 30,000-member Yamaguchi-gumi's code bans recruits from throwing cigarette buts on the ground, making grand entrances in hotels, trains or golf-courses, or giving out business cards with the gang's symbol. A gang spokesperson explained, 'The basic idea is not to inconvenience the public' (Kohut and Sweet 1994).

It can be appreciated from these snippets that Japanese business society is one where the feudal values of fealty, the personal basis of obligations, and the reluctance to allow public law into the private demesne all flourish. As Japan's multinationals acquire Western business groups, the Japanese expatriate manager class starts to resemble the medieval Normans in their separation from the society of the acquirees and their attempts to mount Japanese business methods on the Anglo-Saxon vernacular.

Yankee Samurai are Americans who are employed by Japanese-owned firms in the United States. Few Yankee Samurai expressed respect for the Japanese employees' strong work ethic and willingness to work long hours, while many expressed resentment. Yankee Samurai are uncomfortable with Japanese 'co-ordinators', often referred to as spies or shadows. Yankee Samurai believe that the personnel rotation policies of Japanese firms keep Japanese employees from really understanding Americans. Japanese management by consensus usually involves only the Japanese managers. Only the Japanese seem to enjoy lifetime employment, and the firm's mission is rarely communicated to the non-Japanese employees (Laurie 1990). There is a strong parallel between these Americans under Japanese management and the British Anglo-Saxons of 900 years ago under the Norman conquest, but it is one that can only be elaborated properly in a far longer work than this paper.

The Korean style of management is credited with much of the success of the country's business ventures. Known as K-type management, its distinguishing characteristics can be summarized as:
1. family or clan management;
2. top-down decision making;
3. flexible lifetime employment;
4. high mobility of workers;
5. Confucian work ethic;
6. paternalistic leadership;
7. loyalty;
8. compensation based on seniority and merit;
9. bureaucratic conflict resolution;

10. close government-business relationship;
11. expansion through conglomeration; and
12. informal bureaucratic standardized system (Lee and Yoo 1987).

Korea has the so far unique distinction of preserving the oath of fealty in its business practices, and of administering it annually. Thus, Korean business is even more feudal than the Japanese but scarcely less successful in conventional economically measured dimensions.

THE FEUDAL PARADIGM

In any system that can meaningfully be termed feudal:

> Public authority has become a private possession. Everyone expects the possessor of a 'court' to make a profit out of it and everyone knows that the eldest son of the court-holder will inherit this profitable right, whatever his qualifications for the work. On the other hand, any important accumulation of private property almost inevitably becomes burdened with public duties. The possessor of a great estate must defend it, police it, maintain roads and bridges and hold a court for his tenants. Thus lordship has both economic and political aspects; it is less than sovereignty, but more than private property (Strayer 1952: 17).

FEUDAL SOCIETY: SOME PREREQUISITES?

From what sort of society does some kind of feudalism evolve? Daniel Bell draws a picture, thus:

> The foundation of any liberal society is the willingness of all groups to compromise private ends for the public interest. The loss of civitas means either that interests become so polarized, and passions so inflamed, that terrorism and group fighting ensues, and political anomia prevails; or that every public exchange becomes a cynical deal in which the most powerful segments benefit at the expense of the weak (Bell 1976: 245).

Some people today write about post-industrial society: the nearer prospect, I fear, is the emergence of a post-society industry. In fact, to a much greater extent than is now imagined, liberal society has already disappeared. Those who persist in framing political and economic discussions in terms of defending and preserving it, in fact, directly contribute to the sterility of intellectual and political activity today (McDermott 1991: 13).

We now discuss the opinion of some writers on organizational behaviour that Western corporations have reached the situation quoted in the previous paragraph.

WESTERN CORPORATE FEUDALISM

Edward Mason (1957) was one of the first Americans to consider whether managers could any longer consider their responsibilities to be of a wholly private nature; America, he said, 'is a society of large corporations ... [whose] management is in the hands of a few thousand men. Who selected these men, if not to rule over us, at least to exercise vast authority, and to whom are they responsible?' He thought administrative hierarchies had replaced the market as society's basic distributive mechanism. When General Electric faced antitrust charges in the 1930s, its Chairman, attorney Owen Young, developed the defence that the modern firm had aggregated wealth to such an extent that it had acquired a public function limiting the owners' rights over that wealth; and, that by divorcing control from ownership, the firm had given its own management an unprecedented degree of autonomy which carried with it the duty of care of any public trustee. He told Harvard Business School class of 1927 that they were public trustees who should be educated as such (Case and Case 1982).

> To the business community and the solicitor, land and capital are equally investments, between which, since they possess the common characteristic of yielding income without labour, it is inequitable to discriminate. Though their significance as economic categories may be different, their effect as social institutions is the same. It is to separate property from creative activity, and to divide society into two classes, of which one has its primary interest in passive ownership, while the other is mainly dependent upon active work (Tawney 1961: 67).

Actually, even as economic resources the resemblance between medieval land and modern capital may be less distant than we generally assume. Early medieval manorial evolution was not a single process of disintegration; great estates were formed and fragmented throughout the period, so resembling blocks of modern capital rather than the inalienable entailed estates of popular imagination (Klingelhofer 1985).

> Property is in its nature a kind of limited sovereignty ... property in things swells, in effect, into something which is sovereignty over persons. 'The main objection to a large corporation', writes Mr Justice Brandeis of the US Supreme Court, 'is that it makes possible—and in many cases makes inevitable—the exercise of industrial absolutism' (Tawney 1961: 77).

Increasingly as it enters 'the government business', the corporation is in the business of refashioning social, health, cultural, and other services not only as commercial products but as products that reflect the corporation's own class, property, power and value relations. All in all then, it is appropriate to view the modern corporation as a fabricator of social relationships, directly, indirectly, blindly and by design, as the case may be (McDermott 1991: 199).

Even Foucault's work is relevant because it suggests that all organizational forms are essentially alike, and, as individuals, we are all imprisoned within an organizational world (Burrell 1988).

These quotations suggest, even if they do not persuade, that the power and influence of modern companies shapes the societies in which they operate. To the extent that this is so, there is the feudal spectre of private power with public duties which the law may be loath to enforce. The relevance of this perspective to business ethics and corporate crime will be argued next.

MODERN BANALITIES

Reich (1987) argues that lack of trust within American business culture is robbing US companies of the flexibility they need to remain competitive. Collective entrepreneurialism—an approach to capitalism in which distinctions between owners and workers are blurred—can create options for companies trying to adjust to economic change. Such a strategy, however, requires a level of trust few American companies can muster. Tacit understandings between employees and managers working together to weather economic hardships are often breached when they become inconvenient. Those who renege on informal agreements may overcome the damage done to their reputations, but those who were betrayed are never as trusting again. Precautions, rules and codes proliferate as trust erodes, and commercial dealings become increasingly constrained by contractual stipulations (Reich 1987).

Rothschild (1985) argues corporate crime is inherent in the free enterprise system. E.F. Hutton's check-kiting operations, Exxon's fraud, Eli Lilly's criminal negligence, as well as the Dalkon Shield and Ford Pinto, are to him only the tip of the iceberg. Greed, ambition and the overriding preoccupation with profit account for much of the criminal activity, but other factors also come into play. Corporations are built on bureaucratic models. The diffusion of responsibility promotes a psychic isolation from the activities of the collective. Nobody in a hierarchy, from the president on down, is immune from pressure, and charges of wrongdoing shock officials, who think of themselves as moral individuals (Rothschild 1985).

Some senior executives are so insulated from financial pressures that they do not realize the effect that their insistence on performance has on many employees. Organizations should not use profits or quotas as the primary basis for evaluation of workers, since this practice can lead workers to fall back on unethical methods of meeting goals. Instead, Hosmer recommends that organizations should put more emphasis on other indicators of performance, such as customer complaints and community attitudes (Hosmer 1987). Any such move would be a move away from scientific Taylorist management towards the 'warm rationality', as Boisot and Child (1988) put it, of fief-based feudalism. More than half of the respondents to a survey by the magazine *Working Woman* believe that business ethics have deteriorated in the 1980s. The majority of respondents said that they had witnessed such foul play as lying to employees, expense-account abuses, and in-office jockeying involving favouritism, nepotism and the taking of credit for other people's work. Almost half have seen sexual and racial discrimination, and just under a third have witnessed lying to make a sale. Nearly 60% of the respondents who don't have a formal code of ethics at their workplace believe that instituting one would be helpful, although fewer than a third of them want the government to regulate ethics (Sandroff 1990). This is the first survey I was able to find where an explicit link was made between reducing malpractice at work and the creation of a corporate 'code', thus echoing the role the medieval Church ascribed to the 'code' of chivalry that it blessed as an instrument to achieve the 'peace of God'.

MENTORS AND MACHIAVELLI

In a *Wall Street Journal* poll ten years ago, the CEOs of Fortune 500 companies named 'integrity' and 'the ability to get along with others' as the qualities most important to success. Ruthless aggressiveness received no mention. A new or young employee can build a reputation for integrity by observing the rules of etiquette. The key principle is to behave as if you are already the boss, not by being aggressive but by being the boss you would like to have. Treat subordinates as people under your protection, not as people who owe you loyalty (Collins 1986). What is striking here is the association of integrity with the suzerain virtues of protective mentoring. In feudalism, knights took on pages and squires. In modern Western business, however, mentors may be selected by their protégé(e)s.

Formal mentor programmes have proliferated in recent years, catering to such diverse groups as disadvantaged students, welfare mothers, corporate executives and university professors. Some studies make loose and inflated claims for mentors, in part because there is no clear definition of the term. A consensus is emerging that sees mentorship as a continuum of developmental alliances, ranging from the intense to the superficial. According to some researchers, a successful mentor–protégé relationship must be based on mutual respect and liking. This assumption sheds doubt on the feasibility of institutionalising mentoring through formal mentor programmes, which have become increasingly popular at major corporations (Hurley 1988).

The importance of mentoring in modern corporate culture is testified to by the seriousness of tone with which popular media treat it. Any ambitious woman who has outgrown her relationship with a mentor needs to free herself from it, advised two writers in *Ms* magazine in 1984. First, recognize the symptoms of a stifling relationship. Then tactfully change it. Regular disagreements with one's mentor are a clue. Change the power balance by behaving like a peer instead of a protégée. Don't ask for advice; make statements; share information. Be sensitive to the mentor whose status is declining in the workplace, but faithful to one's own needs. Individual interests may emerge; share them but pursue them independently. Seek new advisers when a work situation changes. Finally, keep emotional demands out of the relationship (Wheatley and Hirsch 1984). Thus the spirit of Niccolo Machiavelli (*The Courtier* not *The Prince*) lives on.

'To seek a protector, or to find satisfaction in being one— these things are common to all ages. But we seldom find them giving rise to new legal institutions save in civilizations where the rest of the social framework is giving way' (Bloch 1961: 147–8). The mentor has not achieved the status of an institution, but already the lawyers and accountants are strengthening the experience requirement of their students as an important step towards institutionalizing mentoring, for the experience requirement involves tying a named practitioner to a content specified mentoring role.

MUSIC AND MOVEMENT

We are almost at the end of this paper's skimming over the various parallels and the few contrasts between medieval feudalism and modern corporate life. On the whole, more similarities than contrasts have been found or, at any rate, have been argued. It may be objected that modern society is not a caste system in the way that feudal society was. Today a working class boy can enter the aristocracy and plutocracy by becoming a rock star. Some may be surprised to learn that in this, too, the postmodern age echoes feudalism. For feudalism was not a caste system. The troubadour Bernard de Ventadorn was the son of a serf, as was Master of the

Troubadours, Giraut de Borneil, as were many others, according to the twelfth-century *Lives of the Troubadours*. Musicians gained access to enemy castles so routinely that lords sometimes disguised themselves as minstrels to spy or invade (for instance, Alfred the Great with the Danes, Olaf the Viking with Athelstan of Brunanburg, and the minstrel Taillefer who rode into battle with William the Conqueror as a sort of medieval Walkman). The first known poem of the first known troubadour, Eleanor of Aquitaine's grandfather, William of Poitiers, occurred within five years of Urban's call for the First Crusade. Bertran de Born asked 'Why do I wish rich men to hate each other? Because a rich man is much more noble and generous and affable in war than in peace.' So important was one minstrel to his master, William the Conqueror, that he was left three Gloucestershire estates (Foss 1975).

FEUDALISM AND FAMILY

Johnson's (1985) thesis asserts that the institution of the family underwent a transformation during the transition from feudal to modern European society, a transformation which involved the differentiation of the family from other social spheres. This change includes the emergence of a specified normative framework appropriate to family role performance and the sentimentalization of family relationships. A set of family changes, predicted by her theory, were confirmed for the English speaking cases. These include:

- The development of domesticity, that is, a rise in psychic and material investment in home life;
- The association of personal virtue with the married state;
- The reorganization of adult family roles, including the centralization of paternal authority and the elevation of the moral status of the wife; and,
- The probable increase in the incidence of companionate marital practices.

Thus, the modern family is a post-feudal creation, an institution 'privatized' by the effects of the Reformation. The Victorian family, with its Victorian virtues and vices, is scarcely compatible with modern corporate life which reintroduces the feudal linkage between work, society, and family in such rituals as the subordinate's dinner for the boss, the business picnic, attendance at the office sports day, etc., all of which transmit to the family relations the polarities and tensions of office relations.

CONCLUSION

Weber (1961) distinguished two types rationalities of institutions: formal and substantive. The difference between formal and substantial rationality is as follows:

Formal rationality is represented by quantitative calculation and accounting. It represents the extent to which provision for needs is, and can be, expressed in calculable terms.

Substantive rationality represents the degree to which supply of resources is shaped under some set qualitative criterion of values, such as ethical, political, utilitarian, hedonistic, feudal, egalitarian or otherwise.

Formal rationality concerns means and substantive rationality concerns ends. Weber describes modern organizations as systems based on formal rationality with no inherent connection to specific substantive ends or outcomes.

The modern corporation fits that characterization and is the one still central to economic theory and most management courses at most universities. The postmodern corporation, as it responds to pressures for socially responsible behaviour and in some cases seeks to evade them, will move away from that characterization towards a substantive rationality whose value content would be reflected in its mission statement, code of conduct and leadership behaviour internally. This paper has suggested some of the ways in which such a move recreates some of the ingredients of feudalism.

REFERENCES

Bell, D. 1976. *The Cultural Contradictions of Capitalism*. New York: Basic Books.

Blish, J. 1968. *Black Easter; or Faust Aleph-Null.* Garden City, NY: Doubleday.

Bloch, M. 1961. *Feudal Society.* London: Routledge and Kegan Paul.

Boisot, M. and J. Child. 1988. The Iron Law of Fiefs: Bureaucratic Failure and the Problem of Governance in the Chinese Economic Reforms. *Administrative Science Quarterly* 33(4): 507-27.

Burrell, G. 1988. Modernism, Post Modernism and Organisational Analysis 2: The Contribution of Michel Foucault. *Organisation Studies* 9 (2): 221-35.

Case, J.Y. and E.N. Case. 1982. *Owen D. Young and American Enterprise: A Biography.* Boston, MA: Houghton Mifflin.

Collins, E.G.C. 1986. Upward Nobility: The Etiquette of Ambition. *Harper's Bazaar* 119 (March): 202ff.

Foss, M. 1975. *Chivalry.* London: Michael Joseph.

Ganshof, F.L. 1951. *Feudalism.* London: Longmans Green and Co.

Heilbroner, R.L. 1976. *Business Civilisation in Decline.* London: Penguin.

Hosmer, L. 1987. Coping with Ethical Decisions (Views of LaRue Hosmer). *USA Today* (August 10): 116.

Hurley, D. 1988. The Mentor Mystique. *Psychology Today* 22 (May): 38-9.

Hyams, P.R. 1980. *King, Lords and Peasants in Medieval England: The Common Law of Villeinage in the Twelfth and Thirteenth Centuries.* Oxford, UK: Clarendon Press.

Ishikawa, K. 1985. *What is Total Quality Control? The Japanese Way.* (tr. David J. Lu). Englewood Cliffs, NJ: Prentice-Hall.

Kohut J. and R. Sweet. 1994. News from the Fringe. *National Enquirer* (April 19): 35.

Klingelhofer, E.C. 1985. *Manor, Vill and Hundred: Rural Development in the Region of Micheldever, Hampshire 700-1100.* Johns Hopkins University Ph.D. thesis.

Johnson, G.D. 1985. *The Privatisation of the Western Family: A Comparison of England, France, and the American Colonies, 1450-1800.* Southern Illinois University at Carbondale Ph.D. thesis.

Johnson, L.L. 1983. *Patronage and Privilege: The Politics of Provincial Capitalism in Tokugawa Japan.* Stanford University Ph.D. thesis.

Laurie, D. 1990. Yankee Samurai and the Productivity of Japanese Firms in the United States. *National Productivity Review* 9 (2, Spring): 131-9.

Lee Sang M. and Yoo Sangjin. 1987. The K-Type Management: A Driving Force of Korean Prosperity. *Management International Review* 27 (4): 68-77.

Mason, E.S. 1957. *Economic Concentration and the Monopoly Problem.* Cambridge, MA: Harvard University Press.

McDermott, J. 1991. *Coporate Society: Class, Property and Contemporary Capitalism.* Boulder, CO: Westview Press.

Neu, D. 1991. Trust, Contracting and the Prospectus Process. *Accounting, Organisations and Society* 16 (3): 243-56.

Rapoport, C. 1991. Good Life After Disgrace in Japan. *Fortune* 124 (July 29): 12.

Reich, R.B. 1987. Enterprise and Double Cross (Excerpt from Tales of a New America). *The Washington Monthly* 18 (January): 13-9.

Rothschild, M. 1985. No Place for Scruples. *The Progressive* 49 (November): 26-8.

Sandroff, R. 1990. How Ethical is American Business? Results of Survey. *Working Woman* 15 (September): 113-4.

Stephenson, C. 1967. *Medieval Feudalism.* Ithaca, NY: Cornell University Press.

Stewart, J.R. 1992. The Work Ethic, Luddites and Taylorism in Japanese Management Literature. *Industrial Management* 34 (6, November-December): 23-6

Strayer, J.R. 1952. *Feudalism in Western Europe.* London: Macmillan.

Sullivan, J.J. 1992. Japanese Management Philosophies: From the Vacuous to the Brilliant. *California Management Review* 34 (2): 66-87.

Tawney, R.H. 1961 [1921]. *The Acquisitive Society.* London: Collins.

Way, K.G. 1986. *Keeping Trouthe: Fidelity and Speech in Chaucer.* Rutgers University Ph.D. thesis.

Weber, M. 1961. *General Economic History.* New York: Collier Books.

Wheatley, M. and M.S. Hirsch. 1984. Five Ways to Leave Your Mentor. *Ms* 13 (September): 106-8.

Zucker, L.G. 1986. Production of Trust: Institutional Sources of Economic Structure 1840-1920. *Research in Organisational Behaviour* 8: 53-111 (JAI Press).

8

PSYCHIC PRISONERS? MANAGERS FACING ETHICAL DILEMMAS: CASES FROM HONG KONG

Robin Snell

ABSTRACT

This paper provides illustrations, taken from the author's own study involving ten Hong Kong managers,[1] of four forms of 'psychic imprisonment' which restrict managers' ability to resolve ethical dilemmas. These are:
1. having limited ethical reasoning capacity;
2. holding stereotypical assumptions about the nature of organizational structures, responsibilities and power relationships;
3. having stunted organizational responsibilities or power;
4. feeling confined by a particular 'moral ethos'.

The first pair of restrictions are psychic prisons internal to the individual. Both are illustrated by an account of the difficulties experienced by one owner-manager (Kevin) in resolving a dilemma concerning his staff. Kevin's difficulties are partially explained with reference to a model of ethical reasoning inspired by Kohlberg's work (but with some significant revisions). A complementary analysis of Kevin's dysfunctional assumptions about organizing and power then follows.

The second pair of restrictions are 'moral mazes', largely residing outside individuals. Two cases illustrate the third restriction: Eric's case is one of limited responsibility within his organization, while Belinda lacks power. Both individuals have a clear sense of what is right or wrong, but Eric fails to assert his position successfully and Belinda has to resign.

The fourth restriction refers to the impact, on members' experience of moral dilemmas, of the prevailing moral ethos; defined as the ethical atmosphere, milieu or climate within an organization. A second Kohlberg-inspired model portrays different types of moral ethos and suggests their likely impact on moral experience, where the ethical reasoning embraced by a moral ethos is respectively 'higher' than, equivalent to, or 'lower' than the ethical reasoning capacity of the individual concerned. Marina's case is one of a manager caught within a lower moral ethos.

The selection of cases drawn exclusively from Hong Kong shows that Western-inspired concepts of organizational behaviour can contribute to the understanding of a diverse set of ethical dilemmas here. There is no intention to imply that psychic imprisonment is a phenomenon unique to Hong Kong.

INTRODUCTORY PREAMBLE: UNDERLYING CONCEPTS

In this paper, I will attempt to explain typical managerial experience of ethical dilemmas by applying the metaphor of the psychic prison to organizational life. My explanations will also draw heavily on Kohlberg's model of stages of moral and ethical reasoning. This introductory section will therefore explain some background concepts and presuppositions on which subsequent analyses are based. Discussion of the concept of moral ethos will come later in the paper.

On Psychic Prisons and Moral Mazes

Applied in organizational analysis, the metaphor of the psychic prison (Morgan 1986: 199-231) holds that there are hidden aspects of organizational life that imprison the minds of members without their knowing. In cognitive terms, members' ability for imaginative and creative problem solving is impaired because of shared mental sets and common stereotypes. In emotional terms, particular patterns of feeling are impressed upon members but other feelings and perturbations are avoided and defended against. These mindsets and emotional patterns are deeply embedded in the social life of organizing.

Jackall (1988) conducted a seminal study of how business and management ethics, as actually practised by managers rather than 'preached' by business ethicists, was a manifestation of psychic imprisonment. He portrayed the worlds of corporate management as having their own sets of language games, embracing their own logics, rules, etiquette, prohibitions, values and taboos. After Jackall, we may view the corporate ethical landscape as a set of moral mazes, orderly yet puzzling; negotiable only by knowledgeable insiders who, in becoming 'expert', risk losing their sense of wider, universally accepted values and principles.

The implication of these perspectives is that at least some ethical dilemmas may stem from individuals getting caught up in 'webs' of assumptions, meanings, relationships, values, deals, politickings, etc., which have a life beyond the conscious control of any one individual involved.

Ethical Reasoning: A Kohlberg-Inspired Model

Kohlberg's seminal research on moral and ethical reasoning (for example, Kohlberg 1969; 1981; Colby and Kohlberg 1987; Kohlberg and Ryncarz 1990) has been widely cited in the social science literature. Kohlberg's model of stages of ethical development has helped to guide research into ethical judgement among managers (see, for example, Trevino and Youngblood 1990; Trevino 1992).

The Kohlberg model holds that the development of moral reasoning capacity in an individual entails progression through a fixed and invariant sequence of six stages. Kohlbergian theory also assumes that once a particular stage has been reached it governs reasoning until a leap of moral imagination carries the individual to the next stage. Essential concerns at the various stages are, in 'ascending' order (and paraphrasing Kohlberg's terminology):

1. punishment avoidance;
2. 'what's in it for me' instrumental calculation;
3. conformity to one's immediate social circle;
4. conformity to law and order;
5. intrinsic motivation to keep to deeper principles because one perceives them to be in the general interest;

6. intrinsically motivated adherence to such principles perceived as ends in themselves.

There are two main reasons to doubt the applicability of these premises to the ethical reasoning of adults who are managers.

1. *Inappropriate target population:* Kohlbergian theory was created to account for the moral judgement of children, not mature adults.

2. *Artificiality:* Kohlbergian theory explains how people tackle hypothetical dilemmas, not real problems of their own.

Specifically, one may be sceptical about the Kohlbergian notion of ethical development operating as a kind of 'ratchet' in the direction of the higher stages. The everyday concept of corruption implies that moral degeneration may take place. Accordingly, Trevino (1986) considerably watered down the Kohlbergian premise of government by a single stage, arguing that it would hold only once Stage Five had been reached; that individuals capable (for example) of Stage Four would be susceptible to situational influences which may 'pull' them down to Stage Three reasoning or lower.

The implications of my own research work (Snell 1994a) are that Trevino's 'revisionist' view does not go far enough. I found that the reasoning used by individual managers for their own dilemmas would typically cover a wide range of stages, including Stage Five. For example, a manager might consider a cocktail of issues when contemplating whether to obey an instruction to dispose of polluted material by means of clandestine 'dumping'. He or she may fear the wrath of the boss (Stage One), acknowledge the need for rules and regulations to restrict action and protect order (Stage Four), and appreciate the value of protecting the physical environment in the interests of humanity as a whole (Stage Five). I also found (Snell 1994b) that when managers addressed hypothetical dilemma cases, their reasoning ranged across the Kohlbergian spectrum. Principled individuals were not consistently principled.

Nor are the Kohlbergian definitions of the particular stages proven. Drawing on literature concerning the ethical implications of self-development in adults (for example, Loevinger 1976), I have developed a model of ethical reasoning that is inspired by Kohlberg's original version, but which differs from it in certain key aspects (Snell 1993: 12-32). The adapted, Kohlberg-inspired, model is presented below in Table 1, along with some broad typifications of how ethical dilemmas may be experienced at the various stages.

I have made two major departures from the original Kohlberg model. The first is away from Kohlberg's insistence on equating all forms of empathy with Stage Three 'niceness'. At Stage Five, I have incorporated the expression of compassion and empathy (human connectedness and not just superficial politeness) toward 'strangers', after Gilligan (1982). Where this we-feeling is limited to the immediate social and cultural circle, it remains at Stage Three. This is an important distinction, given the increasing globalization of industrial production and trade. The second departure in my model is at Stage Six, which gets away from the exclusive Kohlbergian preoccupation with justice and human rights. Commentators on postmodern philosophy, such as Soper (1991), have detected some drift towards the acceptance of open-endedness, of not knowing for sure which principles provide ultimate foundation for the rest. I have, accordingly, adopted the view of theorists such as Fisher et al. (1987) who emphasize the importance of principled self-questioning, dialogue, irony and respect for open-endedness.

Researchers have found (Trevino and Youngblood 1990; Weber 1990, 1991, 1993) that the majority of managers reason at Stages Three or Four. I have shaded parts of Table 1 to suggest the most common type of dilemmas that may be expected if their findings were to be extrapolated to Hong Kong.

PSYCHIC IMPRISONMENT: AN ILLUSTRATIVE CASE STUDY (KEVIN'S CASE)

The case presented in this section illustrates two forms of psychic imprisonment. Kevin is owner and managing director of a small company that he set up when he was 34 years old and which now has eleven staff. He tells his story about a dilemma concerned with choosing between two loyal members of staff.

Four years ago, this company started with three staff, one in promotion, the other two in design. The two designers really helped me a lot. They were very important to me, and were both enthusiastic.

Table 1: A Kohlberg-Inspired Typology of Ethical Dilemmas

Stage of development of ethical reasoning	Value and limitations of reasoning at this stage	Typical dilemma associated with competing claims at this stage	Typical dilemma entailed by pressures or temptations to enact a lower stage
1. Avoid punishment; obey those in authority.	No value other than to the individual or their 'master'. Self-centred, pre-conventional reasoning. No sense of social responsibility or obligation. Adherents require constant supervision and monitoring.	If I do X, I may get caught and be put in prison. If I don't do X, my boss will fire me.	
2. Seek personal gain; avoid losing out.		To get best commission for myself, using my client's money, do I go for low risk-low return or high risk-high return?	If I do X, I might make a lot of money for myself, but if I get discovered, I may go to prison.
3. Earn the approval of others around you or attached to you by being nice to them and by fitting in with their expectations.	A form of conventional morality. Adherents may serve family, friends and even employers well, but may 'bend the rules' and/or discriminate against outsiders if they know no one will find out.	A favoured customer has asked me to offer special terms; if others discover this they will be offended that I have not helped them also.	I know that my friends and family would be ashamed of me if they found out that I did X, but I stand to gain a great deal by doing it.
4. Conform to rules, laws, codes and conventions.	Conventional morality. Adherents can be trusted to maintain rules, keep promises, honour contracts, etc. They lack moral imagination and forget what the rules were intended to achieve, nor address new circumstances nor special cases.	I may be caught between a supplier asking me for a 'special commission' to meet a deadline, and a client demanding that I keep my promise to fulfil his/her order in time.	I can make everyone involved happy by turning a blind eye to the regulations.

Table 1   (cont.)

5. Follow principles based on respect for people and their rights, other organisms, the greater good, a strong sense of empathy and compassion for the human condition (strangers included) etc.	Post-conventional morality. Adherents have stronger and more rigorous ethical principles than are required by law or convention. Others may find this uncomfortable or even oppressive, or argue that it is not good for business.	My principles are in conflict. My supplier breaks no laws, but I worry about environmental pollution and poor standards of safety. I may withdraw my business, but if I do it may result in further unemployment in a locality where there is great poverty.	I am tempted to adopt lower standards (i.e., merely comply with the law) on occasion, in order to maintain a level playing field with competitors who simply keep within the law.
6. Continually question your own actions and principles.	A form of post-conventional morality. Adherents will take no ethical position for granted and will actively question their own every move. Possibly more suited for a life of contemplation?	I constantly strive for the highest ethical standards, but everything I do is problematic. There are no clear 'right answers' or solutions. Every dilemma resolved leads to further dilemmas.	Rather than constantly questioning, and agonizing over values and principles, I prefer to commit myself to some specific cause.

Before I hired them, both of them had been students of mine and had very good potential. They had studied in the same class, and had a good relationship with one another. We struggled hard together when the company started. We worked overnight for six days a week. We had such a close relationship that we seemed like brothers. They came to my house to repair my hi-fi!

As time went by, we got more clients and I couldn't approach all my clients in person. I also had to assign my designers to talk directly to suppliers. The title of designer was not sufficiently representative for them to use when they were dealing with the photographer, so I wanted to promote one or the other of them to creative director. Deciding which one should be promoted was such a dilemma that it took me half a year to decide. The dilemma was that I had to choose which one to keep, because I knew that the one who hadn't been promoted would resign. I didn't have pressure from my staff, and felt no responsibility for their feelings. What made it so difficult was that I would really miss having both of them together.

Before I announced my decision, the one whom I had decided to promote said that he had had no expectation for promotion, and that if the other one left, he would have to take up all the work.

It was a matter of subjective judgement on my part. The design profession is not like sales, where performance is assessed by the figures. Eventually, I promoted the one whom I liked more. This was mainly because of personal interest. We have a similar creative style and I don't need to spend much time directing him. Staff with a different style require constant instruction and supervision. My staff have the right to create their own design pattern, but within my boundary! I want my clients to recognize our characteristic production. I am not unique in this. Most of my contemporaries in the design profession started their own company with their name on it and we can't bear to have a different style attached to it.

The one who left has a good relationship with me now. He came back to visit us regularly and joined our Christmas parties and gatherings. I have the feeling that I forced him to go. When he resigned, I searched for jobs for him as compensation. The job I introduced to him offered better prospects than remaining in our company, and I was concerned that it would provide a suitable environment for him.

If I came across the same case again, I would handle it differently. I would promote both of them, let them head up two different teams. I don't know why I didn't think of this at that time. However, I don't think this case will happen again. My other employees do not share the same experience as we had at that time. I can promote anyone as I like without explanation, just like others do in the business.

I handled this case quite well, no one has any hatred for me. But the company lost a talented member of staff. I intend to expand my business in some other location, and had tentative discussions with him. He is willing to come back to work with me, although it would have to be in a different location.

Restriction One: Limited Ethical Reasoning Capacity

A major theme in this account may be encapsulated in Kohlbergian terms as a dilemma of 'interpersonal concordance'; Kevin is imprisoned by the internal contradictions of his own Stage Three ethical reasoning. Having (it appears) to choose between two protégés for one senior position, Kevin, who strives to be a 'nice' paternalistic boss, realizes that the feelings of one party or the other will inevitably be hurt. Kevin procrastinates because he cherishes the social harmony that exists between all three parties and does not want to destroy it. In the end, he manages to limit the emotional 'damage' of his decision but fails to achieve a satisfactory result, inasmuch as he loses a valuable staff member.

Kevin would have had more options had he been able to draw on insights from the next stage up. A Stage Four perspective would have given him the choice of drawing up a clear statement of the requirements of the new post, that is, some ground-rules against which to assess each candidate. This would have provided a relatively 'objective' and orderly basis for making and justifying a decision. In Kevin's case, however, there is another problem ...

Restriction Two: Stereotypical Assumptions About Organizational Structures, Responsibilities and Power Relationships

An analysis of ethical reasoning in Kohlbergian terms alone fails to provide a complete explanation for Kevin's dilemma. He claims that the decision cannot necessarily, even from a professional point of view, be made objectively because of the prevailing emphasis, within the industry, on aesthetic judgements. Given a vacuum of objectivity, he believes he has no choice but to impose his own subjectively derived aesthetic standards, but also worries that this may result in his being perceived as the maker of arbitrary, unfair decisions.

Further analysis reveals two underlying issues on which Kevin implicitly and unconsciously took a position. One concerns the narcissism of owner-management. Kevin owns the company; it embodies his own personality, his own aesthetic judgements. Its integrity must be preserved even if, in so doing, harmonious working relationships are jeopardized; plurality of styles cannot be tolerated. Perhaps, unconsciously, Kevin was looking for an excuse to get rid of the staff member whose style did not conform to his own?

Or perhaps Kevin was able to avoid narcissism, but may yet have been temporarily blinded by his assumptions about organizing, and hence may have missed the obvious point that there was no need to choose one staff member over the other? His presupposition of the need for hierarchical structuring is a typical one among owner-managers—and it may be difficult for Kevin to conceptualize alternatives.

Had Kevin been conscious and explicit about his position on these two underlying issues, to do with house-style and basic organizing principles, he would have seen the dilemma as an existential choice between either forming a pyramidal, monolithic organization structure that would deliver his own stylistic stamp, or forming a flatter, pluralistic structure with a diversity of styles. His psychic imprisonment means that he automatically accepted the former option as the only possible choice.

MORAL MAZES: RESTRICTIONS RESIDING OUTSIDE INDIVIDUALS

Kevin's case highlights his own internal psychic prisons. 'Neurotic organization' theory (Kets de Vries and Miller 1984) suggests also that in time a 'compulsive' culture may develop in Kevin's company, and that future employees may face dilemmas of standing up for their professional integrity versus satisfying their boss's implicit subjective preferences. In other words, Kevin's future employees may find themselves caught up in moral mazes created by Kevin. Eric's case, which follows, exemplifies what may be a common source of ethical dilemmas among subordinate staff.

Restriction Three: Stunted Organizational Responsibilities or Power

Eric works as Administration Manager for a trading company with twenty staff. During his three years' service, one of his dilemmas was as follows.

My boss became an agent for a client in the United States whom he had known for many years. The client informed us that he had got *an order for several hundred thousand PVC toys, and would like us to quote a price for them. My boss quoted one on the basis of the photo that the client had submitted. On receiving a sample of the toys, my administrators discovered that the price quoted previously had been too low, and that it should have been US$1 instead of US$0.70. However, the client insisted on the initial price, refused to negotiate with us and requested to talk to our boss directly. We tried to persuade our boss to amend the price before the order was confirmed, otherwise, we would suffer a loss in that transaction. However, my boss didn't take any action at that time. We didn't know our boss's baseline. We were in a difficult and helpless situation.*

Six months later, the client confirmed the order. My boss had forgotten what had happened, but on being reminded he realized his mistake. We decided to explain the situation to the agent during his visit to Hong Kong. However, the agent still would not accept any increase in the price. I again suggested to my boss not to accept the order. However, he felt obliged to live with the mistake he had committed and kept his promise on the first order, which was for 200,000 pieces and would result in us suffering a great loss. As a partner in our business, I think it was unfair and lacking in mutual benefit for the client to insist on that business order, since he knew very well that we would be in deficit. We had, in addition, also quoted the wrong price for the mould-making. The client pointed out that he had a right to earn profits and that any loss on our part was nothing to do with him.

I think both parties were in the wrong. My boss didn't follow the rules for quoting the price, and failed to take appropriate action afterwards. He pointed out that it was his own money at stake, but I didn't agree with his way of handling things. He didn't want to be a dirty hand and spoil the relationship between him and the client. The client took advantage of us and took us for fools. He knew very well about our difficulties but forced us to keep to the price, even though he had no legal basis.

In spite of these grievances, I carried on handling the order since it also involved a third party—the buyer. It's our responsibility to fulfil the buyer's need after receiving the purchase order.

If the same situation were to happen again, the process and outcome may be similar. My boss always stresses that he is the one who owns the company. We can only advise him to take action sooner, and I have to follow the rules even if there are better ways to handle the case and even though my moral responsibility is to fulfil the organization's need to the best of my abilities.

Through this case, I learnt not to trust people and that our own interests have to be protected. A small company can easily go bankrupt because of wrong decision making and needs clear baselines, or we will be worn out bit by bit and overtaken by others.

Eric's dilemma stems from not having the authority to put into practice his own Stage Four concern for the legitimate interests of his employing organization. The agent will only do business with Eric's boss. Eric is disturbed by the failure of his boss (the owner!) to follow rules designed to ensure that the company achieves fair business agreements. Eric urges him to reconsider the deal but fails. It appears that the owner then forgets about the case completely until it is too late to renegotiate. One can only speculate why the owner failed so dismally to protect his own interests. Maintaining face? Some other undeclared interest? As it turned out, Eric found a loophole through which he could escape from the dilemma:

When payment was due, the agent explained that the client had run into cash-flow problems, could cover payment for only a proportion of the items ordered, and therefore had no option but to reduce the order correspondingly. I took this opportunity to point out that any departure from the initial agreement would render it null and void. I cancelled the order and we sold off all the items on the Hong Kong market and in the end broke even on the episode.

Probably more often the escape from a dilemma of disempowerment requires resignation. Belinda was in her twenties when she faced the following ethical dilemma.

When I worked in a hotel, one boss showed particular interest in me. I felt under a lot of pressure once he expressed this interest. He was very explicit, so everyone knew about it.

I knew that in material terms I could get anything I wanted from him. He let me decide the rate of my annual increment. But I didn't want to give anything in return, and it went against my ethics to manipulate him, so I chose to leave.

I rejected him for two reasons. First, I believed that I had sufficient ability to do the job and get what I wanted without recourse to such means. I had already achieved quite a lot in my job and I had no need to use a relationship with him as a means to go further. Secondly, if I used such a method I would lose the respect of my colleagues. I did not want my reputation to be spoiled. I regard colleagues as part of the same 'family'. I spend more time with them than with my husband. I only have two hours a day with him. If staff recognize your commitment to the job, they in turn will do everything in order to fulfil job requirements.

Another consideration was business travel, which I had to do all the time. Given that my boss had special fondness for me, how should I behave? How should he behave? That was a problem.

Of course, if I had the same fondness for him, that would have been another story. I enjoyed the projects that I was involved in, but I didn't regret my decision to resign from that post, or feel that I was losing anything. I would not have been happy continuing to work in such an environment, and would not have felt free.

As I grow older, I know how to handle such things. I believe that if I don't want to have something like this, it will not happen, otherwise there must be something wrong with me. Nobody will continue to fight a losing battle. I won't give myself any excuses. I know how to control myself.

Belinda's preoccupation with maintaining a decent reputation is a sign of Stage Three ethical reasoning. That the only obvious means of preserving her reputation required her to resign from the job reveals the lack of a recognized base from which to assert her rights against the assumed prerogatives of a male superior. Her case, along with that of Eric, is evidence that ethical dilemmas faced by middle or junior managers may sometimes stem from the mistakes, oversights, or ill intentions of seniors with power over them.

MORAL ETHOS

Another source of disempowerment, or strong constraint on moral action, may be moral ethos, defined as the social climate predisposing members of an organization toward adopting and enacting some particular ethical standards and deflecting them away from others.

In Jackall's (1988) sociological study of three large US corporations, moral ethos referred to the managerial morality implicitly emerging as people interacted to conduct their business. Lavoie and Culbert (1978) and Petrick and Wagley (1992) identified six types of moral ethos, matching with the original Kohlberg stages. My revised map of moral ethos corresponds to the Kohlberg-inspired model in Table 1. It is the basis of Table 2 (see also Snell 1993: 85-100). I used this to illuminate and differentiate between six reported cases from the social science literature (see Snell 1993: 101-27). My current research has begun to measure moral ethos via a questionnaire with six scales corresponding to the logics of: fear; advantage; members only; official regulation; quality/principle orientation; soul-searching.

Caution is due. Besides the two reasons for doubt and scepticism mentioned earlier in this paper (inappropriate target population and artificiality), two more may be added:

1. *Ungroundedness*. The maps have been drawn up *a priori*, from Kohlberg-inspired theory, and are not based on empirical research into organizational life.
2. *The fallacy of reification*. Kohlbergian theory itself was developed for individuals, not for organizations as entities.

To understand fully a moral ethos, quantitative data must be interpreted in conjunction with qualitative data gathered through interviews, observation, documentary evidence, etc. The work of Jackall (1988) and Toffler (1986) suggests that the moral ethos of organizations in the West emphasizes Stages Two and Three. Preliminary indications regarding moral ethos in Hong Kong are that Stages Two, Three, and perhaps Four are prevalent. If most Hong Kong managers reason at Stage Three or Four, then perhaps we may find that the shaded areas in Table 2 portray the most common kinds of ethical experience here.

Restriction by Moral Ethos

The next case demonstrates the focusing (hence also limiting, imprisoning) effect of a moral ethos. The prevailing ethical reasoning-in-use and resulting social atmosphere may channel members' attention and emotional energy towards particular concerns and preoccupations. At the time of interview, Marina was 32 years old and had worked in her industry for three years, having

Table 2: Different Types of Moral Ethos and Their Impact on the Ethical Experience of Members at Particular Stages of Ethical Reasoning

Prevalent stage of ethical reasoning within the moral ethos. (Characterized by ...)	Typical impression on a member accustomed to the 'next highest' stages of ethical reasoning	Typical impression on a member capable of or accustomed to compatible ethical reasoning	Typical impression on a member accustomed to or only capable of the 'next lowest' ethical reasoning
1. Fear-ridden; oppression, coercion, violent conflicts, unquestioning conformity to rigid command.	Under pressure (threats, blackmail, etc.) to carry out or collude with certain actions. Is prepared to put up with this as long as he/she gets something out of it, too.	Just does what he/she is told, no questions asked, and hopes that he/she comes to no harm.	
2. Advantage-driven; grafting, 'horse-trading', secretive scheming, sour anarchy, obsession with profits, bottom lines, meeting targets with no other questions asked.	Would like to work with people he/she can look up to or trust, but can't do that here because all they seem to care about are their own interests, sometimes balanced against narrow outcome measures. Sometimes feels disgusted with this; regards it as not a 'nice' place.	Makes sure, as best s/he can, that s/he gets a fair deal from others — you scratch my back, I'll scratch yours. Recognizes that others seem to have the same approach. Is prepared to cut corners, as long as s/he is not taken for a ride and made to take the rap if s/he gets found out.	Likes the clear targets, but often worries about the lack of precise instructions for meeting them. Is scared because many people have been fired or have come under legal scrutiny, doesn't want to be the next. Is therefore careful about where s/he takes orders from.
3. Members only; paternalism, cliquish bonding, concern for style, image, impression management, the need to fit in, being good to fellow 'insiders' and by indifference toward 'outsiders'.	Wants fairness and proper consistency. Gets disturbed by subtle biases against certain types of personnel, applicant or client, and by bending of rules and relaxation of standards to favour some at the expense of others.	Doesn't like everything here, and feels some people have not been treated at all well, but has learned to fit in and accept that certain things are not his/her concern. No particular complaints.	Seems to have difficulty fitting in, because others sense that he/she behaves selfishly and is only a 'team player' when it suits him/her to be one.

Table 2   (cont.)

4. Regulated; the need to abide by strict rules and procedures, emphasis on the 'correct' way of handling cases, subject to auditing and accountability.	Appreciates the need for rules and procedures, to help prevent abuse, corruption, etc. Concerned that others forget or fail to understand the underlying principles that the rules are designed to protect. Worries about the failure to adopt a more actively principled approach.	Very comfortable with having an orderly set of rules and procedures and wants to protect them. Regards their enforcement as a matter of principle in itself. Sometimes disturbed by anomalies and loopholes in the rules. Wary of establishing precedent.	Unhappy about the cold and impersonal nature of the rules, when they fail to favour friends or associates. Looks for loopholes or bends the rules to favour those to whom he/she wants to give a 'good turn'.
5. Quality and principle-driven; open dialogue but 'right-on' rigour, mutual attune-ment and alignment around a clearly articulated and publicly defended set of core values.	Occasionally detects, and gets perturbed by, a sense of 'groupthink'. Unhappy about others' tendency to accept some values without question.	Highly committed to the mission, values and products or services of the organization. Ready to argue for and justify such work, and to encourage other organizations to adopt similar values.	Complains that colleagues go too far and expect too much. Disturbed by the mess and disorder caused by constant demands to change rules and procedures or address new problems.
6. Soul-searching; humility, thoughtful and rigorous self-regulation, ongoing dialogue about and critical questioning of guiding principles.		Feels challenged by being a member but contented by that challenge. The only ethical position taken for granted is the requirement to scrutinize his/her own assumptions and actions constantly.	Gets impatient and frustrated by the lack of interest by the organization to align itself behind any particular 'cause' or movement. Wants to put ethical principles into practice.

previously worked with a major competitor of her current company.

Almost every company has confidential information that it is afraid to release. In our industry, there are several competitors and the tendency is to buy information, to find every way to get information. Sometimes we have been astonished to read leaked information in the newspapers.

One big dilemma stemmed from when I was involved in a particular project. We did not want to announce the details in advance, because a competitor would probably have been able to put a stop to it. So we decided to keep all the information confidential and release it only one week before completion. There were only ten people at the meeting where we discussed the details but the information appeared in one of the newspapers the next day.

The company suspected that there was a spy and we made jokes about the possibility of telephone bugging. The information was reported in such detail that people suspected that some form of bribery had been involved.

I found out later on that somebody had been blaming me for the leak. I knew nothing about it at the time, but the company had compiled a list of suspects, and my name had been at the top. Other people's suspicions had been aroused because I had a good friend who worked on that newspaper, and who had given me a Christmas card at a social event. I only found out about this afterwards, through my head of dept. How stupid of me not to have realized!

To resolve the matter, the news reporter concerned agreed to give our boss a chance. If he mentioned a name who hadn't leaked the information, she would say no, otherwise she would keep silent. Eventually, the truth came out and the informant resigned.

After this incident, I began to wonder whether this industry was too complicated and not worth working for. I also wondered why I had been the suspect. I felt that this industry was too dirty. I thought of resigning because I had the feeling that it was just like a Triad society. There are too many tricks. Having had several experiences like this, I have come to trust nobody at work. The one whom you trust may be the one who wants to take over your post. People pay more attention to manipulating human factors rather than to the work itself.

It was so uncomfortable to find out that my peers had been suspecting me without my knowing it. I don't think it's right for people to jump to conclusions so quickly. It requires time and patience. If I had been the boss in this case, I would have asked all those involved to come in, and give them a chance to explain. Then I would have used my judgement to find out the truth. I would have kept the enquiry open.

The incident reminded me that we have to see things from many different angles. Even if we have a bias against somebody, we still have to recognize their strength. It also showed me that I had problems with the impression that I was giving other people. I believed that I had expressed myself clearly and directly, but the outcome showed that I had to think something over before I said it. Having been hurt several times, I understand the need for wisdom in human relationships. It is worth providing training in the form of workshops in office communication skills, so that communication problems can be shared internally.

Marina's preoccupation with her own reputation (how dare they suspect *her* of unauthorized disclosure of information! How stupid she was not to realize that she had been the prime suspect!), her distaste for the 'dirty', ugly office politics, and her regret at not being able to trust people at work are all Stage Three concerns. Towards the end of the account, her allusion to the need for interpersonal skills training suggests a desire for more orderly communication channels, and possibly reveals an ability for Stage Four ethical reasoning. Her overall emotional state, however, is bound up with the failure of her Stage Three needs for 'nice' human relationships. The moral ethos depresses her ethical reasoning, orienting it toward Stage Three. Within the moral ethos itself, Stage Two ethical reasoning appears to prevail: that someone has sought personal advantage by 'selling' their integrity is not an isolated incident. Marina's mention of 'Triad society', tricks and manipulation sums it up.

The implications of the case are:
–   if a moral ethos in which a manager operates is some way below his or her corresponding ethical reasoning capacity, the manager will feel distressed and morally imprisoned; and
–   may reason and act 'below capacity' in terms of ethics.

CONCLUSION

Four kinds of restriction on managers' ethical reasoning and action have been highlighted. Further research may bring more restrictions to light, but enough work has been done to warrant the following observations regarding implications for business ethics in Hong Kong:

1. While there may be some need to improve ethical reasoning capacity by providing training for managers in ethical rules and principles, this is only a small part of the story.
2. Attention must be paid to 'systemic' pressures and dynamics mitigating against ethical behaviour by otherwise well-intentioned managers.
3. The way individual managers (and their bosses) think about organization structure and responsibility may be at least as important a factor in governing ethical conduct as their ethical views and perspectives *per se.*
4. Secondary socialization may serve to 'depress' ethical conduct. In some organizations, even if 'lower' norms are not internalized, capacity for the highest levels of ethical reasoning may be decommissioned.

NOTE

1. The research on which this paper was based was funded by City Polytechnic of Hong Kong Small-Scale Research Grant 903-208, and was carried out in three phases. First, ten Hong Kong managers were interviewed regarding ethical dilemmas that they had experienced. Second, an ethical reasoning questionnaire was developed, drawing on cases from the first phase, and administered to 86 postgraduate management students. Third, a moral ethos questionnaire was developed and distributed to employees in two organizations. The author extends his thanks to Leung Lai-Kit, Kitty, who as Research Assistant conducted, translated, and transcribed all the interviews in the first phase, and helped in the analysis of the second phase. He also thanks Leung Wing-Gi, Gigi, Research Assistant, for help during phases two and three.

REFERENCES

Colby, A. and L. Kohlberg. 1987. *The Measurement of Moral Judgement: Theoretical Foundations and Research Validations, and Standard Issue Scoring Manual* Volumes 1 and 2. Cambridge, MA: Harvard University Press.

Fisher, D., K. Merron and W.R. Torbert. 1987. Human Development and Managerial Effectiveness. *Group and Organisation Studies* 12(3): 257-73.

Gilligan, C. 1982. *In a Different Voice: Psychological Theory and Women's Development.* Cambridge, MA: Harvard University Press.

Jackall, R. 1988. *Moral Mazes: The World of Corporate Managers.* New York: Oxford University Press.

Kets de Vries, M. and D. Miller. 1984. *The Neurotic Organisation.* San Francisco: Jossey-Bass.

Kohlberg, L. 1969. Stage and Sequence: The Cognitive Developmental Approach to Socialisation. In *Handbook of Socialisation Theory and Research.* Ed. Goslin. Chicago: Rand McNally: 347-480.

Kohlberg, L. 1981. *Essays on Moral Development. Volume One: The Philosophy of Moral Development.* San Francisco: Harper and Row.

Kohlberg, L. and R.A. Ryncarz. 1990. Beyond Justice Reasoning: Moral Development and Consideration of a Seventh Stage. In *Higher Stages of Human Development.* Ed. Alexander and Langer. Oxford, UK: Oxford University Press.

Lavoie, D. and S.A. Culbert. 1978. Stages of Organisation and Development. *Human Relations* 31(5): 417-38.

Loevinger, J. 1976. *Ego Development: Conceptions and Theories.* San Francisco: Jossey-Bass.

Morgan, G. 1986. *Images of Organisation.* Beverly Hills, CA: Sage.

Petrick, J.A. and R.A. Wagley. 1992. Enhancing the Responsible Strategic Management of Organisations. *Journal of Management Development* 11(4): 57-72.

Snell, R.S. 1993. *Developing Skills for Ethical Management.* London: Chapman and Hall.

Snell, R.S. 1994a. Adapting Kohlberg: Mapping How Managers

Use Soft Ethical Reasoning for Their Own Dilemma Cases. Under review for *Human Relations*.

Snell, R.S. 1994b. Does Lower-stage Ethical Reasoning Emerge in More Familiar Contexts? Under review for *Journal of Business Ethics*.

Soper, K. 1991. Postmodernism, Subjectivity and the Question of Value. *New Left Review* (March-April): 186.

Toffler, B.L. 1986. *Tough Choices: Managers Talk Ethics*. Chichester, NY: John Wiley.

Trevino, L.K. 1986. Ethical Decision Making in Organisations: A Person-Situation Interactionist Model. *Academy of Management Review* 11(3): 601-17.

Trevino, L.K. 1992. Moral Reasoning and Business Ethics: Implications for Research, Education, and Management. *Journal of Business Ethics* 11: 445-59.

Trevino, L.K. and S.A. Youngblood. 1990. Bad Apples in Bad Barrels: A Causal Analysis of Ethical Decision-making Behaviour. *Journal of Applied Psychology* 75: 378-85.

Weber, J. 1990. Managers' Moral Reasoning: Assessing Their Responses to Three Moral Dilemmas. *Human Relations* 43(7): 687-702.

Weber, J. 1991. Adapting Kohlberg to Enhance the Assessment of Managers' Moral Reasoning. *Business Ethics Quarterly* 1(3): 293-318.

Weber, J. 1993. Exploring the Relationship Between Personal Values and Moral Reasoning. *Human Relations* 46(4): 435-63.

9

CORPORATE ETHICS AND INTERNATIONAL BUSINESS: SOME BASIC ISSUES

Klaus M. Leisinger

INTRODUCTION

Questions about the ethical justification of human activity have occupied philosophers since time immemorial. Whether Laozi, Confucius, the writers of the Gospels, or Fathers of the Church like Augustine or Thomas Aquinas: they all have comparable concepts of what is good and bad human behaviour and what constitutes sensible human existence. Those of us wishing to discover suitable working principles can refer to Immanuel Kant, Max Weber or Hans Jonas. One way or the other, no one today can claim that there are no interesting impulses for appropriate ethical reflection. However, anyone who examines the current social and environmental situation in the world is liable to be disappointed about the influence that the accumulated moral-philosophical wisdom is having in practice.

Since the mid-1970s and increasingly since the beginning of the 1990s, the ethical perspective has been moving more and more to the forefront of social thought. Every significant profession and every institution that thinks anything of itself has its 'something ethics' to proclaim, and environmental ethics, media ethics, research ethics and even corporate ethics are the consequences. The latter has recently, along with environmental ethics, gained most in significance. There are now a great number of national and international books, seminars, symposia, professorships, ethics networks, and journals exclusively devoted to business ethics. There can be no doubt that not only is 'ethics' 'in', but so too is business ethics.

Why should this be so? Has there been a fundamental shift in social value systems and has the 'worth' of ethical argument increased as a result? That would be an explanation, for when traditional ways of life and institutions are no longer taken for granted, philosophical ethics, guided by the idea of sensible human life, seeks generally valid arguments about good and just behaviour in a methodical way. There is no need to point out that we are living in a time of great social change. If social change were to move in the direction of higher morals, then all social groups and institutions—including business enterprises—would be faced with new legitimation demands. Economic performance alone is no longer enough to give businesses legitimacy. Non-economic demands, for example, the sustainable fulfilment of social and environmental responsibility in industrialised and developing countries, have been increasing their significance for legitimation for many years.

Or does the new interest in ethical debate stem from a publicly perceived violation of old 'unspoken grounds for legitimation'? Is ethical thought so vehemently in demand because existing morals are in such dire straits? There is at least the suspicion that those who talk a lot about ethics may be on a rather shaky moral footing themselves and are using ethical alibis to appease a critical public. Looking over what has passed for 'market economy' in many Eastern European countries following the demise of communism, one almost finds oneself agreeing with this argument.

Philosophical reflection is without doubt a fulfilling and intellectually challenging matter, also for those that bear responsibility in corporations. But if one wishes to do more than just get traditional moral philosophical knowledge over to people or preach romantic idealism, then ethics, including corporate ethics, must come down from its lofty realm of 'ideas' or 'values' and establish itself in day-to-day reality. Acting responsibly would then not mean swearing allegiance to higher notions of approvable behaviour, but would emerge from a very worldly setting in which a corporation's or individual's activity has to be based on *real* people with all their strengths and weaknesses, not on *ideal* people that we would all like to have but seldom meet.

Acting *responsibly* always and primarily means acting *intelligently*, that is, carefully weighing up the benefits and harm that one's own actions can bring. All moral activity occurs on the basis of a balance between the realization of interests and the avoidance of physical, social, or even state sanctions—not to mention those in any afterlife. Here I share the view of the German philosopher and business consultant Rupert Lay, that people—privately, in corporations or other institutions—usually tend to act according to the principle of 'marginal ethics'. In other words, they are prepared (consciously or unconsciously) to pay a mental, social, emotional, and financial price only in so far as they can expect a marginally higher mental, social, emotional, and financial return, at least in the long term (Lay 1993: 15ff). I also share his conviction that an institution's efforts to go beyond the level of marginal ethics leads to a higher common good, and that, in the final analysis, this again has positive effects for the institutions concerned.

From this perspective, much of what is called 'unethical conduct' is primarily unintelligent, occasionally even stupid, behaviour that focuses on supposed short-term advantages without considering mid- and long-term consequences. The impotence of ethics is shown in the fact that most people choose to maximize their own benefits when economic and political decisions have to be made, and are only prevented from acting against the common interest by governments branching out into many walks of life. A reflection on corporate ethics must always bear this in mind, and precisely because it must always aim higher and dig deeper than merely avoiding unintelligent behaviour. Intelligent thinking will help to reduce selfish tendencies in our societies. To assume that altruism and a holistic world-view are predominant human characteristics would be unrealistic.

I share the view of the German philosopher Vittorio Hösle, that it is impossible 'to eradicate egoism; and one should not try to achieve the impossible, because it detracts from attaining really important things; and one should be sparing with one's energies, for they are limited' (Hösle 1991: 99ff). The figure of Don Quixote might be ridiculous, but it still has something noble, for it reminds us that ideals constantly transcend reality without losing their validity as regulatory ideas. But if such a 'Don Quixote' had management responsibility in a corporation, this nobility would quickly pale and give way to the ridiculous.

There are two reasons that make it worthwhile to reflect on business ethics. One is that social change in the direction of a higher social and moral order is not only urgently necessary but also possible. The other is that moral enthusiasts who run the risk of foundering when faced by institutional resistance are—at least in my value judgement—more attractive and the lesser evil than thoughtless administrators of the status quo. The latter alternative reminds me of Hannah Arendt, who spoke of the 'banality of evil' during the Eichmann trial in Jerusalem: she found that behind atrocity was not demoniac evil, not unconscious hatred, but no deeper motives at all—just thoughtlessness, a failure to think, and dull observance of routine behavioural rules (Arendt 1964).

So as not to be misunderstood—I am not comparing those in responsible positions in corporations and authorities with a national socialist mass murderer. But if there is a lack of thought in situations deciding the life and death of millions of people, how much more probable is it in situations which are not of such vital significance? I presume that also today, the analysis of a situation in which an individual's action turned out to be 'evil' will probably more often point to thoughtlessness, taking things for granted that should not be taken for granted at all, to self-justifications and clichés, than to circumstances where someone who really knew better was acting in an evil and destructive way.

THE PERCEPTION OF CORPORATE ETHICS

Society's Perception

If one consults the Holy Scriptures for the answer to the question of whether profit-oriented activity is compatible with behaviour pleasing to God, then one will find little comfort in Ecclesiasticus, for instance: 'A merchant shall hardly keep himself from doing wrong; and an huckster shall not be freed from sin. Many have sinned for a small matter; and he that seeketh for abundance will turn his eyes away' (Eccles. 26: 29-27: 1). Even more modern commentaries on the compatibility of profit and morals are rather sceptical. It is said that the Austrian social critic Karl Kraus, in answer to a question from a student as to how one could study business ethics, declared that one could not, one had to decide on one or the other.

As regards the social acceptance of corporate ethics, too, matters look rather bad; in the last ten to fifteen years, society's image of private industry, and particularly of large corporations, has become shaped by sceptical unease. Many believe that a corporation cannot simultaneously have high principles and high profits. In fact, there is an increasingly common view that many corporations are ethically irresponsible, pursuing their profits unscrupulously at the cost of the environment and the safety and health of consumers.[1] The perception of the commitment of multinationals in developing countries seems especially critical.[2]

This view has also had repercussions for the public's image of executives. In a Gallup poll (August 1985) on the ethical standards and honesty of various professions in the United States, the following rankings emerged (Jones and Gautschi 1988: 231):

1.	clergymen	67%
2.	druggists/pharmacists	65%
3.	medical doctors	58%
4.	dentists	56%
5.	college teachers	54%
6.	engineers	53%
7.	police	47%
8.	bankers	37%
9.	TV reporter/commentators	33%
10.	journalists	31%
11.	newspaper reporters	29%
12.	lawyers	27%
13.	executives	23%

There are no comparable polls for the European Union, and so hypotheses on the rankings of European professional groups cannot be considered here. There are, however, more and more pessimistic hints: recent and highly successful German publications refer to German executives as 'pin-striped flops', and accuse them of 'growing criminality' (Ogger 1992: 67) and in connection with corporate executives, state attorneys speak of a 'particularly dangerous power potential' and the 'criminality of the economically powerful' (Eidam 1993: vii).

Another survey in 1990, focusing on business students (AIESEC 1990), brings little cheer either. In answer to the question 'How ruthless are you prepared to be to get to the top of your chosen career?', 2% answered 'extremely ruthless', 14% 'very ruthless', and 39% 'moderately ruthless'. The same MBA students had a more than sceptical opinion of the moral state of the modern business world: 5% thought it had no morals at all, and 35% thought it had 'very few' morals.

Executives' Self-perception

But evident problems emerge too when management circles themselves are asked directly: in 1977, Brenner and Molander published a study where 43% of the executives interviewed felt compelled to resort to practices they considered shady, but apparently found necessary for the survival of their companies and hence their own careers. One of the reasons underlying the sad state of schizophrenia in this US study was a performance appraisal system that concentrated almost exclusively on short-term cost-cutting, sales-boosting, profit-raising action, irrespective of its long-term social and therefore also economic effects (Brenner and Molander 1977).

Various more recent studies of executives' moral perceptions of themselves confirm the existence of conflicts (for example, Vitell and Festervand 1987). Executives often feel their decisions to be a choice between commercial necessity within the time limits of the profit and loss account and the demands of their conscience (see *Management Vissen* 1988). A study by the Düsseldorf Institut für angewandte Marketing-Wissenschaften (IFAM: Institute for Applied Marketing Science) revealed an interesting distinction: lower level executives showed great interest in ethical questions (Hochstätter 1990: 38).

An attitude familiar from the psychology of repression and projection is interesting in this connection: problems tend to be seen as having external causes (for instance, low moral standards in society), but positive solutions are sought internally, here from executives (Vitell and Festervand 1987).

CORPORATE ETHICS AS A MATTER OF LEADERSHIP

Presumably, no one would argue that there should be an 'either/or' relationship between ethical corporate conduct and the pursuit of profit. What the former Federal Chancellor of Germany, Helmut Schmidt, had to say from a politician's point of view is also of great significance for executives: 'We must all ask ourselves how we get from the state we are to the state we ought to be. Whoever tries to solve this question by proposing the shortest possible route from a purely practical point of view can end in ethical disaster.'

How can a business enterprise respond successfully to the day-to-day challenge of corporate ethics? In my view, with various instruments on three levels: firstly, common sense or 'moral reason', secondly 'corporate codes of conduct', and thirdly, comprehensive personnel policies and holistic management development.

Moral Common Sense

The following rules of thumb, which Goodpaster (1984: 6) referred to as 'moral common sense', are significant here:
−   Avoid harming others.
−   Respect the rights of others.
−   Do not lie or cheat.
−   Keep promises and contracts.
−   Obey the law.
−   Prevent harm to others.
−   Help those in need.
−   Be fair.
−   Reinforce these imperatives in others.

At first glance, these 'commandments' are so convincing that further comment seems superfluous. When examined more closely, however, the picture is not so simple. Up to this point, we have dealt only in very general terms with corporate ethics, as the chemical, pharmaceutical, or the agrochemical industries do not need their own ethics. Moral common-sense rules of thumb can, however, be discussed using practical examples of the chemical/pharmaceutical industry.

Avoid harming others

As said before, there is no need for a *special* ethics of the pharmaceutical industry. However, there are some important structural differences between the pharmaceutical industry and others. Drugs are not commodities in the sense of other consumer or investment goods. They are used because people are sick or in pain, or because they have physical or mental disorders, or because they are dying. 'Consumer sovereignty'—the freedom to choose or refuse a product—is limited in this industry's market. The resulting ethical challenge for the pharmaceutical industry, therefore, is pronounced.

Similarly, the pharmaceutical industry's assessments of drug safety and risk/benefit evaluations have particularly fateful properties: if the company's specialists or managers err, they err not just for themselves and their company, they err for the sick people, who are at their mercy. Particularly obnoxious are double standards in safety for production or products, product information (indications, warnings on side-effects), product quality and everything else which is significant for the health or even the maintenance of human life.

Respect the rights of others

A great deal of the responsibility for the global environmental equilibrium rests with a small rich minority of about 15% of the world's population. Their alarming ability to consume resources and create waste is responsible for about 80% of the global environmental problems, including the potential greenhouse effect and the depletion of the ozone layer.[3] Per capita emissions of carbon dioxide and other greenhouse gases of US-Americans, Germans or Singaporeans is about 10 to 20 times higher than those of Indians and Chinese, and about a hundred times higher than those of the people in Bangladesh. The same picture arises if we look at the per capita consumption of nonrenewable resources. Clearly, the 10% to 15% 'rich' people—and among them, you and me—live unsustainable lifestyles if it comes to energy consumption, consumption of non-renewable resources, water consumption or pollution. Major ecological systems would probably already have collapsed, if all human beings had performed the same lifestyle.

Living the way we normally live is known to be harmful to future generations as it leaves them with reduced options and curtails their chances for human development. This faces all of us with a problem of intergenerational justice and with a moral issue, because in contrast to former generations we know the consequences of our actions and we have the political, technical and economic means for a change of course.

In cases like this, ethical decisions are supposed to be simple, the basis was formed in almost all early cultures as a 'golden rule', which, in the Gospel according to Saint Matthew, is formulated as 'all things whatsoever you would that men should do to you, do you even so to them' (Matt. 7: 12). And yet, there are no signs of a turn of the tide with regard to lifestyle change on the part of the rich minority, that is, us.

Do not lie or cheat

The 'three dogs theory' may be helpful to illustrate how one can easily fall into one's own trap: a man rings at your door and complains that your dog has bitten him. Your first answer according to the theory is: 'I do not have a dog!' That is the moment when your dog comes running around the house, barking loudly. You now refer to the 'second dog theory' and say: 'I do have a dog, but it does not bite.' That is unfortunately the moment where your dog bites the man again. You then have to refer to your third and last dog theory: 'I do have a dog, it does bite once in a while—but it does not hurt!' Your credibility, of course, fades away with every theoretical reorientation, as you are clearly only admitting what has already been proven. Furthermore, a 'supposition gap' arises: even after you have said everything you know, everyone still keeps waiting for the 'fourth dog theory'.

An accident that went into legal history as the 'Carnival Monday Case' shows the practical relevance of the 'three dogs theory': after an incident, the company concerned announced that the 'yellow rain' which had fallen over residential areas of a town on a morning in February 1992 was 'not particularly toxic'. After complaints from the neighbourhood, the quantities were adjusted upwards and after investigations by Greenpeace it finally had to be admitted that there were 10 tonnes of chemicals and at least eleven different substances involved, among them o-nitrianisole, which can cause cancer (see Eidam 1993: 191, 403, 421).

A similar series of events is conceivable in connection with information about unexpected side-effects of a drug. 'Do not lie or cheat' in practice means not only 'tell the truth, the whole truth, and nothing but the truth', it also means the acknowledgement that if you do not (yet) know something, you admit this freely and promise clarification.

Keep promises and contracts

This commandment can be viewed from the perspective of the employee, but also from the other perspective, that of the corporation. An example could be the employees' working ethos: to paraphrase a quote from the late John F. Kennedy, one might suggest, 'Don't ask what your company can do for you, but what you can do for your company.' Solidarity means the morally qualified, essential, and active dependence of the individual on the community and vice versa.

Obey the law

Imagine you are travelling in a poor country in Sub-Saharan Africa, or Southeast Asia, or Latin America. And imagine further you become seriously ill. And imagine further still, that you are very lucky—you find a well trained physician who can diagnose your illness and knows how to treat it. If he or she gives you a prescription, it is highly probable that you do not know anything about the substances prescribed, unless you yourself are a physician or a pharmacist. But you recognize the name or the logo of the manufacturer, and if you can tie the name or the logo to a well-known, reputable pharmaceutical manufacturer, almost certainly you will feel relieved. You will expect that the worst will soon be over and you will be on your way to recovery.

Would you fear that such a pharmaceutical company might have high ethical standards to govern its action at home but would conceal dangerous or lethal side-effects of its products in a poor country? You probably would not be troubled by such worries.

Your gut feeling would tell you to trust the decency and the moral common sense of a widely respected, honourable company.

Would you fear that such a drug firm would communicate openly and honestly with government authorities, the health profession, and patients in their own country—for example, the United States, Germany or Switzerland—but would allow serious inconsistencies or omissions to mark its communication in a developing country? You probably would not be troubled by such concerns. As a matter of fact, with widespread poverty, illiteracy, sickness and hunger, and with the pronounced scarcity of physicians, nursing persons, and pharmacists—all influencing drug safety in many parts of the Third World—you would probably assume that a reputed company would try even harder to maintain the safest possible use of its products. Yet, again and again, publications demonstrate that there is reason for worry (Silverman et al. 1992).

Particularly for companies doing business in developing countries, the commandment 'obey the law' is not sufficient to prevent harm to people and society. Many Third World countries do not yet have state-of-the-art legislation (for example, in product safety or environmental protection); or they may for various reasons be forced to tolerate social injustices which would not be allowed in industrialized nations (for example, child labour, dismissal of pregnant women, etc.). Developing countries may be what Myrdal call 'soft states' (Myrdal 1964), where the letter of the law has little to do with legal reality, because laws that have been passed are not enforced with the necessary consistency.

Perceived responsibility on the basis of better insight or knowledge must lead to appropriate action even where country-specific legislation does not require it. Particularly in areas like product, industrial and environmental safety, social welfare obligations, correctness and completeness of information, standards that satisfy the stringent requirements of total responsibility must hold sway. Double standards would have doubly fatal consequences, not only for the corporation but also perhaps for the health and quality of life of people now or in generations to come. One point that would have to be addressed more profoundly in this connection concerns the differences in stringency between the registration conditions in various countries.

Prevent harm to others

The safety of application of pesticides is a matter of widespread concern. Particularly in countries where illiteracy and other social conditions of poverty are pronounced, there is considerable worry about their public health impact (see, for example, WHO/UNEP 1990). And yet, safely and effectively used, pesticides can reduce losses due to insects, diseases, and weeds, thus increasing income for the farmer and output of food for the nations concerned (see Gunn and Stevens 1976).

How far does the ethical responsibility of a specific agrochemical corporation reach? Certainly, an individual corporation cannot run literacy and training courses for hundreds of thousands of people working in the rural areas of the developing world. It is also certain that a company's ethical responsibility goes further than only selling its products to the next wholesale agent. Hence, more ought to be done—but how much more? The answer to that question depends very much on the specific social, economic, and political framework of a specific country, and on the economic feasibility for the company concerned. Co-operation with the state extension services and the manufacturer's associations is almost always part of an appropriate answer.

Ethical reflection is needed on top of technical and economical considerations. Ciba's way to tackle the problem has been to run KAP-studies (knowledge, attitude, practice) on the safe and effective use of plant protection products in India, Zimbabwe and Mexico in order to develop tailor-made education and training programmes. The objective is to produce a pilot project from which others can learn and which others can repeat elsewhere. Another approach might well be to withdraw certain products from a country's market, if all a company's endeavours do not lead to a measurable improvement of the public health impact of its products.

Help those in need

In my understanding of the social division of labour, it is not a primary function of business enterprises to become involved in charitable activities. As far as this is concerned, I firmly believe in subsidiarity and am convinced that global human development needs in the first place good governance and equitable economic relationships worldwide. Nevertheless, I am pleading for every social institution to do what it can from a humanitarian point of view. Ciba has been involved for years in numerous projects for the people living in poverty through the Ciba-Geigy Foundation for Co-operation with Developing Countries.[4]

Be fair

Here again the application of the 'Golden Rule' is an important point in question. It opens a variety of reflections, for example, with regard to one's attitude towards colleagues on the same hierarchical level (key word: mobbing) and with regard to those who have lower ranks in the company (key words: respect, freedom, dignity). Let us share two short case studies:

Suppose you have just heard that one of the most important members of your staff is prepared to leave your department in order to accept a position in another department within your company. The new job would be a challenge and provide excellent career opportunities. You have no doubt that your employee would fit in very well and would be able to meet the requirements of the new position. At the same time you would lose your best team member and your department's performance would suffer seriously, and so would your bonus. The person would be very difficult to replace.

That person's potential new boss has asked for your opinion and has made it clear that your input will be crucial for his or her decision to offer the job to your team member. Will you be fair and give your honest opinion and provide a strong recommendation? Or will you want to keep your staff member and hence mislead the inquiring person?

Or suppose you have a staff member who has been a consistently poor performer, in spite of your best attempts to help. This person has informed you that he or she has applied for a job outside the company and asked you to give him/her references.

Will you give your honest judgement and run a risk to keep the person for the rest of your corporate life or will you recommend him/her against better knowledge and get a chance for making him/her leave the company? It is obvious, that the commandment 'be fair' can be quite a tough one to follow.

The consequences of the commandment 'be fair' for the pharmaceuticals industry here could, for example, be debated on the principle of 'acting on suspicion', that is, when a corporation learns that one of its products, whose safety has up to now been mostly beyond doubt, has been associated with incidents that do not tie in with experience to date. Waiting until the ultimate scientific proof is available would go against the principle of justice discussed here.

Reinforce these imperatives in others

How can a corporation reinforce its moral imperatives in others? Should it have the courage to assume leadership responsibilities in ethically relevant questions, or should it seek conformity with convention, as often happens in practice? Ethical guidelines of business associations are often the lowest common denominator and mostly fall short of what an individual corporation would be prepared to do with regard to higher ethical business standards.

The dilemma that arises when individual corporations obviously impair the whole image of the entire industry must also be considered here: should one stay quiet and thus become a silent accomplice, or should one take the problem up and run the risk of being accused of washing one's dirty clothes in public?

Corporate Codes of Conduct for Sensitive Matters

Not everything that is legal is legitimate. An internationally active corporation, which has to function in different legal and social frameworks and which strives for uniform ethical standards, is well advised to develop codes of conduct for its sensitive activities. There is no *a priori* harmony between corporate or individual profit and what is to be preferred from a social point of view. Indeed, there is a whole set of potential conflicts that a corporation needs to think about how to minimise.

Corporate codes of conduct are defined here as standards of behaviour which a corporation adopts without being compelled to by law, but which then become binding on all employees, in order to minimise potential conflicts arising from undesirable effects of normal business activity on society and environment. Such corporate codes of conduct make it clear that the management of the corporation is not indifferent to how business goals are achieved.

As a kind of negative ethics at least, corporate codes of conduct rule out what the corporation believes to be clearly unacceptable behaviour. As the German satirist Wilhelm Busch said, 'All the good beneath the sun is always bad you haven't done.'

Of some importance here is the question of whether one should almost imperialistically enforce one's own standards in cases of doubt, or whether one should opt more for an 'ethical relativism' that argues for doing what the Romans do when in Rome. Even though one can concede *a priori* that many traditional ways of thinking and behaving are based on sound assumptions, there are a number of situations where a corporation should have the courage to apply its own standards and philosophy and not that of the different social and cultural framework of the host country.

Sensitive areas might be, for instance, marketing, information policy, environmental protection, animal experiments, research policy or other areas for other fields. Ethically acceptable manoeuvrability must be clarified and its effects on people, environment, and society analysed. In a phase of evaluation and weighing up, the desirable and undesirable must be defined and formulated.

In practice, it happens again and again that types of behaviour occur in a corporation which the corporate codes of conduct in force would forbid. Pitt and Groskaufmanis (1990: 24) have developed criteria which can increase the practical effectiveness of internal codes of conduct.

Criteria for the formulation of corporate codes of conduct

- The principles of the code must be tailored to the specific corporate culture—merely taking over general codes is not enough.
- The code of conduct addresses those activities of the corporation which are particularly sensitive or which concern the greatest vulnerability (legal, socio-political and other).

Criteria for the implementation of corporate codes of conduct

- First, a communication programme must ensure that all persons affected by the code of conduct actually know and understand it. It is not enough merely to distribute it, the content should be explained and someone made available to answer questions.
- There should be at least one person who may be approached in confidence (ombudsperson).
- Employees should certify in writing that they have read, understood, and complied with the code of conduct in their work.

Criteria for the enforcement of corporate codes of conduct

- Work with codes of conduct only makes sense if the managers concerned are accountable for its objectives.
- Audit committees, ombudspersons, a hot line, or other means should ensure that employees can have their concerns taken up by the appropriate office.
- Violations of the code of conduct must be investigated and resolved. The message should be clear and leave employees in no doubt: violation of the code leads to penalties, including dismissal, irrespective of whether the violation had positive or detrimental consequences for the corporation.

As not only corporations but probably all the world's institutions have a tendency to be self-referential, that is, to live in a rather closed value and interest system, it is important that corporate codes of conduct are based on a broad social consensus. They should therefore not only reflect the philosophy of corporate management, but should, prior to their adoption, be seriously challenged by external, independent review and as far as possible result from a consensus based on dialogue.

In his discussion of the state (*politeia*), Plato (1991: 298) posits a hierarchy of behaviours by means of which 'insight into things' can be gained or the way to truth be found. At the top is 'understanding', followed by 'sense' (thought). Even today, in many situations it seems valuable and appropriate to draw attention to this hierarchy.

In order to be able to represent a point of view on a fairly firm footing, all the relevant facts have to be collected and illuminated and evaluated from different angles. This needs discussions on a broad basis to take account of all the pluralistic opinions and interests that there are. In view of the urgency and the complexity of many of today's problems, thinking in old terms of right/left categories is no longer of much help. Ideological lines of demarcation or fundamentalist rejections do not improve the quality of solutions; on the contrary, prejudice acts like a wall, preventing our awareness of certain things.

If conflicting opinions (acceptable in form but hard in content) are considered a narcissistic offence in a company, then that company lacks more than just an opposition culture and ability to cope with conflict. Openness to pluralistic opinions is one of the essential conditions for the most comprehensive perception possible of reality. Especially for the social acceptance of industrial behaviour, whose complexity and benefit-risk ratio is not easy for the lay public to grasp, the search for consensus in dialogue is vital for survival. A corporation that is not prepared to talk runs the risk of soon having no more say.

Many expert and socio-political positions that were represented only by fringe minorities ten or fifteen years ago now belong to 'sound common sense'. If one reads the publications of some companies on environmental protection and compares them with the earlier manifestos of 'green' groups, one finds astonishing similarities; however, years of environmentally inappropriate behaviour have already passed. The same can probably be said of other specialized fields within the chemical industry. Social learning time can be shortened through adequate dialogue to the benefit of all.

Decision-making processes are difficult when they involve informed opinion outside the company that wishes to include its concerns and interests in solutions, but has other criteria than the economic and bases its judgement on other value systems.[5] On the one hand, dialogues are 'open processes', that is, it cannot be planned how they will develop and the effects and consequences are visible only to a limited extent. On the other, dialogues do not automatically lead to agreement, and run the risk then of overflowing endlessly and getting involved in controversies that are less and less relevant, instead of working out an acceptable practical compromise for both sides. Dialogues are particularly vulnerable if one or the other side sets itself up as morally superior or butts into other worlds normatively without sufficient expert knowledge.

Nevertheless, controversies must be argued out. Although the final decision on corporate policy lies within the corporation itself and cannot be transferred outside, the harmonization of controversial views is more sustainable through discussion than through power. All those involved must refrain from claiming superiority, think over their own positions, and if necessary revise them. Openness and pluralism are required, though not arbitrariness or cheap 'tolerance' to avoid arguments. True dialogue, in this case, differs from manipulative persuasion and modern advertising by dealing critically both with the necessity of acting in an economically reasonable manner and with wider public interests.

Dialogue with various social groups, and being prepared to listen to the opinions of people from a completely different world of thought who base their concepts of ethics on other systems of values can improve the quality of all types of solutions, not only those of corporate codes of conduct. Socrates' distinction between truth and certainty still has great meaning today: people can be very sure of their opinions and consider this subjective certainty to be the objective 'truth'. The view of others who do not share this certainty are not 'untrue' or 'mistaken'; rather, one certainty is opposed to another.

Corporate codes of conduct are obviously not standardised 'instructions on ethical dealing' that can always clearly determine what is ethically acceptable. Rich (1987: 18) in particular points out that basic ethical questions are, 'when they become concrete, always questions to which there is no single, smooth answer which will harmonize the conflict and calm the troubles.' Nevertheless, guidelines such as those outlined here can give the employees of a company a basis for setting priorities when commercial decisions have to be made under time and financial constraints.

Corporate codes of conduct like this and their constant monitoring provide no guarantee that commercial ambitions will be realised. As the Swiss philosopher and pedagogue Johann

Heinrich Pestalozzi said 200 years ago, no type of government is any good if the people are a real bad lot. Werner Lachmann (1987: 10) placed these thoughts in a context of commercial structures that function as well 'as the people who work in them.' It should be added that the best policies and codes of conduct are only as good as the executives who implement them. Of greatest significance for the realization of commercial goals is therefore the selection of suitable personnel.

Personnel Policy and Management Development

At the beginning of the twentieth century, Max Weber, the eminent German sociologist, pointed out the particular responsibilities of leaders with the following words: 'People who must make political or economic decisions on matters that affect other people's lives will, unless they have lost all reason, find themselves forced more and more to evaluate not only their ethical motivations, but also their decisions' likely consequences based on their knowledge and conscience.' In a political context, Henry Kissinger pointed out that practical politics is always in danger of being overtaken by events and becoming thoroughly unprincipled, and declared that it was very difficult to carry out practical politics successfully without strong moral conviction. The same applies to managers in businesses and other institutions.

I am not so naive as to believe that ordinary mortals are capable in everyday life of emulating the ideal described in the Sermon on the Mount or important scriptures from other religions. But if we are convinced that profit, sales or other commercial successes can never be ends in themselves, but are only legitimate if they serve people and society, then the criteria for personnel recruitment and the content of management development should be extended idealistically.

Before discussing these two issues more deeply, however, yet another problem area has to be addressed: do institutions like corporations (or trade unions, parties, churches, etc.) allow the people who work in them sufficient responsibility of their own? Or do they limit the development of their people, including their moral development, in an illegitimate way?

The question of 'structural violence' in institutions

The concept of 'structural violence' was developed by the Norwegian peace researcher Johan Galtung (1971, 1975) in connection with unjust feudal systems, unequal power relationships, and the unequal chances of life for the people concerned, especially in developing countries. According to Galtung, structural violence exists when people are prevented from developing (in body and in mind) by the social system they find themselves in. In contrast to personal violence, which can be attributed to actual people, structural violence functions anonymously.

This discrepancy between people's total potential and the possibility of its realization has been brought into the debate on business ethics by Rupert Lay (1993: 9), the German philosopher and business consultant. He sees a 'monstrous process of dehumanization'. As 'the morals we have do not regulate how institutions should treat people, only how people should treat people', he believes individuals are suffering disadvantages in the face of the might of institutions, which is growing, in his view, to 'monstrous' proportions. According to Lay, it is institutions and their 'system agents' that are jeopardizing people's chances of survival in this world, not people.

In another connection, Foucault (1976: 220-50) points out that power in an institution is very rarely determined through forced internalization of (written and unwritten) regulations and the 'means of good conditioning'. This conditioning has a standardizing, prescriptive and normalizing effect on the people concerned: it may not always produce eager obedience, but at least makes for behaviour conforming to the system in the pre-legal sphere.

There is a significant element of outside determination resulting from the given institutional framework in every decision made within an institution. Morally speaking, institutions are unusual phenomena. As Donaldson (1982) once said, they have—unlike real people—no pants to kick, no souls to damn, no consciences to keep them awake all night, and nobody to throw into jail. A large number of empirical studies have suggested that people in groups behave differently from when they are by themselves. There seems to be a greater readiness to take risks when responsibilities are not directly attributable, and opportunism and disregard of one's own misgivings seem to increase when most of the other members of the group ally themselves to positions opposed to one's own. This can lead to decisions qualitatively inferior to those based exclusively on one's own moral judgement.

To 'domesticate' institutions with inherent potential for structural violence (instead of domesticating constructively critical employees), Lay (1993: 36-71) proposes making every effort to make institutions 'open systems' with 'open moral', that is, in permanent communication and interaction with their social environment, and put them in a position where they can constructively approach needs other than their own system's ones.

In this sense, within an implicitly given coordination system of standards and recognized yardsticks, 'open' corporations give their employees the freedom of action necessary for *directed autonomy*. They also create the conditions needed, including training opportunities (empowerment). Corporations (and other institutions) which, as open systems, expose themselves to correcting external influences and whose decision-making processes are based on a participatory leadership style and are thus subject to the control process of a pluralistic company-internal 'public', have good prospects of gaining constructive impulses from the field of tension between their own and outside influences.

But, even then, each and every corporation will need people in it who not only are easy to manage, because they have the 'secondary' virtues so beloved of all institutions (for example, obedience, diligence, honesty, reliability, punctuality, love of order, cleanliness), but also distinguish themselves through primary critical virtues.

The significance of primary virtues

Even the classical literature on ethics provides us with an almost complete picture of the ideal personality and desirable characteristics of those bearing responsibility, for (desired) 'requirement profiles' of 'emperors', 'kings', 'generals', 'governors', or even 'managers' too, have been roughly comparable since time immemorial. It is worth looking back here, at the 'way' proposed by Laozi (1985), the sayings of Confucius (1987), the esoteric Indian doctrine of the Upanishads (1986) or Plato (1991), who (in his *Politeia*) describes reason, justice, courage, and thoughtfulness that have matured to wisdom as the most important virtues. In more modern times, the remarks of Max Weber (1988) on 'politics as a profession' could be taken as reference for the necessary virtues of leaders.

'Primary virtues' are now considered to include not only the traditional 'cardinal virtues'—justice, courage, moderation and intelligence—but also those basic attitudes associated with the concepts of civil courage, ability to cope with conflict, tolerance and capacity for constructive disobedience (cf. Lay 1993: 22). Of particular significance in this connection, and by a long chalk not only for corporations, but for institutions of all kinds, is civil courage as it is practiced.

The dangers associated with a lack of civil courage are pointed out by Hösle (1991: 21) in connection with the political paradigm shift during the Gorbachov era in the former Soviet Union: 'People pretended to accept certain principles, even though inside themselves they had long rejected them; they knew that those they spoke with had rejected them too. They participated in communication rituals nonetheless ... in which each of them solemnly swore the truth of those principles, and in which everyone knew, but no one said, that the emperor was naked.' Not that everyone should be born a hero of resistance in totalitarian systems. In a comparable context, Joachim Gauck, the federal officer responsible for the state security files of the former GDR, pointed out to the Zeit Symposium on the occasion of the seventy-fifth birthday of Helmut Schmidt that the first step to resistance was to learn to refuse enthusiasm. This applies not only to totalitarian states but also to institutions of every kind.

As regards 'structural violence' in totalitarian social systems, Gauck is rather pessimistic. He believes that 'cultivation of subjects [is] feasible', and adds,

> proven means of achieving success in cultivation—use of fear, and power resources of a power centre that relativizes itself as little as possible—masking of the power relationships actually existing through accompanying organizational measures, ... denial of actual relationships. Naked lies are recognisable—skilful rationalization, levelling-down, and trivialization are more efficient (Gauck 1991).

For the less mortally dangerous civil courage as practised in corporations, the courts signalled over twenty years ago how those bearing responsibility are expected to act. In the order to stay the proceedings in the Contergan trial, the Court of Aix-la-Chapelle recorded the following in connection with personal guilt as a result of a lack of civil courage on the part of the accused employee of the company concerned:

> Even personal difficulties do not mean that you were unable to take more extensive action. In view of the significant danger of serious injury to health threatening a not inconsiderable number of people (even though their number might be relatively small compared to all those using the drug), you must be expected to put up with personal difficulties if necessary. This is not an unreasonable demand. The health of a large number of people would otherwise be put at risk (Schmidt-Salzer 1979: 481ff, 1982: 271ff).

Analysis of all larger-scale catastrophes in recent years shows that, long before the *Challenger* tragedy, the Chernobyl catastrophe, or the Exxon-Valdez disaster, there were critical voices and warnings about the weaknesses that later came to light through the disasters. These were either ignored or swept under the carpet. More civil courage at all levels, in the form of binding but tough defence of the relevant criticism, has great weight among the desirable characteristics of those bearing responsibility. The lessons of the 'Milgram-experiments' conducted at Yale University (New Haven, USA) in the early 1960s, where obedient participants of the experiment were ready to inflict potentially fatal injuries upon defenceless fellow human beings, teach a valid lesson on the value of constructive disobedience.

An ambitious recruitment policy can influence whether those who work for a corporation and represent it internally and externally have certain essential personality characteristics. At best, it discovers personalities with the personal qualities we would wish in people on whose decisions our own well-being and that of our families depend. They would be leaders who are aware of their full responsibility for everything that they do or do not do: people with virtues like modesty, sensitivity, a consciousness of social responsibility, and ability to view things as a whole. In this connection, Max Weber's (1988a: 551ff.) distinction between 'ethics of attitude' and 'ethics of absolute ends' is still as relevant as it was.

Management development

Whether such primary virtues are teachable or learnable is a moot point. Since Immanuel Kant, great moralists have repeatedly professed themselves rather sceptical about the improvability of people (Kant thought 'nothing straight can be fashioned out of the warped wood of which people are made').[6]

This is no reason to throw in the towel, however. The inclusion of ethical matters in educational plans has produced a number of positive experiences (cf. Nelson and Obremski 1990; Johnson 1985). Normative orientations in connection with corporate decisions are teachable and learnable, albeit not so easily as the orthodox content of internal or external training schemes. Despite the difficulties related to this kind of training, I consider reflection on questions of sense and value to be exceptionally significant for a corporation's long-term prosperity, as important lodestar knowledge can be transmitted: lodestar knowledge about the possibilities and limitations of human action and ability, not in the sense of a finalized doctrine, but as an approach that argues with reason.

There are nowadays various answers to the question of whether religion should play a part in the debate about business and corporate ethics. On the one hand, what Max Weber (1988b: 237) said around 80 years ago is still true: that no business ethics (and therefore also no corporate ethics) have ever been determined *solely* by religion. On the other hand, as Weber mentions as well, one (*one* being the operative word) of the determinants of business ethics (and therefore also corporate ethics) is the religious certainty of how life should be led (ibid.: 238). For many authors concerned with corporate ethics, ultimate ideological certainties, certainties about the essentials of human existence, its 'whence' and 'whither' is fundamental, despite the erosion of the perceived obligation of religious commandments in many Western societies.[7] In more profound debate and reflection on ethics, I believe the discussion of ultimate points to be unavoidable.

All the same, there is no need to introduce religion into corporate ethics. Although in our culture the Christian Church still has the main responsibility for the transmission of moral values, from its own understanding and from outside perspectives, reference to religious norms, responsibility before God, the obligation to settle one's account in the afterlife, and to fear of one's Creator today, bounce off the protective secular wall of enlightenment. In view of the erosion of religious consciousness and orientation that has been found among business leaders (cf. Kaufmann et al. 1986), too much weight on religious criteria could be mistaken for a 'Sunday sermon' or cant, and damage the whole exercise.[8]

As, in the end, the practical consequences for day-to-day work of reflection on business ethics are more important than the single and specific content of that reflection, it will probably have to be decided from case to case how religion is to be approached. Anything that might result in a specific public failing to take the matter seriously should in the interests of practical expediency be left out. In cases of doubt, take Max Weber's (1988b: 14) advice: 'Anyone who wants a sermon should go to the conventicle.'

There can be no doubt about the value of case studies (for instance, the parable of the Sadhu: see McCoy 1983) and the subsequent debate on the ethically relevant problems involved (see Tyson 1990). Case studies gain in quality when ethical dilemmas are considered and due attention paid to complex processes in which overall decisions are split into many single ones. It can be shown in such cases that the ethical problems in the single steps in a process are negligible, but when added together they can be so problematic that the conclusion has to be drawn that every single step needs to be considered in the light of the whole.

In the course of the discussion of case studies, a desirable side-effect can be the elimination of prejudices about colleagues: surveys have found again and again that individuals believe they are far more ethical in their behaviour than their colleagues (see McDonald and Zepp 1988; Ferrell and Weaver 1978; Pitt and Abratt 1986). Female managers, by the way, also largely regard themselves as more ethical than their male colleagues (Kelley et al. 1970). The resulting attitude that 'everybody does it' could lead to justification of ethically questionable dealings, especially so if they are regarded as 'necessary' for career advancement. This could cumulate in a downward process that will harm everybody in the end. Case studies on ethical matters could also tend towards a solution of the prisoner's dilemma, by, for instance, making clear what options are open and the consequent advantages and disadvantages for each of those concerned.

In this connection, the concept of situational ethics is highly significant: there are no moral principles which apply in all circumstances. Even the commandment 'Thou shalt not kill' does not apply in any absolute sense in emergencies or to fend off greater harm. Books and guidelines provide no general pointers as to what is ethically good in a particular situation, only notional ones. Moral decisions are always questionable, and their quality depends on the highly specific circumstances and the information and decision-making aids available at the time. As, in the vast majority of cases, no final decisions can be taken about the 'good' versus the 'bad', rather, the lesser evil found by carefully weighing up all the factors involved, the debate on situational ethics has to be sustainable. This also applies to the general discussion of ethical matters in management development. A quick wipe over does not do justice to the complexity of ethical questions, and will also not succeed in changing the behaviour of the people concerned. This should, however, pose no insurmountable problem, for the cost of ethical training is well worth it. It helps to preserve value and increase the value of human working power, and thus eventually also improve our commercial effectiveness.

Performance appraisals

The implementation of the maxims of corporate ethics in everyday practice is not a 'matter for the boss'; it has to be carried out at all levels. It will, however, probably get no further than good intentions if the tip of the corporation hierarchy fails to internalise and live plausibly by suitable criteria and take them into account in employees' performance appraisals.

In most cases, this means that the catalogue of performance appraisal criteria and the incentive system has to be extended. Moral standards are also more effective the more adherence to them is checked up on and observance of them rewarded or non-observance sanctioned. As long as employees are measured by short-term financial results only, in ethically ambivalent situations they could see themselves compelled to choose between their consciences on the one hand and their careers and financial benefits on the other.

Increasing weight should therefore be given in performance appraisals to accomplishments in product safety, environmental protection, information policy, fairness in leading people, and other areas that are not immediately related to economic efficiency. Ethical conduct should lead to promotion wherever possible, even if the economic effects are detrimental in the short-term. And *vice versa*: the significance of ethical standards must also become visible in a corporation by sanctioning employees who violate them by demotion or, if the violation is serious enough, by dismissal, even if the corporation obtained short-term commercial benefits from it.

It is admittedly not always easy to discover criteria to evaluate ethical conduct. Can the fact that a sales manager failed to achieve his or her targets or exceeded cost budgets be attributed to ethical reservations or is this just an excuse for insufficient commitment? Is it possible for the inefficient or idle employee to exploit the system and the hard worker to be left behind? These loopholes will not be easy to close, but it should be possible to do so.

GOOD ETHICS ARE GOOD BUSINESS

Why should a company consider ethics in directing its behaviour, on top of law, self-interest, and convention? The worst conceivable result of high moral standards would be competitive or other tangible detriment because the special efforts and costs a company attaches to ethical consideration result in net disadvantages for it. There are a number of indications that the short-term profit from ethical conduct does not exactly burst into the limelight or even show clearly measurable financial disadvantage. It would be dishonest to exclude these effects as an option in action on corporate ethics.

On the other hand, there are many empirical examples in which unethical corporate behaviour caused a great social outcry and intervention from the authorities, and presented no favourable options even in the short term (see Swanda 1990). In these cases it is easy to show that unethical conduct can be a burden on a corporation and that high ethical standards can be seen as an asset.

A second conceivable possibility is that financial disadvantages due to investments over and above those required by law (for instance in environmental, social, or safety areas) or withdrawing from sale for ethical reasons could be compensated and balanced out by non-financial advantages (for instance, the company's reputation). The problem here is that investments and falling sales are easier to measure than increased opportunities from an enhanced reputation.

At least for enlightened corporations, commercial success now means more than just how big the year's profit is. Profits to companies are like food to people: an absolute necessity, without which they die. But only a few sick people would consider eating to be the central or only purpose of life. The reputation of a company is one of its most valuable assets, even if it does not appear directly in the balance sheet (Swanda [1990] therefore suggests that 'goodwill' should become a balance-sheet item). The verdict of the public depends significantly on the company's perceived contribution to socially valued ends. Meeting customer requirements in the extended sense, that is, acting in a socially and environmentally responsible way and using energy and non-renewable resources wisely, are important blocks in the mosaic of commercial success.

A third possibility is that ethical dealing might be worthwhile from both the financial and non-financial points of view. I personally tend to see this as the most probable, at least in the mid- and long-term, for the following reasons.

Reduction in the Cost of Friction with the Social Environment

First and foremost, ethical conduct brings reductions in the cost of friction with the social environment (for private individuals and institutions). For corporations, social friction costs arise where behaviour which is legal but seen as illegitimate or unethical leads to calls for boycotts from church or other organizations. Whether a critically committed public demonstrates in front of the works gates, charitable organizations set up wailing walls, or the media 'put on pressure' through critical reporting, for the corporation concerned, this means loss in social recognition. Whether this leads to a fall in the share price or physically measurable sales losses occur or not is of secondary importance. Criticism 'from outside' generally means that management capacity is taken up with defensive activity and is therefore not free for the shaping of the future. Intelligent corporations forbid dealings that could provoke negative social reactions.

On the other hand, there is growing evidence that a corporation's 'image' can become a competitive advantage because a 'positive coefficient' arises (Global Business Relations 1990). This can become a decisive market advantage where a corporation offers products and services that are comparable in quality and usefulness with those of other companies. In the United States, there are a number of indications that so-called 'green consumers' represent an increasingly important niche in various sales markets, and companies that are environmentally exemplary and go beyond the minimum legal requirements can gain market advantages.

Employees' Motivation

Other costs can arise through friction with one's own employees. The fact that a company is the focus of public criticism (but also in a situation where employees see that colleagues are promoting their careers in an unethical way) can have disastrous results for morale and job satisfaction in a corporation. In the mid- and long-term, this can lead to valuable employees looking for other work and leaving the corporation. As employees are a corporation's most valuable 'capital', this alone is reason enough why unethical conduct cannot lie in a corporation's interests.

Various empirical studies (Vitell and Davis 1990; Hoffmann 1986) reveal a positive correlation between ethical conduct in a corporation and job satisfaction. Where top management is seen as giving strong support for ethical conduct, job satisfaction increases together with the degree of employee identification with the corporation. Everything points to the conclusion that a positive reciprocal relationship exists between 'job satisfaction' and 'ethical conduct'. Applied business ethics become a component of 'corporate identity', the totality of value systems, thought, and decision patterns, modes of behaviour and structures within a corporation that transmits a positive 'us-feeling' to employees and thus boosts motivation to work.

The fact that corporate behaviour which is at least frictionless but wherever possible goes beyond marginal ethics also prompts customers to buy and motivates serious investors to purchase shares, and that the direct neighbours (residents, communities) look to the corporation with pleasure and pride, reinforces employees' positive identification. What Jakob Burckhardt (Griechische Kulturgeschichte, quoted in Riklin 1987) formulated for individuals also applies to whole corporations: they are not just what they are, but also what they have set themselves as ideals. Even if they do not emulate these 100%, a part of their being is marked by the mere fact of wanting to.

There are a number of indications that corporations whose ethical conduct is considered above reproach are seen as more attractive employers than those which have been publicly criticized due to failure to recognize their responsibilities or even due to wilful damage to the welfare of the community or the environment. A poll of business studies students carried out in 1990 revealed that 66% considered a 'job that makes sense' an important criterion in choosing an employer. This can hardly be true of companies where Greenpeace demonstrates in front of the factory gates or churches call for a boycott.

Corporations are now no longer measured on what they produce, but on what they present. The strength of such trends can of course change again, especially when the labour market develops unfavourably for those seeking employment. But an increasing number of citizens, whether as employees or consumers, are taking ethical viewpoints seriously—more seriously than ten or twenty years ago.

Protection of Commercial Freedom

Many of those with responsibility in corporations are complaining about an increasing and already too dense jungle of laws, stipulations, and directives. Commercial freedom, the complaint goes on, can no longer exist within the ever narrower straitjacket of state regulations—too many rules endanger the industrial success. There is a good deal of evidence that such complaints have a grounding in reality in many respects, and that 'less state' can have an enlivening effect on corporate commitment.

Freedom is, however, always freedom as ethical duty and may thus be demanded only as a correlate of responsibility. Anyone who wishes to help avoid further regimentation of the economy and correct inappropriate legal developments must offer plausible proof of ethically responsible conduct.

Ethically responsible corporate dealings mean dealings beyond the *status quo*, active shaping, and forward-looking ethical equilibration. Whoever maintains a running battle on the basis of current law to defend positions that might have been based on a consensus many years ago but which are now regarded as illegitimate and will be even more so in the future, is not being businesslike but negligent. Such companies support those social forces that demand more controls, narrower legislative chains, and thus more state bureaucracy.

Business Ethics as Comprehensive Competitive Advantage

Innovation, efficiency, effectiveness, the ability to utilise market potential optimally, recognise the signs of the times, and the art of saving costs and expense in the right place at the right time will continue to be of the greatest importance alongside all the other corporate virtues. However, an additional element will gain in significance: applied business ethics. It will become more and more a new, solid basis for competitive ability, breaching the limits of classical markets. The more affluent a society is, the more significant non-material values become. Corporations that act in a visibly ethical way will be preferred by informed consumers more and more. This fact will become a problem for those corporations that ignore moral aspects, and for others it will be an opportunity to get to the very top.

NOTES

1. See *Business Week* (1989). According to a representative survey conducted by the Düsseldorf Institut für angewandte Marketing-Wissenschaften (Institute for Applied Marketing Science) in the

German Federal Republic in 1989, the large chemical companies seemed to come in for particularly heavy criticism: one of the questions was, 'Which company is especially irresponsible, immoral, unethical?' 18.8% of those questioned named BASF, 18.2% Bayer, and 12.6% Hoechst. Nevertheless, there were some positive indications: 5.2% considered BASF 'particularly exemplary'; Bayer achieved 2.4% and Hoechst 1.9% here. See *Wirtschaftswoche* 1990.

2. See, for instance, Turner (1973); Senghaas and Menzel (1976); Villamil (1979). For an opposite view, see, for instance, Pausenberger (1982); Silverman et al. (1982); Buko Pharma Kampagne (1982); Bühler (1982); Müller (1983); Hartog and Schulte-Sasse (1990), and the literature given there. But see also Silverman et al. (1982).

3. For the respective statistical evidence see World Resources Institute (1994).

4. The report of the Ciba-Geigy Foundation for Co-operation with Developing Countries may be ordered from the Company's postal address (CH-4002 Basel).

5. With all the differences in value systems, at least a minimal consensus about commonly accepted values is necessary, otherwise a dialogue can achieve no constructive results. Fundamentalist positions of 'never' and 'no way' can never lead to compromises.

6. See Kant (1968: 41). In the same essay, however, there is an indication of a desire for moral schooling. 'We are cultivated to a high degree through art and knowledge. We are civilised almost to excess with all sorts of social respectability and courtesies. But there is still a long way to go before we can consider ourselves moral' (ibid.: 44).

7. For instance, Herms: No rationale for action without religion. See Herms (1989: 86). Max Weber (1988a: 550) considered the weight and the significance of ethics in the Sermon on the Mount to be 'a serious thing ... It is no joking matter. The same applies to it as has been said of causality in science: it is not a taxi you can stop when you like to get in or out. On the contrary: all or nothing, that is its meaning, if anything more than trivialities are to come out of it.'

8. In a seminar held by the Gesellschaft für Ethik, Bildung und Management (Society for Ethics, Training, and Management), however, it became clear that it would be socially advantageous if the Christian Churches were to regain a greater share in the 'religion market'. In some business circles, new age tendencies with their vagabond attitude to religion are unmistakable. These tendencies are a sign that business managers are breaking out of the process of increasingly secular orientation with its inescapable power of the

externally material over people. The resulting 'disorganized religiousness' beneath the high religions is however characterized by an inability to formulate a generalizable doctrine that could act as a basis for social systems. Furthermore, it lacks rational control by the public.

REFERENCES

AIESEC (Association Internationale des Étudiants en Sciences Economiques et Commerciales). 1990. *Profile: Tomorrow's Managers: Sheep, Horse or Wolf?* Brussels: AIESEC.

Arendt, H. 1964. *Eichmann in Jerusalem: ein Bericht von der Banalität des Bösen [Eichmann in Jerusalem: a Report on the Banality of Evil].* Munich: Piper.

Brenner, S.N. and E.A. Molander. 1977. Is the Ethics of Business Changing? *Harvard Business Review* 55 (January-February): 57-71.

Bühler, M. 1982. *Geschäfte mit der Armut [Dealings with Poverty].* Frankfurt am Main: Medico International.

Buko Pharma Kampagne (ed.) 1982. *Gesundheit und Arzneimittel in der Dritten Welt [Health and Pharmaceuticals in the Third World].* Bielefeld: Bundeskongress Pharma Kampagne.

Confucius. 1987. *Gespräche [Analects / Lun Yü].* Cologne: Eugen Diedrichs. (Diedrichs Gelbe Reihe).

Donaldson, T. 1982. *Corporations and Morality.* Englewood Cliffs, NJ: Prentice-Hall.

Business Week. 1989. May 29: 29.

Eidam, G. 1993. *Unternehmen und Strafe. Vorsorge-und Krisenmanagement. [Ventures and Strife. Preventive and Crisis Management]* Cologne: Carl Heymanns.

Ferrell, O.C. and K.M. Weaver. 1978. Ethical Beliefs of Marketing Managers. *Journal of Marketing* 47 (July): 69-73.

Foucault, M. 1976. *Überwachen und Strafen- die Geburt des Gefängnisses. [Surveillance and Punishment- the Birth of the Prison]* Frankfurt am Main: Suhrkamp.

Galtung, J. 1971. Gewalt, Frieden und Friedensforschung [Violence, Peace and Peace Research]. In *Kritische Friedensforschung [Critical Peace Research].* Ed. Senghaas. Frankfurt am Main: Suhrkamp.

Galtung, J. 1975. *Strukturelle Gewalt, Beiträge zur Friedens- und Konfliktforschung [Structural Violence: Contributions to Peace and Conflict Research].* Reinbek: Rowohlt.

Gauck, J. 1991. *Die Stasi-Akten : die unheimliche Erbe der DDR [The Stasi Files: the Chilling Legacy of the GDR].* Reinbek: Rowohlt.

Global Business Relations (ed.). 1990. The International Business Issues Monitor. *Monitor Bulletin* No. 90-19. New York.

Goodpaster, K.E. 1984. *Ethics in Management.* Boston, MA: Harvard Business School.

Gunn, D.L. and J.G.R. Stevens (eds.). 1976. *Pesticides and Human Welfare.* Oxford, UK: Oxford University Press.

Hartog, R. and H. Schulte-Sasse. 1990. *Das bundesdeutsche Arzneimittelangebot in der Dritten Welt [Supply in the Third World of Pharmaceuticals by the Federal Republic of Germany].* Bielefeld: Bundeskongress Pharma Kampagne.

Herms, E. 1989. Der religiöse Sinn der Moral: Unzeitgemäße Betrachtungen zu den Grundlagen der Ethik der Unternehmensführung [Religious Aspects of Morality: Timeless Observations on the Foundations of the Ethics of Business]. In *Unternehmensethik [The Ethics of Enterprises].* Ed. Steinmann and Löhr. Stuttgart: C E Poeschel.

Hochstätter, D. 1990. Lorbeer und Mammon [Laurels and Mammon]. *Wirtschaftswoche [Economic Weekly]* January 26 (No. 5): 38.

Hoffmann, M. 1986. What is Necessary for Corporate Moral Excellence? *Journal of Business Ethics* 5: 233-42.

Hösle, V. 1991. *Philosophie der ökologischen Krise [The philosophy of ecological crisis].* Munich: Beck'sche Reihe.

Johnson, H. 1985. Bribery in International Markets: Diagnosis, Clarification and Remedy. *Journal of Business Ethics* 4: 447-55.

Jones, T.M. and F.H. Gautschi. 1988. Will the Ethics of Business Change? A Survey of Future Executives. *Journal of Business Ethics* 7: 231-48.

Kant I. 1968. Ideen zu einer allgemeinen Geschichte in weltbürgerlicher Absicht [Thoughts on a Common General History from the Viewpoint of a World Citizen]. In *Schriften zur Anthropologie, Geschichtsphilosophie, Politik und Pädagogik I*

[Writings on Anthropology, Philosophy of History, Politics and Pedagogy I]. Ed. Weischedel. Vol. XI. Frankfurt am Main: Suhrkamp Taschenbuch Wissenschaft.

Kaufmann, F.-X., W. Kerber and P.M. Zulehner. 1986. *Ethos und Religion bei Ethik [Ethos and Religion in Ethics]*. Munich: Kindt-Verlag.

Kelley, S.W., O.C. Ferrell and S.J. Skinner. 1990. Ethical Behaviour Among Marketing Researchers: An Assessment of Selected Demographic Characteristics. *Journal of Business Ethics* 9(8): 681-8.

Lachmann, W. 1987. *Wirtschaft und Ethik [Economics and Ethics]*. Stuttgart: Hänssler Verlag.

Lao-tse. 1985. *Tao te King*. Zürich: Diogenes Verlag.

Lay, R. 1993. Dis Macht der Moral. *Unternehmenserfolg durch ethisches Management [Success in Business Through Ethical Management]*. Düsseldorf: Econ Taschenbuch Verlag.

McCoy, B.H. 1983. The Parable of the Sadhu. *Harvard Business Review* 61 (September-October): 103-8.

McDonald, G.M. and R.A. Zepp. 1988. Ethical Perceptions of Hong Kong Chinese Business Managers. *Journal of Business Ethics* 7: 835-45.

Management Wissen. 1988. No.12 (December): 52-65.

Müller, M. 1983. *Heile und Herrsche*. Berlin: Staatsverlag der deutschen demokratischen Republik.

Myrdal, G. 1964. *Economic Theory and Under-Developed Regions*. London: G. Duckworth.

Nelson, D.R. and Obremski, T.E. 1990. Promoting Moral Growth Through Intra-Group Participation. *Journal of Business Ethics* 9: 731-9.

Ogger, G. 1992. *Nieten in Nadelstreifen. Deutschlands Manager im Zwielicht. [Pinstripe Blues: The Twilight of the German Manager]*. Munich: Droemer Knaur.

Pausenberger, E. 1982. *Entwicklungsländer als Handlungsfelder Internationaler Unternehmungen [Developing countries as Operating Areas for Multinational Companies]*. Stuttgart: CE Poeschel.

Pitt, H.L. and K.A. Groskaufmanis. 1990. Why a Corporate Code May Not Protect You. *Across the Board* Ed. Conference Board. May: 22-25.

Pitt, L.F. and R. Abratt. 1986. Corruption in Business: Are Management Attitudes Right. *Journal of Business Ethics* 5: 39-44.

Plato. 1991. *Der Staat.* (The Politics/Politeia). Munich: Deutscher Taschenbuch Verlag/Artemis, Bibliothek der Antike.

Rich, A. 1987. *Wirtschaftsethik: Grundlagen in theologischer Perspektive [Business Ethics: Theological Foundations].* Volume 1. Third edition. Gütersloh: Mohn.

Riklin, A. 1987. *Politische Ethik [Political Ethics].* Vorträge der Aeness-Silvius-Stiftung an der Universität Basel [Produced by the Aeness-Silvius Foundation of Basel University]. Basel: Helbing and Lichtenhahn.

Schmidt-Salzer, J. 1989. *Entscheidungssammlung Produkthaftung [The Product Responsibility Decision Collection],* Volume II. Heidelberg: Verlagsgesellschaft Recht und Wirtschaft.

Schmidt-Salzer, J. 1989. *Entscheidungssammlung Produkthaftung [The Product Responsibility Decision Collection],* Volume IV. Heidelberg: Verlagsgesellschaft Recht und Wirtschaft.

Senghaas, D. and U. Menzel (eds.). 1976. *Multinationale Konzerne und die Dritte Welt [Multinational Companies and the Third World].* Opladen: Westdeutscher.

Silverman, M., P.R. Lee and M. Lydecker. 1982. *Prescription for Death: The Drugging of the Third World.* Berkeley, CA: University of California Press.

Silverman, M., M. Lydecker and P.R. Lee. 1992. *Bad Medicine: The Prescription Drug Industry in the Third World.* Stanford, CA: Stanford University Press.

Swanda, J.R., Jr. 1990. Goodwill, Going Concern, Stocks and Flow: A Prescription for Moral Analysis. *Journal of Business Ethics* 9: 751-9.

Turner, L. 1973. *Multinational Companies and the Third World.* New York: Hill and Wang.

Tyson, T. 1990. Believing that Everyone Else is Less Ethical: Implications for Work Behaviour and Ethics Instruction. *Journal of Business Ethics* 9: 715-21.

Upanishaden. 1986. *Die Geheimlehre der Inder [The Secret Teachings of the Indians].* Cologne: Eugen Diedrichs (Diedrichs Gelbe Reihe).

Villamil, J.J. 1979. *Transnational Capitalism and National Development.* Atlantic Highlands, NJ: Humanities Press.

Vitell, S.J. and D.L. Davis. 1990. The Relationship between Ethics and Job Satisfaction: An Empirical Investigation. *Journal of Business Ethics* 9: 489-94.

Vitell, S.J. and T.A. Festervand, 1987. Business Ethics: Conflicts, Practices and Beliefs of Industrial Executives. *Journal of Business Ethics* 6: 111-22.

Weber, M. 1988a. Politik als Beruf [Career Politics]. In *Gesammelte Politische Schriften [Collected Political Writings].* Ed. Winckelmann. Fifth Edition. Tübingen: UTB/J.C.B. Mohr (Paul Siebec): 505-60.

Weber, M. 1988b. Die Wirtschaftsethik der Weltreligionen: Vergleichende religionssoziologische Versuche [The Business Ethics of The Religions of the World]. In *Gesammelte Aufsätze zur Religionssoziologie I [Collected Essays on the Sociology of Religion I].* Ninth edition. Tübingen: UTB/J.C B. Mohr.

Wirtschaftswoche 1990. January 26 (No. 5): 35.

World Health Organization (WHO)/United Nations Environment Programme (UNEP). 1990. *The Public Health Impact of Pesticides Used in Agriculture.* Geneva: WHO.

World Resources Institute (ed.). 1994. *World Resources 1994-95. A Guide to the Global Environment.* Washington, D.C.: Oxford University Press.

10

BUSINESS VALUES: A STRATEGIC IMPERATIVE FOR THE COMING DECADES[1]

Arthur Yeung and Jenny Yeung

INTRODUCTION

In the 1980s, research in business values and culture reached an unprecedented climax. Innumerable theoretical and empirical studies encompassing almost all researchable topics in business values and culture were conducted, focusing on such areas as definition issues, theoretical perspectives, methodological approaches, typological schemes, traits of successful values, organizational outcomes and the creation, development and change of business values (Allaire and Firsiroto 1984; Deal and Kennedy 1982; Gregory 1983; Hofstede et al. 1990; Kilmann et al. 1985; Louis 1985; Ouchi 1981; Ouchi and Wilkins 1985; Peters and Waterman 1982; Schein 1985; Smirich 1983). As succinctly expressed by Hofstede (1986: 253), since the early 1980s, organizational culture and business values 'had acquired the status of dominant buzzword in the US popular and academic management literature.'

However, in the 1990s, articles on business values have been declining rapidly in the United States, both in number and importance. In their place, new waves of management research focusing on organizational learning and reengineering have been superseding, in importance, research on business values. The present article represents an attempt to refocus research interest back towards a subject which has ever-increasing relevance in the 1990s. Continued neglect of the multi-faceted field of business values would be a serious disservice to the corporate world, as many corporations are grappling with the challenges posed by business values in a rapidly changing business environment.

A recent study of ten major corporations worldwide—AT&T, British Airways, Broken Hill Proprietary, Daimler-Benz, EDF/GDF, Fiat, Kao, Siemens, Ssang Yong, Union Carbide—confirms the importance of business values in corporate restructuring and transformation (Ready 1993; Yeung and Ready 1994). Of the 1,213 executives who responded to the study, two-thirds believed that their corporations were in the midst of a transformation in culture, mindset and strategy. More importantly, these executives considered the ability to 'articulate a tangible vision, values and strategy' as the most important leadership capability (out of 45 leadership capabilities) for their effectiveness within corporations over the following three years. Clearly, business values remain a vital challenge that many corporations are wrestling with in their journey of corporate renewal and transformation.

In an effort to reassert the pivotal role of business values for both academicians and managers, the present article explores three major questions:

- Why do business values continue to be an important imperative in the business world of the 1990s and beyond?
- How do corporations institute new business values?
- What are possible new directions in the study of business values?

Both literature review and in-depth case studies provide the basis for our investigation of these issues. First, the importance of business values is examined from a theoretical perspective, based on an analysis of business environment trends in the 1990s. Second, based on in-depth interviews with ten senior executives, case studies of two corporations—American Express and Levi Strauss and Co.— offer insightful anecdotes and ideas about the role of business values in these corporations and how new business values are being adopted.

The accumulated impact of these two avenues of investigation points to the vital and dynamic role business values are playing in the life of corporation. When well integrated into the fabric of organizational processes and behaviour, business values are proving fundamental to corporations' capacities for:

- co-ordinating increasingly complex business operations in a global environment;

- balancing employee empowerment and needed organizational controls in an age of information technology;
- delivering responsive and tailor-made services to demanding customers;
- winning employee commitment to achieving both short- and long-term corporate goals.

BUSINESS ENVIRONMENTS AND BUSINESS VALUES

Business values have been commonly referred to as a specific mode of conduct or end-state of existence that is organizationally preferable to an opposite or converse mode of conduct or end-state existence (Rokeach 1973). Business values can be terminal or instrumental (Rokeach 1973), desired or desirable (Hofstede 1984), emerged spontaneously from employees or managed carefully by management (Schein 1985). But for purposes of the present paper, the term 'business values' will be used to refer to those business priorities, standards, and principles which are carefully crafted and managed by top management to the success of corporations. At the outset, it must also be noted that business values and business culture are inextricably related, as business values are the building blocks of business culture itself. Unlike other management tools, business values are people-focused, 'soft', implicit, subjectively defined, and difficult to change (Hofstede et al. 1990). Having clarified our conceptualization of business values, this section examines why business values will continue to be a business imperative in the present decade and beyond.

In the 1990s, four major business environment trends are exerting a deep impact on how corporations worldwide operate and how business values contribute to organizational success. They are: the intensified globalization of enterprises, an accelerated development in information technology, the heightened expectations of customers, and the increased importance of knowledge workers (Fortune 1993; Howard 1990). In response to these immense challenges and opportunities, many corporations are reevaluating their fundamental approach to values in business practices and processes. The catalyst for such efforts is to manage better the competing demands of change and continuity, global integration and local flexibility, customer responsiveness and corporate efficiency, employee empowerment and managerial control. Traditional organizational practices through formulaic strategic planning, rigid hierarchical control, and standard policy/procedural systems have proven inadequate and ineffective (Bartlett and Ghoshal 1990; Evans 1992; Howard 1990). Increasingly, corporations are realising they must rely on business values to guide and shape employees' beliefs and behaviour. Creating core values which strike a responsive chord in employees' hearts and minds is the key to employee commitment, co-ordination and control. It is through shared business values that companies can truly empower employees, strengthen their capacity to organize horizontally around key business processes, and share information freely with their colleagues and co-workers. Without a set of commonly shared values to guide employees from within, companies are reluctant to relinquish their traditional safeguard mechanisms against possible destabilization.

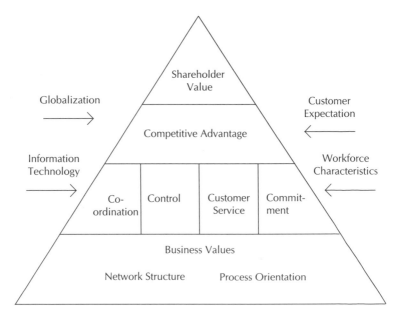

Figure 1: Business Environment Challenges and Emergent Organizational Model

Figure 1 illustrates how corporations utilize business values—in conjunction with other innovative organizational design such as network structure and process orientation—to build a more flexible, responsive and customer-focused organization that will develop competitive advantage and deliver higher shareholder value in the face of the four business environment challenges. The relationship between these challenges and the role of business values within corporations are further discussed below.

Globalization of Enterprises

To capture international market opportunities and reap vital production advantages in different regions, large corporations are increasingly organizing on a global basis in order to gain competitive advantages. While such globalization represents an unavoidable business reality, it also poses tremendous organizational challenges to corporations in co-ordinating and integrating their business operations (Bartlett and Ghoshal 1990). Confronted by multidimensional co-ordinative requirements (based on functional competence, products, markets, and geographical regions), formal organizational structures (including matrix structures) quickly reach their limits in handling such organizational complexities (Evans 1992). Shared business values provide the underpinnings which enable corporations to deal successfully with the complexities of globalization. By instilling and integrating corporate values and philosophy, rather than implementing corporate policies and practices, on a worldwide basis, corporations allow managers to cope more flexibly with tremendous variances in business environments on the one hand, while maintaining strong organization co-ordination on the other.

Development of Information Technology

While globalization presents a host of organizational challenges for corporations, advancements in information technology provide an enormous opportunity for corporations to redesign and reengineer their core processes (Hammer and Champy 1992). The integration of computer and communications technology—including integrated databases, expert systems, hand-sized cellular computer terminals, point-of-sale information systems—all offer a wide range of applications for the reconfiguring of organizational operations. Such integration enables first-line operators and managers to be more responsive to customer requests and deliver better products and services (Hammer and Champy 1992). However, by putting information into the hands of those who are closest to products and customers, corporations are diffusing their power by allowing employees and managers alike to make more decisions on the spot. Traditional controls by supervision and structure become ineffective. As expressed by Bob Haas, CEO of Levi Strauss & Co., in an empowered organization where power is diffused, control needs to be conceptual (by core business values) rather than structural (by rigid structures) (Howard 1990).

Heightened Customer Requirements

The globalization of enterprises and the impact of advanced information technology have driven changes not only in the ways businesses are co-ordinated and employees are managed but, more importantly, in how customers are treated. With a wider choice of products and services because of global competition and an almost endless access to market information, customers today can exert more power than ever before over suppliers, expecting them to deliver better customer value. It is no longer sufficient for a company to provide high-quality or low-cost products; customers are now demanding tailor-made services and quick responses. Increasingly, the ways in which customers are treated and served are becoming competitive differentiators, given the fact that high-quality products or low-cost products are taken for granted in today's markets. People, not just products, are the new source of competitive success in the global marketplace. Business values that orient managers and employees towards being more customer-focused are not simply business considerations but business necessities.

In addition, corporations are developing a heightened sensitivity to customers' concerns with environmental and human rights issues. Managers are realizing that ethical corporate values and practices will better satisfy customers expectations and, in the long term, will result in stronger market competitiveness. Integrity, environmental consciousness, corporate citizenship, and so on, are business values that are being emphasized in many corporations.

New Generation of Workforce

With the widespread applications of information technology in business operations and the economic development of many countries, both the demographics and psychographics of employees are changing dramatically. First, corporations are employing more and more knowledge workers who are better educated (Drucker 1988). To utilize fully the potential of knowledge workers, the traditional management approach of 'checking your head at the entrance' that characterised the industrial age is no longer feasible. In the post-industrial information age, corporations require adding value not only through the 'hands' of workers, but through their minds and hearts as well (McDonald and Gandz 1992). By formulating a set of core values that appeals to employees' aspirations, corporations can gain the commitment of their employees (Howard 1990). Second, as societies become more affluent, employees' work ethics and attitudes also inevitably change. Even in Japan, employees become less automatically loyal and less willing to put in long hours at work unless strong motivating factors exist. With large-scale downsizing taking place in the United States, Europe and probably Japan, employees are becoming more cynical and distrustful toward management. As a result, rallying employee loyalty and regaining employee trust and respect have become new challenges for many corporations worldwide. Many companies find the need to alter both their organizational design and their management philosophy in order to offer more job challenges, pride, ownership and satisfaction for employees in the workplace. Employee commitment from within—through identification and internalization of business values—rather than control from without has become crucial (Walton 1985).

BUSINESS VALUES IN ACTION

Based on the analysis of business environments, we believe that business values will become increasingly important in the corporate world in the coming years. However, we are still not clear in two important issues: (1) how business values actually affect day-to-day business operations and decisions; and (2) how business values are being instituted in corporations. To fill the gap, we supplemented the research findings with two case studies based on our recent in-depth interviews with senior human resource executives at American Express and Levi Strauss & Co. (LS&Co.). In each company, we interviewed four or five senior executives. Each interview lasted for about one hour. Although the two companies are completely different in their product lines, customer base, and business operations, business values play a central role in both corporations. Both corporations are also successful and represent key players in their respective industries.

American Express

After enduring some financial difficulties several years ago, American Express, with the advent in 1993 of new CEO, Harvey Goulb, is undergoing major restructuring. Recognizing that it is fundamentally a service company and its sustainable competitive advantages derived from the ways its employees interact with customers, American Express has formulated six core business values—client focus, quality, integrity, teamwork, people orientation and good citizenship—to guide business decisions and shape employee behaviour. Unlike most companies where business values are used to support business strategies, American Express uses business values to determine its actual business portfolio, that is, what businesses it should be in. Those that are not consistent with the core values (see above) of American Express are targeted for divestiture.

The culture of the retail stock business is an illustration. As explained by Joe Kielty, Executive Vice-President of Quality and Human Resource, 'the business behaviour that typify generally across all of our business, in the way that customers are treated, in terms of treating our employees with dignity and respect as an individual, are necessarily violated through the way that subculture "retail stock business" operates.' Employees who aggressively exert pressure to meet quotas—by making dinnertime telephone solicitations, coercing individuals who lack the appropriate profile to last to buy stocks, etc., are clearly not upholding the core business values of American Express. 'Those folks don't care. They have their sales quota. The rest of the company, in terms of the way we treat a customer or client on a daily basis, is absolutely violated,' elaborates Joe Kielty. Business values, not simply business opportunities, are key considerations before American Express is willing to put its logo behind a business venture.

In addition to long-range strategic business decisions, the new core values affect business behaviour of managers and employees on a day-to-day basis. What differentiates American Express from other companies is that it has instituted an elaborate and highly innovative parallel structure to hold its values in place and to make managers and employees accountable for their behaviour. First, the company revamped its performance appraisal system to include both G-ratings (that is, goal accomplishment) and L-ratings (that is, leadership behaviour consistent with business values). Employees are now evaluated not only on what they have accomplished but also on how they accomplished their goals. As a matter of fact, L-ratings may be even more important because they directly affect the career development of employees within American Express. Employees who rate low in L-ratings can be terminated or demoted, while employees who rate low in G-ratings can still have a chance to improve their performance through training and development activities. Second, to encourage senior managers to demonstrate leadership behaviour consistent with business values and to hold them accountable for the business behaviour within their units, the bonus of managers is directly tied to results of periodical value surveys in their units. Employees' perception of general business behaviour and the upholding of business values in a unit affects the amount of bonus their unit managers receive. Third, to help senior managers identify their weaknesses in leadership behaviour in relation to business values, personal feedback reports based on upward feedback of subordinates are provided. These reports serve as an action plan for senior managers to improve their business behaviour.

By using core business values as a blueprint for strategic business decisions and day-to-day business behaviour, American Express is transforming itself and melding its disparate business units into a single-minded, customer-focused powerhouse. Indeed, business values, and their resulting impact on people (customers as well as employees), are regarded as the most important sustainable competitive advantage for American Express.

Levi Strauss & Co.

Like American Express (LS&Co.), the largest casual apparel company in the world, is also value-driven. However, it has demonstrated its concern with values in quite different ways. After assuming the position of president in 1984, closing twenty-one plants and laying off 6,000 employees due to excess capacity, and launching a successful leveraged buyout to turn LS&Co. into a private company in 1985, Bob Haas, the current Chairman and CEO, and his senior management team, turned their energies toward the development of long-term business values.

In 1987, the company hosted a retreat meeting for the top management team. After being faced with an intriguing question posed by Bob Haas: 'What do we want to be remembered for in LS&Co.?', the top management team engaged in deep reflection and discussion that resulted in the issuing of two important texts: the Mission Statement and the Aspiration Statement. These two statements, together with the Business Vision Statement developed later, outline why LS&Co. is in business (Mission Statement), what it wants to be (Business Vision Statement), and how it can accomplish its goals (Aspiration Statement). These three statements together form the core corporate values and 'glue' for the entire company. Since the formulation of the Mission and Aspiration Statements in 1987, LS&Co. has achieved its sixth straight year of record sales in 1992, with sales reaching US$5.6 billion and earnings US$360.8 million. Clearly, the benefits are not only in the creation of aspirational work environments for employees, but also in economic success.

The corporate values articulated in these three statements have been taken exceptionally seriously by managers and employees alike at LS&Co. Starting from Bob Haas and the executive management committee, top management 'walk what they talk' in developing an ethical, responsible, and successful company that attempts to meet the aspirations of employees, stockholders, customers, and suppliers. As a result, key business decisions are based not only on cost, efficiency, convenience, or competitive pressures, but are also heavily influenced by corporate values. In fact, in many instances, LS&Co.'s decisions are more influenced by these values than financial considerations *per se.* Among its value-driven initiatives are the following:

- LS&Co. recently announced its decision not to use contractors in China as a result of that nation's pervasive violation of human rights. In deciding this issue, top management debated for twenty days, considering the viewpoints of various sources, including China experts, political prisoners and others. The degree of top management attention devoted to such ethical issues as this has rarely been seen in other companies.

- When LS&Co. learned that its two contractors in Bangladesh employed workers under the age of fourteen, LS&Co. intervened. While the employment of under-age workers clearly violates corporate guidelines, LS&Co. also understands that these female children play an important part in supporting their families in that region. If these under-age workers were to lose their regular jobs, they might become prostitutes instead. Faced with this ethical dilemma, LS&Co. worked with the contractors to create an education programme for the workers. As a result, LS&Co. now pays for the tuition, books, and uniforms for these workers until they reach the age of fourteen. In addition, the contractors agree to continue paying these children their salaries and benefits while they attend school.

- When some employees complained to top management that LS&Co. was discriminating against gay and lesbian employees by not paying benefits to their partners, LS&Co. adhered to its Aspiration Statement and approved the Domestic Partner Policy (giving benefits to gay or lesbian partners of employees), even though it costs the company a substantial amount of money.

- After employees complained about the difficulty of balancing their personal and professional lives, LS&Co. responded with a flex-time programme and a four-and-a-half day working week programme.

Clearly, the corporate values of LS&Co. have become a potent way of affecting the beliefs and behaviour of many employees at LS&Co. How has LS&Co. managed to achieve this kind of impact? Sue Thompson, Director of Human Resource Development, suggested that 'the corporate statements have come from the hearts of the top management. It is an inside-out programme'. As a result, top management can naturally and comfortably walk what they talk and serve as a strong role model.

In addition, human resource programmes have played a strategic role in developing and reinforcing strong values among employees. Starting from the top, every employee has to go through a three-module training programme called Core Curriculum, a programme which has proved to be a major force in communicating corporate values to employees. It includes three components: Leadership Week, Valuing Diversity and Ethics. In the Leadership Week programme, twenty employees go through a one-week, intensive, and experiential programme that discusses and debates the core values of the Aspiration Statement. A senior manager, a business manager, and a consultant facilitate the meeting. After the week, every participant signs his or her name on the Aspiration Statement to signify his or her commitment to the statement. The Valuing Diversity programme is a three-day workshop in which the biases, stereotypes and prejudices of employees are frankly explored and approaches formulated to overcoming negative attitudes. Finally, the Ethics programme reviews and discusses the code of ethics at LS&Co., such as honesty, promise-keeping, fairness and integrity.

The Core Curriculum has proved to be a key component in communicating corporate values to employees. Findings of employee surveys indicate that employees have increased their understanding of the Aspiration Statement over the years. Along a five-point scale (1 = to very little extent; 5 = to a very large extent), employees' understanding of the Aspiration Statement has increased from 2.75 in 1987 to 3.09 in 1989 and 3.65 in 1992. It is fascinating to note that employees generally accept the Aspiration Statement as consistent with business success.

In addition, employees are appraised and rewarded based on their adherence to the Aspiration Statement, one of the four components that are evaluated in the newly designed pay system called 'Partner in Performance'. Under the new pay system, employee performance is explicitly linked with their adherence to six core values in the Aspiration Statement. In other words, what one has achieved and how one has attained goals are equally important in performance appraisal.

Corporate values are also driving large-scale organizational restructuring at LS&Co., specifically, through the Alternative Manufacturing System (AMS) and Customer-Supplier Service Chain (CSSC) restructuring. In the apparel industry, the piecework pay system has long been extremely prevalent for production workers. To derive high efficiency, work has been divided into many small tasks where production workers repetitively engage in one of these tasks. To earn more money, production workers need to repeat the same motions, resulting in common health problems such as repetitive motion injuries. Clearly, the old system is contrary to the 'new' belief in the importance of creating a healthy work environment, both physically and psychologically.

To address the problem, LS&Co. has redesigned its production jobs and organised workers into self-managed work teams, of about thirty-five employees, to create garments from start to finish. Instead of payment based on piece rates, team members are now paid an hourly salary, plus incentives. The incentives are calculated based on the performance of the team, plant, supply-chain, and company. To implement AMS, a significant amount of training is conducted in basic skills for effective teamwork, including leading meetings, participating in meetings, setting requirements, problem solving, team building, communications, etc. Typically, it takes about five years to make the work teams fully functional. Although a lot of time and significant costs are involved in implementing AMS, LS&Co. and its employees have reaped great benefits from the new system: production lead-time has been greatly reduced (from 26.4 days in 1991 to 16.3 days in 1992), flexibility has been enhanced, costs have decreased by 10%, product quality has been increased, employees' quality of worklife has been improved, and repetitive motion injuries have decreased. AMS is an excellent illustration of how business considerations and Aspirational values converge.

According to Sue Thompson, Director of Human Resource

Development, 'Do what we told our customers' is one of the driving forces that has initiated the largest scale restructuring in LS&Co.'s history: the Customer-Supplier Service Chain restructuring. 'Customer interviews indicate that customer service is the number one concern to many retailers. Our products are not delivered 100% accurate and on time. We are only delivering 85% to 90% accurate and on time. It is very hard to further improve the ratio given the current organizational design', says Donna Goya, Senior Vice-President of Human Resource at LS&Co. Moreover, LS&Co. is facing tough competition from companies like VF Corporation and Gap in their distribution channels. Given the premium pricing and quality strategy of LS&Co. products, LS&Co. must improve its relationships with retailers in order to compete successfully for shelf space. Starting in 1991, LS&Co. has been reengineering its CSSC in order to be more process-oriented, functionally-integrated, and customer-focused. Up until now, the initiative is still actively ongoing with a strong commitment and resource support from top management.

Clearly, business values play an important role in the reengineering effort. While this reengineering initiative will strengthen the competitive conditions of LS&Co., it is their corporate values in promise-keeping and integrity that help justify large-scale restructuring like this when the corporation is extremely successful and profitable. By adhering to its corporate values, as outlined in the Aspirations Statement, the Mission Statement, and the Business Vision Statement, LS&Co. is truly a value-driven organization that continually strives to find innovative ways of improving its relationship with all its constituents, from stockholders, and employees, to customers, consumers and suppliers.

When we compare American Express with LS&Co., we observe a lot of similarities between two companies. Both companies have been very successful in instituting business values in their corporations and practising those values in their corporate life. Unlike many companies that have invested enormous time and resources to formulate a set of high-sounding business values that are hardly remembered by employees and managers alike, American Express and LS&Co. are unique in the sense that they are able to put those business values in place and ensure managers and employees live out their business values. There are three key factors to their successful institution of business values. First, the new business values have been not only formulated and supported by their top management but consistently demonstrated in their behaviour and decisions. Second, both companies have made their business values actionable by translating abstract business values into observable behaviour. Figure 2 depicts the two-step process involved: (1) from business values to thoughts and emotions, and (2) from thoughts and emotions to actions and behaviour.

Without making business values actionable, companies can hardly reinforce abstract business values (such as customer orientation, corporate citizenship) in employees' behaviour. Third, both American Express and LS&Co. have used extensive human resource practices (performance appraisal, rewards system, training and staffing) to evaluate and influence employees' behaviour. By translating business values into observable behaviour and holding employees and managers accountable for their own behaviour, business values have become a potent force in shaping employee beliefs and behaviour in both companies.

POSSIBLE DIRECTION FOR FUTURE RESEARCH

Based on the analysis of business environment trends and the two case studies, this paper argues that business values play a crucial role in the business world, from both conceptual and empirical perspectives. While business values are increasingly replacing formal structures as a co-ordination and control mechanism, they are also driving strategic business decisions in major companies like American Express and Levi Strauss & Co. However, the decreasing focus on business values and culture in American business journals reveals a striking discrepancy between research attention and the actual importance of business values. Although extensive research was conducted in business values and culture in the 1980s, we believe there are still important research areas to be explored in the 1990s and beyond. Three possible directions for future research are suggested.

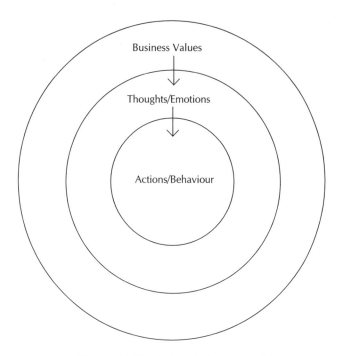

Figure 2: Making Business Values Actionable

First is the value intensity question. While corporations are inculcating and instituting business values to enhance co-ordination, commitment, and control, it is important to ask what will be the appropriate degree to which values should be emphasised and shared in the workplace. Conceptualizing business values as a 'glue technology' (that is, a strategy to enhance corporate cohesiveness), Evans (1992) argues that corporations run the risk of being over-dosed by business values, in addition to sometimes being under-dosed. Empirical research indicates that such a possibility does, in fact, exist (Yeung 1990). When corporations share too much of their mindset towards business values, their innovativeness and adaptability may suffer. Assuming intensity level is a real concern to corporations, then how can corporations know where to set boundaries and what are some possible mechanisms to prevent over-indoctrination? Evans' (1992) duality theory and Quinn's (1993) competing values approach represent possible avenues for future research. By skilfully balancing competing and conflicting values, corporations may alleviate the trap of being overwhelmingly rigid in any single set of business values. Research into how companies have done this or could do it would be of value to the business and academic communities.

Second is the cultural integration question. When global corporations expand their operations worldwide, to what extent should they apply their business values on a consistent basis? Given the fact that business values may differ significantly between Anglo-Saxon and Asian countries (Redding 1987; Wong 1983) and between well-developed and developing countries (Kedia and Bhagat 1988), should the business values of global corporations be adaptive to different countries or consistent on a global basis? Or should corporations develop two-tiered business values, including both globally generic values and regionally specific values? Cultural conflicts in business values may emerge in ways of managing foreign employees, and conducting business with foreign customers and suppliers. A dramatic example is the pervasive corruption problem in Asian countries. How should corporations behave in business environments like this when corporations, as a whole, emphasize integrity and ethical business behaviour?

Third is cross-cultural research in business values. Let us talk about the case of Asia. Clearly Asian business values, especially in Chinese societies, play an important role in business success (Redding 1987). However, it is also evident that Chinese business values are very different from those in the United States and Britain (Wong 1983). Chinese business values are typically utilitarian, outcome-oriented, family-related and seldom explicitly articulated. In contrast, business values in American corporations are more explicitly articulated, more formal, and balanced between behavioural and outcome orientation. In addition, the ways business values are socialised in Chinese societies are quite different from Anglo-Saxon countries. Useful comparative studies in the antecedents, contents, and consequences of business values in different countries are still lacking, in spite of some pioneering studies in this area (England 1975; Hofstede 1984).

CONCLUSION

The four business environment trends—globalization of enterprises, advances in information technology, burgeoning customer expectations, and changing characteristics of the workforce—have been serving, and will continue to serve, as catalysts for corporate transformation. They are also the spur for the development of business values: values which can galvanize the workforce to pressing organizational goals and facilitate the co-ordination of increasingly complex business operations. Unquestionably, business values will continue to play a dominant role in corporate restructuring. They will become vital aspects of emerging organizational design—more decentralized, more flexible, and more responsive to ever-increasing customer expectations.

For these reasons, the complex issues involved in the formulation and institution of business values must be addressed by managers and explored in academic research. Only in this way can corporations achieve their fundamental goals, best serving the needs of customers, employees and stockholders. Indeed, the cultivation of strong business values is a strategic imperative for international corporations striving to distinguish themselves in today's intense global arena.

NOTE

1.   The case studies quoted in this paper are part of a larger research project funded by the Executive Education Research Centre of the University of Michigan. We gratefully acknowledge the significant contribution of Wayne Brockbank at the University of Michigan and Schon Beechler at Columbia University to the research project.

REFERENCES

Allaire, Y. and M. Firsiroto. 1984. Theories of Organisational Culture. *Organisational Studies* 5: 193-226.

Bartlett, C. and S. Ghoshal. 1990. Matrix Management: Not a Structure, a Frame of Mind. *Harvard Business Review* 68 (July-August): 138-45.

Deal, T. and A. Kennedy. 1982. *Corporate Cultures: The Rites and*

Rituals of Corporate Life. MA: Addison-Wesley.

Drucker, P. 1988. The Coming of the New Organisation. *Harvard Business Review* 66: 45-53.

England, G.W. 1975. *The Manager and His Values: An International Perspective from the United States, Japan, Korea, India, and Australia.* Cambridge, MA: Ballinger.

Evans, P. 1992. Management Development as Glue Technology. *Human Resource Planning* 15: 85-105.

Fortune Magazine. 1993. Special issue on managing change, December.

Gregory, K. 1983. Native-view Paradigms: Multiple Cultures and Culture Conflicts in Organisations. *Adminstrative Science Quarterly* 28: 359-76.

Hammer, M. and J. Champy. 1993. *Reengineering the Corporation.* NY: Harper Business.

Hofstede, G. 1984. *Culture's Consequences: International Differences in Work-Related Values.* CA: Sage.

Hofstede, G. 1986. Editorial: The Usefulness of the 'Organisational Culture' Concept. *Journal of Management Studies* 23: 253-7.

Hofstede, G., B. Neuijen, D.D. Ohayv and G. Sanders. 1990. Measuring Organisational Cultures: A Qualitative and Quantitative Study Across Twenty Cases. *Administrative Science Quarterly* 35: 286-316.

Howard, R. 1990. Values Make the Company: An Interview with Robert Haas. *Harvard Business Review* 68 (September-October): 132-44.

Kedia, B. and R. Bhagat. 1988. Cultural Constraints on Transfer of Technology Across Nations: Implications for Research in International and Comparative Management *Academy of Management Review* 13: 559-71.

Kilmann, R.H., M.J. Saxton and R. Serpa (eds.). 1985. *Gaining Control of the Corporate Culture.* San Francisco: Jossey-Bass.

Louis, M. 1985. An Investigator's Guide to Workplace Culture. In *Organisational Culture.* Ed. Frost, Moore, Louis, Lundberg and Martin. Beverly Hills, CA: Sage.

McDonald, P. and J. Gandz. 1992. Identification of Values Relevant to Business Research. *Human Resource Management Journal* 30: 217-36.

Ouchi, W. 1981. *Theory Z: How American Business Can Meet The Japanese Challenge.* Reading, MA: Addison-Wesley.

Ouchi, W. and A. Wilkins. 1985. Organisational Culture. *Annual Review of Sociology* 11: 457-83.

Peters, T. and R. Waterman. 1982. *In Search of Excellence: Lessons from America's Best-Run Companies.* NY: Warner.

Quinn, W. 1993. *Morality and Action.* Cambridge, UK: Cambridge University Press.

Ready, D. 1993. *Building a Competitive Capabilities Profile.* Working paper, International Consortium for Executive Development Research (October).

Redding, G. 1987. The Study of Managerial Ideology Among Overseas Chinese Owner-managers. *Asia Pacific Journal of Management* 4: 167-77.

Rokeach, M. 1973. *The Nature of Human Values.* New York: The Free Press.

Schein, E. 1985. *Organisational Culture and Leadership.* San Francisco: Jossey-Bass.

Smirich, L. 1983. Concepts of Culture and Organisation. *Adminstrative Science Quarterly* 28: 339-58.

Walton, R. 1985. From Control to Commitment in the Workplace. *Harvard Business Review* 63 (March-April): 77-84.

Wong, S.L. 1983. Business Ideology of Chinese Industrialists in Hong Kong. *Journal of the Hong Kong Branch of the Royal Asiatic Society* 23: 137-71.

Yeung, A. 1990. *Cognitive Consensuality and Organisational Performance: A Systematic Assessment.* Ph.D. Thesis, University of Michigan.

Yeung, A. and D. Ready. 1994. Leadership Capabilities of Global Corporations: Balancing Business and Cultural Imperatives. Paper under review. *Human Resource Management Journal.*

11

ETHICAL ATTITUDES TO BRIBERY AND EXTORTION

Jack Mahoney

INTRODUCTION

Bribery is a source of considerable concern in many quarters of the globe, as events and scandals in various countries in the last twenty years have shown. Reasons for its common ethical condemnation are examined, as well as attempts made by international agencies to outlaw the practice. A distinction is drawn between bribery and extortion, and conditions are explored under which payment of extortion may be considered morally justifiable. However, situations of social change or transition call for particular resistance to practices of bribery and extortion. Such resistance requires governments and businesses to take all possible practical measures within their respective spheres of influence. It also often calls for a considerable degree of moral courage on the part of individual managers.

ETHICAL ATTITUDES TO BRIBERY AND EXTORTION

Among the topics suggested for treatment at this international conference by its organizers, that of managerial responses to corruption, presents considerable intellectual as well as ethical and moral challenges. I intend to explore one particular expression of corruption, by offering some reflections on Ethical Attitudes to Bribery and Extortion. I propose first to review various approaches to bribery and the reasons why it is judged to be unethical in principle and calls for international action; then to consider whether an ethically meaningful distinction can be drawn between bribery and extortion and under what conditions; and finally to review what steps might be taken by governments, businesses and managers, faced with the prospect of bribery and extortion in varying situations.

Bribery is a topic which greatly concerns business people who are interested in the ethical conduct of business. I understand bribery to be the providing of an inducement to influence an official improperly in the exercise of their duties. Modern business history contains no lack of national and international bribery scandals to keep the subject before the public eye. In my own country of Great Britain, the death in July 1993 of T. Dan Smith recalled for many people what amounted to a national crisis in the 1970s over the disclosures and trials of Smith and his co-conspirator, the architect and public building contractor, John Poulson, whose 'systematic web of corruption' involved bribery at every level of British society and led to a Royal Commission and the resulting requirement for Members of Parliament to list their business interests (Fitzwalter and Taylor 1981: 216).

In those years, of course, it was the tidal waves of bribery scandals in the United States which seized the world's shocked headlines. As the Watergate investigations into domestic political payments by major corporations began also to uncover large overseas bribes, it became evident that considerably more was at stake for US business than re-electing President Nixon. So much so that when the US government invited voluntary disclosures from American corporations the consequence was, as Clinard noted in his 1990 study of *Corporate Corruption*, that more than 450 large US corporations, mostly *Fortune* 500s, ultimately disclosed to the Securities and Exchange Commission during the late 1970s and early 1980s illegal or questionable payments abroad, totalling more than US$1 billion and paid either as direct bribes to foreign government officials or through foreign corporate 'sales agents' (Clinard 1990: 121; Kline 1985: 24).

The tentacles of US overseas bribery spread throughout the globe at the time, and to countries as far apart as Japan, the Middle East and The Netherlands, rocking the political structure of several countries (Noonan 1984: 652-80). Yet it was by no means the only cause for concern at the time about bribery in the world of business. In Hong Kong also the 1970s saw major steps being taken to cope with the problem, by the introduction in 1971 of the Prevention of Bribery Ordinance, to be followed three years later by the establishment of the Independent Commission Against Corruption (ICAC). On that period an interesting commentary was offered on 26 January 1994 by the Chief Secretary, Mrs Anson Chan, when she observed in the debate in the Legislative Council to review the ICAC's powers and accountability that: When the ICAC was established twenty years ago, Hong Kong was very different from what it is today. In the 1960s and early 1970s ... the community was in danger of becoming resigned to corruption. Today things are very different. Our community demands and expects clean government. Far from being resigned to corruption, it now shows a high degree of intolerance of corruption' (*South China Morning Post* 1994, cf. Lee 1981).

Italy, too, is a country where, as we are increasingly learning today, bribery has been systemic for decades. The corruption scandals first broke in Milan in early 1992, and the increasing revelations of bribery throughout many sectors of Italian society, including its major political parties and its major business companies, do not yet appear to have exhausted the uncovering of what *The Economist* (1993b) described as 'the rot ... in the pillars of Italy's establishment'.

Depressing as the apparently widespread incidence of bribery in business is, nevertheless there is also some ground for encouragement in recognizing that influential parties in at least some major societies are not prepared to countenance it, and that they take determined steps to counter its presence, as in Hong Kong in the 1970s and Italy today. Of course, the major step was taken in the United States, with the passing in 1977 of the Foreign Corrupt Practices Act (FCPA) to prohibit American corporations from offering or making payments to officials of foreign governments (Donaldson 1989: 31). Nor was the United States alone in its aim to influence the international scene in commercial bribery. Various worldwide bodies also began to attempt to control the phenomenon, as we shall see, and all this local and internationally concerted action to combat the practice naturally leads into a consideration of why there should be such universal condemnation, at least in theory, of the offering and accepting of bribes.

Commercial bribery can be faulted ethically on three general grounds: as being bad for business, bad for the participants, and bad for the society in which it occurs. The arguments against bribery as being bad for business are headed by the consideration that in seeking unfair advantage over others the practice undermines the whole philosophy of the market as a system in which success depends on the notion of fair competition. The leading business ethicist, De George (1993: 104), sums it up: 'Bribery is a way of getting preferential treatment.' Moreover, by its bid for a virtual monopoly it can result in the inefficiencies which are widely recognized as characteristic of monopolies (Velasquez 1992: 196). As Nobel Laureate Gary S. Becker observed, bribery usually does considerable damage, including the extracting of monopoly prices and misusing time and resources which could be better used to produce useful goods and services (Becker 1994: 8).

Again, by its need to cultivate secrecy, bribery introduces a note of public surmize and suspicion about various transactions, driving out certainty from exchanges, and at the same time deceiving investors as to the true state of the market. By diverting negotiations away from being product-related to being determined by the size of the bribe 'it seriously distorts the decision-making process' (Moody-Stuart 1993: 27), ignoring product quality, satisfaction and often safety, and also often increasing costs and thus adversely influencing production.

Bribery can also have harmful consequences for those actively involved in the transaction. Not only does it involve stealing from their owners and possibly violating company policy as well as the law, with the danger of blackmail and the continual risk of detection, shame and punishment; the colluding in dishonesty and the conspiring to defraud also constitute a fundamental breach of trust and dereliction of duty.

Finally, bribery is regarded as on various grounds harmful to the society in which it takes place. There is the economic loss of taxes on the money and activities which can be involved. Another is noted by Shleifer and Vishny (1993: 19) in their suggestion that 'many poor countries would rather spend their limited resources on infrastructure projects and defence, where corruption opportunities are abundant, than on education and health, where they are much more limited' (cf. Moody-Stuart 1993: 28-30). More generally, the lying, dishonesty and other crimes entailed in promoting or covering up a culture of bribery are not only profoundly dispiriting to a citizenry in simple human terms of the collective quality of social life. Bribery and extortion are particularly harmful to the poor in any society, who cannot afford the additional costs to be paid to obtain simple justice (*The Economist* 1988). For the practice can become addictive for the individual and contagious to others. It was not without reason that George Moody-Stuart (1993: 3) wrote, from a lifetime's experience of business, of 'the invasive cancer of grand corruption.' And even on a more petty scale the practice can easily become endemic and provide a breeding ground for other antisocial practices, so tainting many other expressions of social life and intercourse.

One particular expression of bribery which is considered especially harmful to a society is that resorted to by multinational or transnational corporations in Third World or less developed countries. In his study of multinational corporations Feld (1980: 1-3) observes that during the 1970s, MNCs, with their immense economic power and financial muscle, became increasingly a subject of controversy. In the developing world such disquiet was compounded by the ability of MNCs at times to engage in large-scale bribery often to the disadvantage of local enterprises. As one Director of Exxon summed up the reputation of the MNC, it was

> viewed by some as an intruder in foreign countries, even an arm of domination by its home country. Others viewed it as an outsider even at home, dangerously lacking the legitimacy that comes with having a firm place among purely national institutions (Coolidge et al. 1977: 29).

In the circumstances it was not surprising that in the 1970s less developed countries in particular were eager for steps to be taken at an international level to curb the power and activities of MNCs by aiming to introduce agreed codes of conduct for them. The best known attempt was that undertaken by the United Nations Economic and Social Council, beginning in 1972, which set up a

Commission on Transnational Corporations to produce an agreed code of conduct on how MNCs should behave in host countries, and also how they should be treated by host governments. In 1976, the Council set up an Ad Hoc Intergovernmental Working Group to consider the Problem of Corrupt Practices and in 1978 this produced a draft International Agreement on Illicit Payments. This draft (para. 20) required MNCs to

> refrain, in their transactions, from the offering, promising or giving of any payment or other advantage to or for the benefit of a public official as consideration for performing or refraining from the performance of his duties in connection with those transactions (UNCTC 1988: 32-3).

It further required MNCs to maintain accurate records of payments made by them to any public official or intermediary, and to make these records available on request to the competent authorities of the countries in which they operate (ibid.: 33). In the event, the Agreement was not, however, accepted by the United Nations General Assembly, and matters have remained unchanged.

Another international approach to regulating the conduct of MNCs in relation to bribes is to be found in the activities of the Organisation for Economic Cooperation and Development (OECD) in the discharge of its role to develop international co-operation among industrialized countries. In June 1976 the OECD Conference of Foreign Ministers adopted a set of Guidelines for Multinational Enterprises (Feld 1980: 108), which stipulated that 'Enterprises should ... not render—and they should not be solicited or expected to render—any bribe or other improper benefit, direct or indirect, to any public servant or holder of public office' (ibid.: 164).

The OECD guidelines had the merit, as Feld (1980: 116) points out, of being 'the first major statement by the industrialized countries of the world about their expectations regarding the future behaviour of MNCs everywhere'. However, the OECD has still not secured complete agreement among the twenty-four participating nations on the means to deter companies from making illicit payments for overseas contracts and to punish those which are apprehended. The US campaign to have other countries follow its own lead in outlawing overseas bribes and to cease allowing them to be tax-deductible at home came to a head in April 1994 at a meeting of the OECD working party on illicit payments. It seems likely, however, that the recommendation to be put to finance ministers for ratification this month (June 1994) will reflect the alternative preference of other OECD countries, including Britain and Japan, that each country should carry out a national review and take appropriate local steps as it sees fit (Waterhouse 1994).

On such illicit payments a much fuller statement than that of the OECD came from the International Chamber of Commerce, whose 1977 *Report on Extortion and Bribery in Business Transactions* (ICC 1977; Kline 1985: 92-3) was the most detailed international treatment of the subject, no doubt because, as Feld observed, 'The ICC, as a nongovernmental organization, had the least obstacles to overcome' (Feld 1980: 108). The Report's explicit concern was 'to set forth the co-operative action that should be taken by governments and enterprises to combat bribery and extortion in business transactions' (ICC 1977: 6). Addressing governments in the first instance and having in mind the aim of international harmonization of standards, the report called on each government to introduce, review or perfect its statutes

> to ensure that they effectively prohibit, within its territorial jurisdiction, all aspects of both the giving and the taking of bribes, including promises and solicitation of bribes, as well as so-called facilitating payments to expedite the performance of functions which government officials have a duty to perform (ibid.: Part II: 1).

The ICC was also able, as the world business organization, to admonish the international business community that it had 'a corresponding responsibility to make its own contribution towards the effective elimination of extortion and bribery' by self-regulation in international trade. To that end it presented for business enterprises a set of *Rules of Conduct to Combat Extortion and Bribery*, which were more stringent than those legally imposed in many countries, but it expressed the hope that the spirit of the Rules of Conduct would be faithfully followed by 'all business enterprises, whether international or domestic' (ibid.: III: Introduction).

With the ICC *Rules of Conduct*, then, we have moved from

exclusive concentration on multinational corporations and the need or the wish to control their behaviour in various countries around the globe, to consider regulation against bribery and extortion on the part of all national governments and business enterprises. Moreover, they provide a useful introduction to an ethical analysis of the whole issue, on which we may now embark. More than one commentator, for instance, on the US FCPA notes that its proscribing of bribes abroad does not include 'facilitating payments' to minor government officials, or in more colloquial terms 'grease' injected into the bureaucratic system in order to lubricate it and ensure its smooth running (De George 1993: 103). As Jacoby, Nehemkis and Eells (1977: 113) point out, 'foreign political payments are made more frequently to induce government employees to perform their official duties than for any other purpose.' In other words, a basic distinction which can cast light on various degrees of moral responsibility involved in engaging in bribery is that between bribing someone to do what they ought to be doing in any case in the line of duty, and on the other hand bribing someone to use their position or power to do what they ought not to do. The distinction does not occur explicitly in the ICC Rules, but it is implied in the Rules' recommendations to governments to criminalize 'so-called facilitating payments to expedite the performance of functions which government officials have a duty to perform' (ICC 1977: II: 1).

Paying bribes just to get normal business expectations fulfilled is what appears to worry many, if not most, ordinary business people who are attempting to run their business with integrity along ordinary decent lines. And certainly the other form of bribery, inducing people to do what is inherently unethical, such as breaking the law, turning a blind eye to defects, condoning tax avoidance or permitting exploitation, appears much more reprehensible conduct than surreptitiously paying people to do their duty. Noonan (1984: 688) captures the essential ethical distinction when he refers to paying bribes for 'the proper performance of a task not its perversion'.

Of even more ethical significance, however, is the further distinction to which this points the way, that between bribery and extortion. For no one would pay a bribe to ensure normal service unless they were being in some way coerced to do so. As the ICC observes,

> public opinion has sometimes tended to assume that corruption is generally initiated by enterprises ... The truth is that much bribery is in fact the response to extortion. Enterprises have too often had the experience, in many countries, of having to choose between giving in to extortion or not doing business (ICC 1977: I).

Noonan (1984: 89, 149) traces back to Roman law and early Christianity a juridical and ethical distinction between the free offering of a bribe and being compelled to pay extortion (cf. Jacoby et al. 1977: 90). The distinction is not always clear-cut and is 'frequently blurred' in reality (ibid: 154). Nor does it imply that the payment of bribes is criminal while the payment of extortion is necessarily exempt from criminal proceedings (ibid.: 176; Noonan 1984: 579-80). Nevertheless, if the handing over of extortion money is essentially compulsory, and is aimed at dissuading someone from inflicting or threatening unjustified harm or damage, either by commission or omission, then the payment of extortion can have a degree of ethical justification which would not apply to the voluntary offer of a bribe. For paying extortion is akin to 'justifiably buying off harassment, paying a kind of ransom' (Noonan 1984: 638), simply in order to go about one's ordinary and legitimate business without fear or hindrance (cf. Velasquez 1992: 196). As De George observes, somewhat grudgingly in my view, 'the coercion mitigates to some extent the culpability of the victim.' Yet he also notes that payment serves to reinforce the practice. 'It acquiesces in evil rather than resisting it. At best it may be the lesser of two evils' (De George 1993: 198, 126). As Noonan also warns, 'the excuse of paying off harassment cannot be invoked in a merely individual situation; the damage to the common good is too great' (Noonan 1984: 695).

If paying extortion in business is to be on occasion ethically justified, on what conditions might this be the case? I suggest that there are four conditions, all of which need to be fulfilled. The first would be that unless one pays extortion there is simply no practical possibility of going about one's business. One is faced with a climate of extortion, or socially deep-rooted practices of being overtly or subtly bullied into submission in a manner akin to the protection rackets which flourished in Chicago earlier this century and, if reports are true, which are present in parts of Northern Ireland today. A second condition would be that the purpose of the payment is to persuade the extortioner to desist or refrain from doing something wrong, that is, from unjustifiably doing or threatening damage. A third ethical condition is that the business which one wishes to conduct is lawful and legitimate, and of benefit not only to its immediate participants but also to stakeholders and notably to the economy and society in which it is conducted. Indeed, this positive benefit of a business to society is the countervailing factor which balances or outweighs the social ill of contributing to the continuance of a practice of extortion. Finally, if one is seeking to do business by surrendering to so socially harmful a practice, then a fourth ethical condition of doing so is to do all in one's power at the same time to combat that practice.

The bribery required as a condition of doing normal business may be due to explicit demands or expectations. It may more subtly result from an inherently unjust market characterized by inequality of access and unfairness in distribution, as has been alleged with regard to modern Russia, where trying to work within such an unethical system can justify taking countermeasures which would not otherwise be ethically acceptable (cf. Filatov 1994: 12). Yet, the case which I have outlined for apparently colluding in wrongdoing by paying extortion under certain well-defined circumstances is not unique. In a wider perspective, there are illuminating parallels between doing business in a society characterized by extortion and doing business in a society, for example, which depends on apartheid, as in South Africa until recently, or doing business in or with a country where there is widespread violation of human rights or a corrupt regime or appalling labour conditions. Such regrettable situations pose the more general ethical question of whether one can ever be justified in doing business in or with a society which contains certain features which one considers unethical or with which one is reluctant to be associated, yet which one cannot ignore.

Is the ethical stance either to avoid all such societies—an almost impossible undertaking—or to deal with them and share their guilt by collusion or at least by association? Or is there a middle way? One lesson which can be learned from the debate over trading with South Africa is that there can be more than one ethical answer to that and similar questions (cf. Williams 1986). The adoption of the Sullivan Code by companies doing business in South Africa indicated that, while the general ethical strategy was to abolish apartheid, there was nevertheless more than one ethical tactic to bring that about. One could either express concerted disapproval from a distance to pressurize the economy and the government by withdrawal, or one could be present in the country trading and at the same time undermining the foundations of apartheid from the inside.

It seems possible, then, to formulate a general ethical principle which can apply to a climate of extortion just as much as to a climate of apartheid or dictatorship or human rights violation: that one can be ethically justified in working in a culture which has certain unethical features, but only on condition that they are unavoidable, at least for the time being, that one is operating for good business and social reasons, and that one is also working to change those unethical features of the culture.

How much can, or should, be done by individual companies to work at changing the climate of extortion in any particular culture then depends on two circumstances: one relating to the power of the company to influence the situation, and the other relating to how much the prevailing social situation can in fact be changed. Clearly, the larger and more powerful a company is, and the more it is likely to profit from trading even when submitting to extortion, the greater is its ethical responsibility to use its power, influence, and profits to remedy the situation, either by refusing to succumb to extortion, or by exposing would-be extortioners, or by pressing government to take effective measures against them. Even companies which are not giants on the commercial scene are not powerless, however, if they can combine their forces to pressurize or work with government. As De George observed, 'official complaints by groups of American companies have changed the practice of bribery in some countries, and collective or industry-wide efforts have proved to be more effective than efforts by individual firms to oppose a pattern of bribery solicitation' (De George 1993: 14).

The other circumstance which affects the moral responsibility of companies to work to combat a climate of extortion depends on how socially entrenched the practice is in the country in question. It is here that one tends to meet a mood of moral fatalism, in the frequently expressed view that extortion is too deep-rooted as a way of life to be significantly diminished, far less uprooted, from a particular society. If this were true, and extortion was literally an irremovable feature of business life in any society, then companies would be exonerated from wasting their resources in attempting to do the impossible, and moral fatalism would appear to win the day. Yet it may be that there are scenarios where a commercial and political renaissance in a country can provide grounds for giving the lie to moral fatalism, or where a society is undergoing or facing a process of transition where the social stakes for the future are so high as to provide an immensely powerful ethical incentive and determination to combat the spread or the further consolidation of extortion.

What has been happening in Italy recently, for example, was well described by *Business Week* (1994) in its statement that 'since a political hack was caught red-handed with US$5,000 in bribes two years ago in Milan, a steamrolling anti-corruption investigation has smashed an entire political regime—and way of life—to bits.' In the estimation of *The Economist* (1994c) in the same week, 'close to 5,000 businessmen and politicians have been arrested on corruption charges over the past two years.' One early result of this 'clean hands' Italian judicial campaign was the issuing in May 1993 of a new 'code of business ethics' by Italy's biggest private company, Fiat, which was being accused of widespread and long-lasting payment of bribes to Italy's various political parties. This set out required behaviour for all the group's employees towards government officials, political parties and civil servants to avoid any form of bribery or kickbacks involving the public sector 'even as a result of illegal pressure' (*The Financial Times* 1993). And this idea of illegal pressure was spelled out in self-justifying detail the following week in the statement of the group chairman of Olivetti, Carlo De Benedetti, providing magistrates with information about the £20bn (US$13.3m) in bribes which his company had paid to political parties over the years. As he explained, 'the pressure from the parties and their representatives in the state entities reached an impressive crescendo ... of menaces and extortion to become in the last few years nothing short of racketeering' (Graham 1993).

Whether Italian business has been the unwilling victim of extortion by the major political forces in the country, as the chairman of Olivetti claimed, or whether, on the contrary, the business leaders were often all too ready accomplices, as accused politicians alleged (Graham 1993), the case can be made that in the past co-operating in extortion in Italy was less ethically reprehensible for a company than straightforward bribing, and that it could have been justified on the conditions which I have just outlined. However, now that the rot has been uncovered and a massive clean-up operation is under way, the overriding ethical consideration for any company is not now to acquiesce fatalistically in the old order, but on the contrary to throw its weight behind the movement for change and to contribute to the continuing momentum and completion of that social revolution.

It may be that the progressive exposure of endemic political and business corruption in Italy was made easier by the collapse of the Soviet Union and the end of any need for a united front to support anti-Communist political and business forces in Italy. At any rate, the disintegration of the Soviet hegemony in Central and Eastern Europe has certainly led to a major transition stage for business there, with enormous future stakes which make it imperative not to surrender to a climate of corruption and systematic extortion. In a recent study on 'Unethical Business Behaviour in Post-Communist Russia', Professor Alexander Filatov analyses the origins and trends in such behaviour, and he diagnoses the current transitional situation as characterized by instability, uncertainty and conflict. It is not therefore surprising if he concludes that 'many experienced Western businessmen know that in order to operate in such distorted market conditions their strategies ... must be pursued without any reference to ethical considerations that govern within fairer economic structures' (Filatov 1994: 11-2). At street level there are also alarming indications in Russia of local economies being effectively controlled by 'mafia chiefs who [impose] gangster-style levies on private kiosks and businesses' (Binyon 1993). In the Ukraine one leading young entrepreneur finds that his biggest running costs are paying corrupt local bureaucrats for government 'licences' and paying interior ministry troops to guard his many pavement kiosks from local gangs (*The Economist* 1994b). On the former Eastern bloc as a whole, the Czech economist, Marie Bohatá, reports that 'the decline in morale threatening former communist countries has been very disturbing ... Corruption, financial deals and "agreed" auctions, in many cases with foreign capital participation, have been growing' (Bohatá 1994: 91).

The European Bank for Reconstruction and Development, in the words of its recent president, Jacques Attali, is all too aware of the need to restructure such economies and of the price which will have to be paid for failure to do so: 'the black market, bribery and corruption' (Attali 1993: 114). All of these observations serve only to confirm the statement made in 1992 by the Director of the US Office of Government Ethics, Stephen Potts, that 'the single greatest threat to the emerging democracies of Eastern Europe and the former Soviet Union is corruption.' They also reinforce his strong admonition to American companies doing business there not to offer bribes and kickbacks to corrupt officials or intermediaries, precisely because such actions may hinder the development of the fragile democracies (Singer 1992: 1).

If it is true, then, that surrendering to extortion is less justifiable in a socially volatile and improving situation, as in Italy, or during an all-important period of transition, as in Central and East Europe, then perhaps a similar conclusion can be drawn with regard to Hong Kong in the light of the major change in its relationship with China which it is preparing to undergo in 1997.

The observation of the Chief Secretary in January 1994 which I have already mentioned, that the Hong Kong community now shows a high degree of intolerance of corruption, appears borne out by a survey conducted in August 1991 among Hong Kong managers and reported in the *Hong Kong Manager* which concluded that 'Hong Kong managers ... have positive opinions of the ethical and social responsiveness of their organizations and feel the organizations they work for are favourably perceived by others' (Migliore et al. 1993: 20). Reassuring as such perceptions about the ethical quality of Hong Kong business are for the present, they nevertheless appear to coexist alongside serious anxieties concerning mainland Chinese companies or individuals. Such was the situation reported from Hong Kong last November by Simon Holberton of *The Financial Times* (Holberton 1993), referring to the recent ICAC finding that corrupt business practices may represent 3% to 5% of the cost of doing business in China, a factor which respondents nevertheless claimed was bearable and not a disincentive to doing business there.

Such anxieties, it appears, can only increase as Hong Kong companies become even more involved with its largest trading partner, and Chinese firms increasingly arrive in Hong Kong. It is expressed baldly in *The Other Hong Kong Report 1993*, which claims to identify 'a perception that corruption will worsen in the run-up to 1997' and which refers to 'the business community's concerns for the difference between anti-bribery regulations in Hong Kong and China' (Choi and Ho 1993: 66, 68). Given that, as *The Economist* (1994a) observed, 'Hong Kongers are increasingly worried about the contagious nature of Chinese business practices', it is not surprising that the focus of the activities of the Independent Commission Against Corruption has shifted from investigating government malpractice to concentrate increasingly on the private sector.

Yet, it can also be noted that it is not only honest people in Hong Kong who are concerned about the future ethical quality of business. In March 1994, Li Peng, the Chinese Prime Minister, described corruption as 'a matter of life and death' for China, and 'the abuse of power for personal gain, graft and bribery' as behaviour which must be 'punished unsparingly' (Poole 1994). As one writer reports the situation, since late 1993 the Chinese government has been campaigning against corruption and business fraud, including bribery, as a serious threat to the Communist Party. In so doing it has also been responding to popular ethical anger and revulsion: 'ordinary Chinese citizens are increasingly disgruntled about petty graft; an anticorruption hotline set up by the Supreme People's Procuratorate has been swamped with calls' (Poole 1994).

If, then, there are certain social situations of revolution or transition in which it is particularly incumbent on business to work for the common good, and to decline to acquiesce in a culture of extortion continuing or becoming entrenched, it then becomes all the more important for governments as well as businesses to take all possible effective steps to combat bribery and extortion within their sphere of influence. Governments can usefully begin by criminalizing the practice and by denying the legitimacy of custom as a justification or mitigation, as was done by the Hong Kong Prevention of Bribery Ordinance (cap. 201, 19). Reference to a *de facto* acceptance of the practice in various societies, which is so regularly appealed to by outsiders, may be sometimes discounted as a need to find an excuse for business failure and partly identified as exaggerated and self-fulfilling rumours, as was noted some years ago by *The Economist* (1988). Yet, in this connection governments can also usefully take positive steps to educate the public on the social and economic damages inflicted by all forms of corruption, as exemplified by Hong Kong's Announcements in the Public Interest to the general public, including new immigrants from China, and as described in the 1992 Annual Report of the ICAC (1992).

More specific and practical steps can and need to be taken at national and international levels, in accordance with what the ICC Guidelines called 'the political will and the administrative machinery' (ICC 1977: I: a). Such steps include anything which, in the words of Husted (1994: 25), will make bribery 'prohibitively expensive', whether this be in financial terms or in any other human or corporate terms. This includes the establishment or strengthening of national background institutions to promote the rule of law and its protection of human rights (cf. De George 1993: 144); intergovernment co-operation and harmonization, as well as appropriate provision for extradition; procedures for regularly disclosing details of relations between public officials and commercial agents; independent review of the award of government contracts, which should not be left to individuals (Jacoby et al. 1977: 245); the requirement of an anti-bribery clause in all major contracts; strict enforcement of auditing legislation; and transparency in the payment of political contributions at least by requiring public record of such payments and public accounting of their receipt. Since bureaucracy can be a labyrinth, especially for strangers, governments should put their own houses in order by radically simplifying regulations in order to diminish the need to resort to bribery and to cut down opportunities for exacting extortion (cf. Shleifer and Vishny 1993: 5). Provision should be made for an adequate salary structure for public officials which will attract suitable candidates and obviate their need to supplement their income by bribery; there should be strict limitation and regular supervision of the discretionary authority of minor officials (Jacoby et al. 1977: 244-5), frequent transfer of officials and agents to prevent long-term relationships being developed, and conflict of interest laws preventing official association or relations with suppliers (Husted 1994: 25). Finally, government should ensure effective prosecution and appropriate penalties, including imprisonment, for convicted companies, top executives and chairmen, and regular publication of the relevant information; and should also encourage freedom of expression in the press and other public media of communication (cf. *The Economist* 1988).

So far as businesses themselves are concerned, self-regulating structures can be introduced and regularly reviewed comparable to many of those enumerated for government. What now appears indispensable are explicit codes of conduct which, in the words of the ICC, 'may usefully include examples and should enjoin employees or agents who find themselves subjected to any forms of extortion or bribery immediately to report the same to senior management' (ICC 1977: art. 10). But in the case of bribery, as in all other business malpractices, it is absolutely essential that codes of conduct have teeth, and that infringement is immediately and publicly penalized. Other possible procedures to delimit bribery and extortion include annual signed statements by CEOs (Moody-Stuart 1993: 59) and all employees; more non-executive directors who are truly independent, who are given an explicit ethics remit and who form audit committees along the lines of the recent UK Cadbury Report on Corporate Governance (Cadbury 1992); a policy that middlemen should receive remuneration which is strictly commensurate with their detailed services and which is not to be shared with others as bribes, or transferred outside the country as accommodation payments (cf. Kline 1985: 133-4); the refusal to countenance 'off the books', or secret, accounts; and strict compliance with the letter and spirit of local laws.

The goal of such governmental and corporate structures and

procedures is to lessen the pressures on companies and individuals and to decrease the occasions for wrongdoing, thus making it that much easier for them to resist temptations or solicitations to bribe. In the same context it will be interesting to follow the fortunes of a new body, Transparency International, which was founded in 1993 for the express purpose of forming a coalition against corruption in international business transactions, particularly in evolving or developing countries. TI is based in Berlin, with many national chapters in the process of being established, and among the means to which it is committed is the creation of what it terms national 'islands of integrity', where honest business practices are encouraged, honest businesses are attracted, and companies which bribe, or attempt to bribe, are exposed and penalized (TI 1994).

All these and other aids and supports to promote and protect ordinary decent business dealings without recourse to bribery and extortion are surely valuable. Yet, ultimately, there can be no substitute for personal self-regulation, or the individual manager's own integrity as he or she goes about their business. At the end of his classic history and analysis of bribery Noonan concludes, 'Human beings do not engage in such acts without affecting their characters, their view of themselves, their integrity' (Noonan 1984: 700). Whether one agrees with so sweeping a judgement or not, the subject of the ethics of bribery and extortion cannot be adequately covered without some concluding remarks on the need for personal business integrity, and particularly, where bribery and extortion are concerned, on the need for the personal quality and the exercise of moral courage.

I began this paper by observing that the subject of bribery and extortion was one which offered considerable intellectual, ethical and moral challenges; and so far we have been concerned with the first two, the intellectual challenge of analysing and understanding the practice and varieties of bribery, and the ethical challenge of evaluating bribery and extortion in terms of whether and why they are wrong. It remains, however, to consider briefly the moral challenge which follows from these intellectual and ethical analyses, namely, the challenge of actually deciding whether or not to behave in accordance with one's intellectual and ethical conclusions about bribery and extortion.

For most practical purposes, the two terms 'ethical' and 'moral' are synonymous, one deriving from Greek and the other from Latin, to refer to the same characteristics of some forms of human behaviour. It is also possible to consider 'ethics' as the more academic term of the two, used to describe the scientific and systematic analysis of various ways of behaving and to deliver a theoretical verdict on them, as we have been doing with reference to bribery and extortion. However, coping with bribery and extortion in business calls for considerably more than intellectual analysis of the issues involved, and a good deal more than just arriving at a judgement in principle on the ethical quality of such behaviour. It also involves personally acting on that analysis and that judgement in particular situations, and facing up in practice to what can thus be properly called the moral challenge of matching one's actions to one's ethical principles.

This is where recent work in ethics to recover the classical notion of moral virtue has much to contribute to our subject, concerned as it is with the character of individuals and their integrity. Such moral integrity, directed at actually behaving ethically, implies the notion of a certain moral wholeness of character and a moral loyalty to one's principles. De George (1994: 4) remarks that 'integrity requires that one have developed ethical views to which one adheres.' In addition to this, however, the idea can often also include an element of moral courage to follow through in putting these ideas into action.

This idea of moral courage as a necessary personal resource for individuals seeking to behave ethically in business was first popularized by O'Toole in his 1985 study of *Vanguard Management* in a chapter entitled 'Moral Courage: The *Sine Qua Non* of Greatness' (O'Toole 1985: 340-71), although he did little more than illustrate it as the leadership quality of taking a public stand on controverted social issues. The subject is usefully deployed in a little more detail by De George in the context of international business, especially when he observes that 'moral courage is central to acting ethically in difficult situations' (De George 1993: 111; cf. 22). Recognizing this traditional philosophical insight into the nature of moral courage can be of particular help to individuals when faced with the pressure of having to decide on occasion whether or not to have recourse to bribes or to succumb to extortion.

Courage in the face of difficulties and dangers is commonly seen as the capacity to cope with the fear which such situations can arouse in us. In his study, *The Anatomy of Courage*, Winston Churchill's physician, Lord Moran (1945), defined fear as 'the response of the instinct of self-preservation to danger', and courage as 'will-power' to handle that instinctive reaction. As such, it may not, of course, necessarily be moral courage. A fraudster may well have the courage to overcome the fear of being caught out; or a cat burglar may need to acquire the courage to overcome a fear of heights. What makes the difference between merely physical or psychological courage and moral courage is when the action which it is feared will lead to unpleasant consequences is itself a moral action, such as telling the truth, or keeping a promise or resisting various pressures to do something one knows or believes to be unethical. In this context it was instructive to read the forthright verdict of *The Economist* (1993a) on the explanations given for the conduct of some members of the British government in the Churchill Matrix scandal involving the sale of military equipment to Iran, that 'nine-tenths of the explanation boils down to cowardice', that is, to the absence of moral courage.

Moral courage, then, appears to be the capacity to do what one judges is ethically called for in spite of one's perception of the dangers and difficulties involved. As such it is an almost routine requirement on the part of people engaged in ethical business. Yet such moral courage to withstand fear seems especially required in situations where the instinct for survival, whether personal or corporate, can exert very considerable pressure on the individual to remove that fear by simply having recourse to bribery or extortion. In such cases, to succumb to offering and receiving bribes is to court the lowest standards of human social intercourse. To exact their contribution is to poison the wells of human and business relationships. To decline or refuse to be associated with bribery, and particularly with routine extortion, can call for the exercise of moral courage to an impressive degree. Yet sometimes the conduct of ethical business calls for no less.

REFERENCES

Attali, J. 1993. The Ethics of European Transition. *Business Ethics: A European Review* 2 (3): 111-6.

Becker, G.S. 1994. To Root out Corruption, Boot out Big Government. *Business Week* (January 31): 18.

Binyon, M. 1993. Capitalism Gone Wild. *The Times* (October 5).

Bohatá, M. 1994. Ethics in the Czech Transformation Process. *Business Ethics: A European Review* 3 (2): 86-92.

Business Week. 1994. March 28: 46-8.

Cadbury, A. (ed.). 1992. *Report of the Committee on the Financial Aspects of Corporate Governance.* London: Gee.

Choi, P-K. and L-S. Ho (eds.). 1993. *The Other Hong Kong Report 1993.* Hong Kong: Chinese University Press.

Clinard, M.B. 1990. *Corporate Corruption: The Abuse of Power.* New York: Praeger.

Coolidge, P., G.C. Spina and D. Wallace, Jr. (eds.). 1977. *The OECD Guidelines for Multinational Enterprises: A Business Appraisal.* Washington DC: Georgetown University Institute for International and Foreign Trade Law.

De George, R.T. 1993. *Competing with Integrity in International Business.* Oxford: Oxford University Press.

De George, R.T. 1994. International Business Ethics. *Business Ethics Quarterly* 4 (1): 1-9.

Donaldson, T. 1989. *The Ethics of International Business.* Oxford: Oxford University Press.

Economist. 1988. Business Bribes: On the Take. November 19: 21-4.

Economist. 1993a. Trading in hypocrisy. December 18: 55-6.

Economist. 1993b. Così fan tutte. October 23: 55-6.

Economist. 1994a. Hong Kong: the Trouble with Caesar's Wife. January 29: 37-8.

Economist. 1994b. Geller the Seller. February 19: 74.

Economist. 1994c. Italian Magistrates: Arresting. March 26: 66.

Feld, W.J. 1980. *Multinational Corporations and UN Politics. The Quest for Codes of Conduct.* New York: Pergamon Press.

Filatov, A. 1994. Unethical Business Behaviour in Post-Communist Russia: Origins and Trends. *Business Ethics Quarterly* 4 (1): 11-5.

The Financial Times. 1993. May 12:

Fitzwalter, R. and D. Taylor. 1981. *Web of Corruption. The Story of John Poulson and T. Dan Smith.* London: Granada.

Graham, R. 1993. Buck Stops at De Benedetti. *The Financial Times.* May 18.

Holberton, S. 1993. Anti-corruption Official Sacked in Hong Kong. *The Financial Times.* November 11.

Husted, B.W. 1994. Honour Among Thieves: A Transaction-Cost Interpretation of Corruption in Third World Countries. *Business Ethics Quarterly* 4 (1): 17-27.

Independent Commission Against Corruption (ICAC). 1992. *Annual Report by the Commissioner of the Independent Commission Against Corruption.* Hong Kong: Government Printer.

International Chamber of Commerce (ICC). 1977. *Extortion and Bribery in Business Transactions.* Paris: ICC.

Jacoby, N.H., P. Nehemkis and R. Eells. 1977. *Bribery and Extortion in World Business: A Study of Corporate Political Payments Abroad.* New York: Macmillan.

Kline, J.M. 1985. *International Codes and Multinational Business: Setting Guidelines for International Business Operations.* Westport, CT: Quorum.

Lee, R.P. (ed.). 1981. *Corruption and its Control in Hong Kong: Situations Up to the Late Seventies.* Hong Kong: Chinese University Press.

Migliore, H.R., R.T. Martin, R.E. Stevens and D.L. Loudon. 1993. Hong Kong Managers: A Survey of Corporate Culture. *The Hong Kong Manager* (July/August).

Moody-Stuart, G. 1993. *Grand Corruption in Third World Development.* York: Quacks.

Moran, Lord. 1945. *The Anatomy of Courage.* London: Constable.

Noonan, J.T., Jr. 1984. *Bribes.* New York: Macmillan.

O'Toole, J. 1985. *Vanguard Management: Redesigning the Corporate Future.* New York: Doubleday.

Poole, T. 1994. Greasing the Dragon. *The Independent on Sunday* (April 3).

Shleifer, A. and R.W. Vishny. 1993. *Corruption.* Working paper No. 4372. Cambridge, MA: National Bureau of Economic Research (May).

Singer, A.W. 1992. Is Corruption a Threat to the New-born Democracies of Eastern Europe? *Ethikos* 6 (1). New York: Mamaroneck.

South China Morning Post. 1994. Accountability of ICAC Comes under Scrutiny. January 27: 6.

Transparency International (TI). 1994. *Transparency International Newsletter* (March). Berlin: Transparency International.

United Nations Centre on Transnational Corporations (UNCTC). 1988. *The United Nations Code of Conduct on Transnational Corporations.* London: Graham & Trotman.

Velasquez, M.G. [1982] 1992. *Business Ethics. Concepts and Cases.* Englewood Cliffs, NJ: Prentice-Hall.

Waterhouse, R. 1994. Britain Spurns U.S. over Bribes. *The Independent on Sunday* (April 3).

Williams, O.F. 1986. *The Apartheid Crisis: How We Can Do Justice in a Land of Violence.* San Francisco: Harper and Row.

12

BUSINESS VALUES AND EMBRYONIC INDUSTRY: LESSONS FROM AUSTRALIA

Stewart Clegg

WHAT IS EMBRYONIC INDUSTRY?

Embryonic industry is new and emerging. Its novelty lies in the application of distinctive practices to production, service or problem resolution in ways that are discontinuous with existing technologies, values, and knowledge. The root metaphor is that of an 'embryo'. If there is not something that is new and discontinuous then there would be no new conception, nothing in embryo. At the core is innovation in products and processes. Innovation is not just technical; it is also organizational and managerial. Effective innovation harnesses technical innovation in products and processes to social systems that can manage, organize and deliver them to markets effectively (Eriksson 1990).

The literature of innovation concentrates upon questions of technological innovation and emphasizes radical transformations of product technology. While new technologies imply what is probably the most potential source of embryonic industry, they are not the only source. In practice, we found, the focus on embryonic industry requires a broader focus than on technology *per se*.

The crucial focus is on technological competence. Three aspects define this competence (Gattiker and Willoughby 1993). First, there are the cluster of 'learning-related' aspects. The second aspect of technological competence concerns the cultural embeddedness of this competence in organizations and countries by individuals and groups. In this research report the priority given to cultural sources of innovation reflects this aspect. The third aspect of the competence is a particular locale. Many of our recommendations, and much of our focus, particularly on 'How to cultivate embryonic industry' through chains, clusters, networks, and strategic alliances, address this issue of relative scarcity and how to overcome it.

For any organization to survive, it must have some distinctive competence (Selznick 1957), those things that it does especially well when compared with its competitors in a similar environment. Within any organization two particular kinds of competence are particularly important: technological competence and cultural competence. Cultural competence refers to the ability to be able to harness and use culturally diverse myths, symbols, rituals, norms, and ideational systems creatively to add value to an organization's activities. Technological competence may be defined, following Gattiker and Willoughby (1993: 463) as the ability 'to receive and use information for solving technology and economic-related problems and opportunities for making appropriate decisions.'

Technological competence, and technology-driven views of innovation, were at the core of the bulk of the research literature that we consulted, perhaps because the focus was on specific forms of innovation that were defined by their underlying technologies (for example, Willoughby 1990, 1992). Yet, as we learnt from the Focus Groups, not all innovation is technology driven.

The relationship between market intelligence and innovation is central to the emergence of successful embryonic industry. Markets are as important as innovation. New markets open not only because of novel technologies; shifts in values and culture also are potent sources of innovation.

EMBRYONIC INDUSTRY CAN BE CULTURALLY DRIVEN

The diversity of cultures offers major sources of value for Australian enterprizes. First, it does so by virtue of the introduction of cultural novelty. Food is the most evident case in point. Socially, innovation comes from cultural diversity just as it comes from a diverse gene pool biologically. The emergence of a 'Mediterrasian' cuisine that is distinctively Australian as a source of culinary excellence has only been possible because of the culturally diverse ethnic traditions represented here. Innovative chefs can draw on the diverse traditions that the application of their skill and their biographies have exposed them to. From the cultural overlays come innovations. Shifts in values that derive from culture create new market opportunities. It is market intelligence that identifies these as opportunities. Innovators respond to these opportunities and, if successful, seed an embryonic industry.

A second major source of value for Australian industry comes from the diversity of the personnel who comprise it. In selling overseas, whatever the product, whether traditional or innovative, Australian enterprises have a remarkable opportunity to do good business through the serendipity of multiculturalism. Australians who are also native speakers of a customer's language have a head start in doing good business in that culture because they already have much of the tacit knowledge and implicit learning that those who are alien can acquire only slowly and painfully. In general, a great deal of learning occurs through making mistakes. In business this can be costly. Multiculturalism presents the possibility of much lower-cost learning. However, diversity requires good management for innovation. Australian enterprises have to learn what a valuable resource their multicultural habitat can be. They must use it and know how to manage it well. Specific recommendations that follow address the issue of diversity.

There is a third important attribute of culture in relation to embryonic industries. Recent studies assess and compare cultural attitudes towards technology. Such attitudes mediate the effective use to which technological innovation may be put (Gattiker and Willoughby 1993; Gattiker and Nelligan 1988; Early and Stubblebine 1989). Evidence suggests that some countries have a more positive governmental and public policy culture with regard to education for technology, such as Germany (Littek and Heisig 1991).

That Australia is now a country of great cultural diversity is axiomatic. Goldstone (1987) has suggested that situations characterized by cultural diversity and ferment are those that most readily foster innovation. Enforcement of a state of orthodoxy, the preservation of tradition as the yardstick of action, the veneration and conservation of the past, these promote nothing so much as intolerance, hostility and resistance to innovation. Pluralism encourages innovation organizationally (Perry and Sandholtz 1988).

In the appropriate conditions, Gattiker and Willoughby (1993: 474) observe, 'if a firm or region can develop technological competence and manage the multicultural workforce successfully, and thereby improve its competitive advantage in global markets, it will ultimately succeed in securing more resources and wealth.'

While this is correct, it underestimates the role that culture can play. While good management of the multicultural workforce is vital, there is more to culture than merely its proliferation across the diversity of employees. There is also the question of cultural identity in the marketplace, the identity of customers and consumers. While in all 'postmodern' societies, by definition these identities will be fragmented, disparate and heterodox, there are potentially profitable points of cultural convergence that can offer competitive advantage on a global scale. We will focus on what we believe to one such unique opportunity for Australia.

Cutting across cultural diversity in Australia are some central, if contested, values. One of these may provide a major source of competitive advantage for embryonic industry in the development of a 'green' profile for Australian enterprises and activities. Successful global examples exist, such as the Body Shop, and in the United States, Redken Cosmetics, who market products that claim to contain 'natural' Australian ingredients.

It is not only in the exploitation of green niches in existing product markets that opportunities present themselves. Additional openings derive from the application of new technologies to the problems of previous polluters or from powering existing applications through new green technologies. An example of successful Australian innovation built on 'green values' is Waste Management and Pollution Control Ltd., a venture that has been established through a Cooperative Research Centre initiative. Its efforts focus on improving water quality, minimizing waste impact on soils and landscapes, minimizing harmful gaseous emissions, and remedying contaminated sites.

Australia does not yet have an international reputation for its application of green values, although the well-publicized role of

Greenpeace as consultants to the successful Sydney Olympic bid is a toe-hold that the country could build on.

EMBRYONIC INDUSTRY REQUIRES A NEW PARADIGM OF MANAGEMENT

The research confirms the emergence of a new paradigm of management, one that theoreticians see as having particular relevance for embryonic industry. Not all practitioners will find the practice of this new paradigm easy, given past habits of power and the reluctance that is often attached to innovation in customers, even for those who make a point of innovation in technical practice.

What one might call a 'female ethos' or a 'feminization of management' clearly is becoming increasingly prominent. This does not mean that the ranks of management are becoming staffed with more women than in the past. The reference is, instead, to the substantive content of management activity, where 'masculinism' characterizes older, military-derived models. To make the point clear, the adoption of such masculinist models could be the hallmark of feminine occupations as much as masculine ones. Nursing, historically, was a case in point (Chua and Clegg 1990). Here the employees were principally women, but the organizational model derived from the male world of the military, with its bureaucratized ranks, uniforms, distinctions and command structure. Certainly, the new paradigm is very different from older models of management derived from the military, through public sector bureaucracies (Weber 1947) and engineering practice (Taylor 1911), in the earlier years of this century.

In this new way of managing, increasing recognition is given to factors such as relational rather than competitive values, the need for firms to seek interdependence rather than dominance in the marketplace, and for business opportunities to be nurtured in an 'emergent' manner through affiliation and co-operation rather than rationality, separation and manipulation, even when this brings together firms who would previously have seen each other as competitive threats. These, taken together, have been felt by many authors to be more characteristic of female than of male behaviour.

Table 1 'Old' And 'New' Paradigms of Management

New paradigm	Old paradigm
organization learning	organization discipline
virtuous circles	vicious circles
flexible organizations	inflexible organizations
management leaders	management administrators
open communications	distorted communication
markets	hierarchies
core competencies drive product development	strategic business units drive product development
strategic learning capacities are widespread	strategic learning occurs at the apex of the organization
assumption that most organization members are trustworthy	assumption that most organization members are untrustworthy
most organization members are empowered	most organization members are disempowered
tacit and local knowledge of all members of the organization is the most important factor in success and creativity creates its own prerogative	tacit and local knowledge of most members of the organization must be disciplined by managerial prerogative

In the past, while formal structures of imperative command crystallized as bureaucracy could aspire to control all that was within the reach of the organization, that control could never be total. The many 'vicious circles' of attempts at control to repair a perceived power deficit by management, leading to increased employee resistance, are well recorded from Gouldner (1954) onwards (see Clegg and Dunkerley 1980). That control will be far less and attempts to achieve it far more inappropriate when the most important relations that the organization enters into are not within its grasp as a legally fictive individual should be self-evident. As networks expand and as markets intrude into organizations, intra-organization hierarchies, and control premised on them, recede in importance. As organizations seek value through the strength of their ties to and networks with other organizations, attempts at imperative managerial control become intrusive and inappropriate. Control through networks, particularly where there is considerable complexity and short span of product life-cycles, means that emergent 'windows of opportunity' require rapid and widespread sharing of knowledge, rather than its concealment from competitors. The old paradigm of management tradition and practice is increasingly obsolete for the managers of embryonic industries.

THE ROLE OF MANAGEMENT EDUCATION, DEVELOPMENT AND TRAINING

Criticism has concentrated on a curriculum that stresses financial calculation over the management of substantive processes (also see Higgins and Clegg 1988). The core of the criticisms focuses on management that is too centred on short-term financial and accounting criteria.

Management education, at every level of provision, if it is to counter these criticisms, should emphasize:

- the centrality of co-operative as well as competitive behaviour both within and between organizations;
- that managing the politics of knowledge are central to successful management;
- that complex problems rarely are amenable to single technological solutions;
- that 'market intelligence' should be the central focus of all management education (Goldman and Nagel 1993).

In terms of the organization of Management Education, a free and competitive market in management ideas and institutions seems to be the best historical model for innovation, rather than founded on the chartering of elite privileges to a small, select number of institutions. After all, it was with these arguments that Adam Smith (1961), in *An Inquiry Into the Nature and Causes of Wealth of Nations*, first mounted his moral case for the supremacy of capitalism as an allocative system over that of absolutism of mercantilism. Competitive markets allow diversity to flourish by affording multiple niches within which innovations might take seed and grow.[1]

An emphasis on networks and alliances as organizational forms, and on collaboration as a management practice, is something that should extend into management education, development and training. Accordingly, universities, technical and further education, professional associations, private training providers, and firms must link in a system that celebrates diversity, accentuates quality, and which formal bodies accredit where appropriate. Australian management education institutions will have to develop skills in order to educate managers appropriately for the twenty-first century. These point, particularly at graduate level, to more varied modes of education delivery and assessment than presently exist. The new styles will involve problem-based learning that is project centred, involving multifunctional teams with cross-cultural work placements in business overseas. Providers will design their curriculum in collaboration with overseas partners to maximize exchange of skills, in both faculty and students. Degrees will require work at more than one institution, cross nationally. However, without some incentives that encourage a focused view on strategic objectives for market place realities, it is unlikely that such initiatives will flourish.

Europe is in the vanguard in these initiatives in terms of institutional collaboration. It occurs both through firms and tertiary institutions. In Germany, conscious internationalization programmes are conducted by banks and large companies as staff move globally to gain comparative experience. Management students in one European institution, De Montfort University in Leicester, UK, spend one semester in Leicester, and two semesters abroad, at a French and Spanish partner institution respectively. There is no reason why Australian universities cannot offer their students the same experience of an international marketplace. Institutional partnering needs careful choice. It is best if the focus of the institutions is complementary rather than overlapping. Doing the same thing twice in different contexts will achieve little.

INTERNATIONALIZING THE MANAGEMENT CURRICULUM

The majority of the texts, cases, and ideas used in current teaching derive from the highly idiosyncratic and individualistically focused Anglo-American culture. Gattiker and Willoughby (1993: 460) observe, writing from Canada and Australia, respectively, that students often write papers

> dealing with technological and cross-national issues based primarily on US-grounded models and studies. Thus, North American ethnocentrism (i.e., the tendency by scholars to overlook the applicability of their concepts and theories beyond their own country and/or culture) will extend into the training of future managers by those learning about technology and cross-national issues through North American 'tinted glasses'.

Management education needs to focus on analysis of comparative management and technical practices, rather than assume that a particular approach that is endemic to a national context is universal. Being English-language speakers in a distinctive but small country, dominated as we are by the intellectual and cultural productions of North America and the United Kingdom, compounds this problem. What is available to us in English may not even be useful in our national context. More attaches to a successful curriculum than retooling American texts with Australian cases. Indeed, all of our research points to the need for cultural relativism and cultural listening rather than unitary models of national or organizational culture.

The curriculum requires stretching to focus much more on a global curriculum and to enable students to learn more of the business recipes used in other countries. Japan is the obvious example, but students should learn about both other societies in our region and from the experience of other small but highly developed countries, such as the Netherlands and the nations of the Scandinavian region. One feature that has been said to characterize firms in these countries is that they are predisposed to 'organization learning' (Clegg 1990; Marceau 1992), a theme that we explore briefly in the next section.

TEACHING ORGANIZATION LEARNING SKILLS

Firms that are not 'agile', that cannot develop new products or services, and that do not attend to their customer needs, will not survive long where they are in increasingly competitive business environments, unsheltered and unprotected. Since the object of innovation is to commercialize products valued by customers, acceleration of the process should not jeopardize the *quality* of the firm's offerings. It requires continuous, open, and timely communication, sensitive to the need to nurture effective teamwork among all members of the firm and its alliance partners to achieve this acceleration. Personnel training and the allocation of sufficient resources to make technologies effective and efficient should accompany the implementation of innovation.

Successful new product performance suggests that product innovation is a learnable activity (Cooper and Kleinschmidt 1986; Dwyer and Mellor 1991). The learning cited by the above authors applies predominantly to production issues. Whether it works equally for product innovation is unclear. Incremental product innovation involves modification to existing products in the context of given levels of technology. Discontinuous innovation often transforms these, as it radically alters technologies, occupational definitions, and the authority relations that existing knowledge relations constitute. There is usually a considerable time-lag as the socio-cultural impact of changes flows through. (The locus of these changes is not necessarily technological. One may think of examples such as the shift to greater diversity in organizations that have been typically mono-cultural or single gender: the armed forces are a case in point. Innovations in traditional organizations will require that more exploratory and far-reaching learning skills develop. Often new socio-cultural management skills will need importation, as the Navy is slowly learning.)

It is not just that firms need to learn from their learning; the experience of learning requires institutional expression if it is to be efficient. Focus Groups, particularly in Brisbane, affirmed the success of learning networks in which entrepreneurs from one industry share experiences. The case in point involved CEOs, collaborating on the basis of openness and trust, sharing experience and commercial information to gain collaborative advantage. This form of cluster learning has much to recommend it as unobtrusive, inexpensive and consistent.

THE ROLE OF THE CEO

Given that innovation is likely to become increasingly important to firm survival over time, learning will assume greater significance, the faster discontinuous futures approach. Top management, in particular, has an important role to play in the acquisition of the learning skills that institutionalize innovation. This role includes linking the organization to key outside contacts that serve as 'learning agents'; cultivation of particular technical skills within the organization; encouraging an innovative mindset among personnel; and locating, defining, and linking skills within the organization and matching skills with the organization's strategic plan. Top management is best able to establish innovation as a central value (McKee 1992). Communication and political skills should lie at the heart of the training that is appropriate for management for the twenty-first century.

The CEOs of twenty-first-century firms should not be afraid to be their own venture capitalists: they should back employee's hunches and fund them. Benetton have done this to great advantage, creating the most global and successful of popular fashion houses. Many of the firms they sub-contract to in Emilia Romagna are of their own creation. CEOs need to be taught to abandon vertical integration and instead to force market relations into the firm, to subcontract extensively, and to create numerous joint ventures and alliances, especially with new firms, where they are in more established industries.

Highly responsive and agile enterprises can sometimes broker roles as 'virtual companies', that exploit transient or niche markets as they emerge, where management achieves a speed and flexibility that matches that of the technologies involved (Goldman and Nagel 1993). Such agile management, characterized by strategic focus on long-term financial performance, seeks opportunities for growth and profit in constant change that flexible management can exploit. Authority diffuses in the agile enterprise rather than being concentrated in a chain of command. Instead of a static corporate structure based on fixed, specialized departments, agile corporations have a dynamic structure, keyed to the evolving needs of cross-functional project teams. They are totally integrated organizations.

Work goes on concurrently rather than sequentially and is not necessarily contained within the envelope of the legally distinct corporate entity. Sub-contractors, partners, customers and end-users interrelate in the concurrent design and production network. Management becomes less and less functionally oriented and more and more the management of diverse project teams, creating new alliances with embryonic industry firms. There are implications of this to apply to corporate governance in management education (but see Mathews 1993). Diversity, in all its characteristics, whether premised on diverse knowledge, whether occupational or particularly, other social identities, is a central issue of heightened salience in contemporary Australia as a multicultural country.

THE MANAGEMENT OF DIVERSITY

There is no Australian culture. Not in the singular. Australian cultures exist. The scene is one of diversity. It is for this reason that in the discussion of 'culture' we wish to break ranks with the predominant wisdom. Since at least Peters and Waterman (1982), when management theorists and practitioners have emphasized the importance of culture, they have done so in terms that eulogize the importance of a 'strong' culture. It has become almost axiomatic to discuss the necessity of having a unitary culture for organizations that are to achieve excellence. Rather than contribute further to a discussion of culture that mistakes the existence of strong symbols and rituals for a sign of unitary culture, rather than as a mechanism designed to try and create one where it is usually absent, we think that such discussion in the context of a culturally diverse society may better orient towards consideration of cultural diversity as a strength rather than a weakness.

Multiculturalism, the widespread use of community languages and the vitality offered by ethnic communities that are not being forced into a melting pot are major advantages. Australian management education can build upon these to gain competitive advantage in the markets that our community languages and cultures represent. If multicultural management is to become a reality in the fastest possible time, then skills adequate to the management of diversity must become a central component of management education, development and training.

It is not only the need to integrate cultural and language elements with the curriculum of management that is important. One of the fastest growing areas in the United States Academy of Management is 'the management of diversity', and we need to develop the same skills here in Australia. A great deal of management is culturally implicit behaviour, as feminist evaluation of the masculinist bias of management has identified (see Barrett 1994). Yet, it is not only gender cultures that are at work in organizations. There are also cultures of ethnicity that require surfacing and managing in their assumptions. The development of the management of diversity is a necessity for the management curriculum, particularly for embryonic industry. This is because, as we have identified, there is a central role for cultural entrepreneurialism to play in developing innovation. Yet, if it is not only to be in the area of ethnic businesses that these innovations occur, then other organizations in Australia will have to develop capabilities that allow them to add the value that cultural diversity makes implicitly available, rather than to resist it in the name of a strong culture—one that would frequently be Anglo-Celtic, whatever else it might be.

While one innovation of the project may have been to consider culture in general as a source of innovation for embryonic industry in Australia, the report also addresses the importance of green values, or a culture that privileges the ecology, as an important component of the context in which embryonic industries will innovate. We wish to endorse the importance of green issues for the management curriculum, and do so in relation to the green credentials of the Olympic bid, noting it as an important opportunity to establish Australia's international green credentials.

Within the management curriculum, green issues ought not to be considered as a separate item, as a green ghetto of knowledge. On the contrary, green issues will impact on many areas of any management curriculum: upon manufacturing management, accounting, and human resources management. Virtually all the substantive disciplines that contribute to management will feel the impact of green values in some way. At present, discussion, curriculum, and textbook inspection suggest that the impact is slow and uneven.

ENVIRONMENTALISM

The green movement may be many things. To some elements in the community it is a source of mischief, an irritation, an unnecessary constraint on economic and community activities. For others it is almost a sacred cause. For embryonic industry it can be an important source of competitive advantage. The values of green culture can be a major push for the adoption of processes that add value, as industries adapt to their demands. An unspoilt environment and ecologically sound produce from it will have a competitive edge in polluted and dense overseas markets. Accordingly, Australian quality should emphasize this advantage and become synonymous with green values. Green management, like green accounting, should become a central part of management education, development and training for the next century.

One of the ways that green management practices will spread rapidly, similarly to many other forms of organization learning, is through organization networks. The whole area of organization networks and their importance as a mechanism for adding value to the organizations that compose them, should be a central thrust of management in the future.

RECRUITMENT TO NETWORKS

Firms that network internationally have access to intelligence on competitors, new technologies, product sources, new product applications and new manufacturing processes.

As McKinsey (1993: 34) noted, it is decreasingly production costs and increasingly factors such as 'product design, technology application, marketing and branding' that drive competitive success.

In scanning the business environment, an initiative, modelled in part on a scheme reported by McKinsey (1993: 56), may be useful. Linking technology and innovation in California is the

University of California Access Model, an information platform that includes information on technology available for licensing in universities and federally sponsored research programmes in progress on the product lines and capabilities of over 39,000 high-tech corporations.

For firms in embryonic industries, the greatest creativity in scanning the business environment often has to be exercised in ensuring that there is a steady supply of an appropriate amount of venture capital. The relation between venture capital and embryonic industry management is two-way. Venturers have to acquire a sound grasp of the management needs of embryonic organizations, striving to innovate in the marketplace. The finance specialism is not a stand-alone set of techniques. Management education needs techniques that allow both venturers and managers of firms in embryonic industries to communicate more effectively.

THE MANAGEMENT OF PROBLEMS AND PROJECTS IN AND THROUGH NETWORKS

Beyond simply putting scientists and technologists together in the same faculties as management academics, the further development of a new paradigm of management requires a shift toward a problem-oriented and project team curriculum that integrates management with other applications, such as science and technology, or design. The specific needs of the successful management of embryonic industries require explicit attention; firms involved in innovation in embryonic industries look nothing like the corporate bureaucracies that are still the model for much management education, with its stress on functional knowledge and location within a predominantly Anglo-American field of practice.

Conventional business knowledge organized in a traditional graduate management mode of delivery is of little relevance to the manager of a firm in an embryonic industry, trying to manage networks and alliances rather more than functional areas or disciplinary problems. Many entrepreneurs in new fields are creative artists, technological innovators, or scientists. Embryonic industry members of our Focus Groups stated that they did not have time to take on a post-first degree management qualification. Where they did, they found much of the curriculum irrelevant for their needs.

There is an additional issue. Management knowledge is required at an earlier stage of their organizational life-cycle: before, rather than after, having had to struggle to run their embryonic firm. Management education at the post-first degree level (in honours and above) needs to shift from the education of individuals into the training of project teams. It should move from a disciplinary to a problem focus. The teams should work on project that require using a range of skills from the team to co-operate with the teachers' design and delivery of the program and instruct students in co-operating in the teachers' resolution of the problems faced. New project-centred and interdisciplinary technology and science degrees focused on the management of projects may be part of the answer. Such an approach should include industry alliance and permit modular training and education by either ally. The University of Western Sydney is conducting, with ANSTOW and ICI, a technology management programme that has many of these features. Importantly, industry and the university developed the programme as a strategic opportunity. For reasons of economy of effort and targeting of critical consumers, within tertiary education, efforts may focus most effectively on honours and graduate students, rather than the general undergraduate student body.

DEEPENING AND EXTENDING NETWORK RESOURCES

More use of the skill bases of under-employed and retired strategic managers in contributing to teaching teams are possible. The Canadian Federal Business Development Bank, for instance, provides training and counselling services at local and regional levels that use such retirees. Technology changes and restructuring have produced in Australia a pool of retired, unemployed or under-employed strategic managers. Educators, firms in embryonic industries, and these managers, would gain.

CONCLUSION

All innovation requires management. By definition, embryonic industries, if not wholly exploratory, are at least stretching frontiers and opening up new niches for innovation. Today, the management of innovation for embryonic industry requires skills that are relatively new and emergent, premised on a paradigm of management that is different in many respects from older habits of command. Innovation is not an isolated attribute possessed by a solitary inventor but an interactive effect. It requires market intelligence to make a creative response to emergent opportunities; the management skills that are appropriate to their realization, and supporting conditions that encourage these opportunities, skills and conditions to flourish. This chapter has outlined how some of these issues are being conceptualized in best practice thinking in influential policy circles in Australia. Perhaps there is something to be learnt from this work elsewhere, beyond the shores of this 'wide, brown, sunburnt land'?

NOTE

1. The market is essential to innovation and it would seem odd to restrict access through a license to practise, something similar to, if not the equivalent of, medieval Tudor 'Chartering'.

REFERENCES

Barrett, M. 1994. The Feminisation of Management. In *Leadership and Management Needs of Embryonic Industries*. Ed. Clegg et al. University of Western Sydney: 184-90.

Chua, W-F. and S.R. Clegg. 1990. Professional Closure: The Case of British Nursing. *Theory and Society* 19: 135-72.

Clegg, S.R. 1990. *Modern Organisations: Organisation Studies in the Postmodern World*. London: Sage.

Clegg, S.R. and D. Dunkerley. 1980. *Organisation, Class and Control*. London: Routledge and Kegan Paul.

Cooper, R. and E. Kleinschmidt. 1986. An Investigation into the New Product Process: Steps, Deficiencies and Impact. *Journal of Product Innovation Management* 3: 71-85.

Dwyer, L. and R. Mellor. 1991. Organisational Environment, New Product Process Activities and Project Outcomes. *Journal of Product Innovation Management* 8: 39-48.

Early, P.C. and P. Stubblebine. 1989. Intercultural Assessment of Performance Feedback. *Group & Organisation Studies* 14: 161-81.

Eriksson, I.V. 1990. Educating End-Users to Make More Effective Use of Information Systems. In *End-User Training*. Ed. Gattiker and Larwood. Berlin: de Gruyter: 59-102.

Gattiker, U.E. and K. Willoughby. 1993. Technological Competence, Ethics, and the Global Village: Cross-National Comparisons for Organisation Research. In *Handbook of Organisational Behaviour*. Ed. Golembiewski. New York: Marcel Dekker: 457-85.

Gattiker, U.E. and T. Nelligan. 1988. Computerised Offices in Canada and the United States: Investigating Dispositional Similarities and Differences. *Journal of Organisational Behaviour* 9: 77-96.

Goldman, S.L. and R.N. Nagel. 1993. Management, Technology and Agility: The Emergence of a New Era in Manufacturing. *International Journal of Technology Management* 8(1): 18-38.

Goldstone, J.A. 1987. Cultural Orthodoxy, Risk, and Innovations: The Divergence of East and West in the Early Modern World. *Sociological Theory* 5: 119-35.

Gouldner, A. 1954. *Patterns of Industrial Bureaucracy*. New York: Free Press.

Higgins, W. and S.R. Clegg. 1988. Enterprise Calculation and Manufacturing Decline. *Organisation Studies* 9(1): 69-89.

Littek, W. and U. Heisig. 1991. Competence, Control and Work Redesign: *Die Angestellten* in the Federal Republic of Germany. *Work and Occupations* 18: 4-28.

Marceau, J. (ed.). 1992. *Reworking the World: Organisations, Technologies and Cultures in Comparative Perspective*. Berlin: de Gruyter.

Mathews, J. 1993. R&D Networks. The Triangular Strategy. *Journal of Industry Studies* 1(1): 65-74.

McKee, D. 1992. An Organisational Learning Approach to Product Innovations. *Journal of Product Innovation Management* 9: 232-45.

McKinsey & Co. Inc. 1993. *Emerging Exporters: Australia's High Value-Added Manufacturing Exporters*. Final Report of the Study by McKinsey & Co. for the Australian Manufacturing Council. Reported in Rennie, M. 1993. Global Competitiveness: Born Global. *McKinsey Quarterly* 4: 45-52.

Perry, L.T. and K.W. Sandholtz. 1988. A 'Liberating Form' for Radical Product Innovation. In *Studies in Technological Innovation and Human Resources. Vol. 1: Managing Technological Development*. Ed. Gattiker and Larwood. Berlin: de Gruyter: 9-31.

Peters, T. and R. Waterman. 1982. *In Search of Excellence: Lessons from America's Best Run Companies*. New York: Harper and Row.

Selznick, P. 1957. *Leadership in Administration*. New York: Harper and Row.

Smith, A. 1961. *An Inquiry into the Nature and Causes of Wealth of Nations*. Indianapolis, IN: Bobbs-Merrill.

Taylor, F.W. 1911. *Principles of Scientific Management*. New York: Harper.

Weber, M. 1947. *The Theory of Social and Economic Organization*. London: Edinburgh.

Willoughby, K.W. 1990. *Technology Choice*. Boulder, CO: Westview Press.

Willoughby, K.W. 1992. *Biotechnology in New York: A Global Industry in a Global Community*. Stony Brook, NY: Center for Biotechnology, State University of New York.

13

DEVELOPMENT IN THE UNDERDEVELOPED WORLD: A NEW CHALLENGE FOR BUSINESS ETHICS

John F. Quinn

ABSTRACT

Business ethics and environmental ethics are inextricably intertwined in the new philosophy of sustainable development. This new philosophy, based upon a partnership between business and government, promises to achieve a more ethical relationship in the way that business is conducted between the developed and the developing world. While using the suggestions of the recent emphasis on business ethics to curb the pursuit of non-sustainable development practices, it also incorporates the suggestions of those who have argued for an environmental philosophy of sustainable non-development.

Sustainable development as a new strategy to conduct business is more than a new way for the industrialized world to increase productivity while respecting nature; it is also a fundamentally different approach to the relationship between the developed and the developing world. I believe that the agreement between the United States, Canada and Mexico, the North American Free Trade Agreement, is such an effort. It is based not upon dependency but the modernization of Mexico, a developing country. This was legally guaranteed by the side agreements on labour and the environment, which will be enforced through the co-operation of a Joint Council of government and business representatives from all three countries.

With the formulation of the United Nations' *Agenda 21*, the world community has realized that sustainable development initiatives, necessary to maintain human survival on Earth, are closely linked to the situation of developing countries and their relationship to developed countries. *Agenda 21* also recognizes the responsibility of Western businesses to assist underdeveloped countries in achieving sufficient and sustainable levels of development. A major concern articulated in the proposal is to tackle the increasing poverty levels in the Third World which are closely related to environmental degradation.

Moreover, simple protectionist approaches to environmental preservation have received increasing criticism from developing countries. The notion of 'We want our turn and when we're rich, we can start worrying about the environment' (Newton 1993: 197), puts increasing pressures toward the North to assist the South in development and not in preservation. The reasons for the increasing disparity between the North and the South have their roots mainly in Western ways of controlling the world market. Low prices for raw materials, increasing debt, and protectionist trade agreements contribute to the desolate situation of underdeveloped nations and their poverty problems.

Moreover, traditional development initiatives, by neglecting cultural and historical differences and solely concentrating on top-down standard economic development, have actually helped to create more inequalities, unemployment and poverty. Traditional development is not in compliance with the requirements of sustainable world business practices as articulated in the literature of sustainable development.

New, alternative development initiatives, on the other hand, foster cultural identity and directly attack poverty by focusing on the satisfaction of basic human needs that are necessary to achieve levels of sustainable development. By using intermediate technologies and local know-how, it becomes possible to promote the use of renewable resources, create employment in impoverished areas, and satisfy local needs.

Moreover, the local and participative organization of development creates the possibility of joint efforts to tackle development problems, in addition to equal distribution of funds and decreasing poverty levels. Although this approach seems most difficult to implement, since it relies heavily on political willingness to give up central power, it aligns with *Agenda 21* and the requirement of international and local co-operation between governments and businesses. Thus the challenge for business ethicists is to encourage traditional businesses to compete with integrity in the industrialized world marketplace, but this cannot be done without sustainable development. Sustainable development cannot take place without a new business ethics in the relationship between developed and developing countries.

INTRODUCTION

In recent years, the industrialized Western world has begun to realize the tremendous negative effects that its resource-consuming lifestyle and growth-centred economic policies have had on the environment. The issue of preventing further depletion of natural resources and maintaining conditions that allow human survival requires business to consider the position of the so-called Third World nations to achieve a solution to these problems as part of an integrated global strategy. Western approaches to development and sustaining a viable environment have received increased criticism from developing countries. However, the position taken by the world community in the United Nations' *Agenda 21* is a first attempt to integrate the problems of underdeveloped nations into a global environmental and business ethic of sustainable development. This would ensure economic development and environmental sustainability as a major business value. How to change course for a business in the developed and developing world is the major challenge for corporations. This paper develops the intersection between environmental ethics and business ethics as a new business focus in the relationship between developed and developing countries.

Sustainable Non-Development

The preservationist view of nature by pointing out the intrinsic value of nature and promoting sustainable non-development as the only option to ensure survival has emerged as a direct response to business policies of non-sustainable development. In its various forms of anthropocentric, biocentric, and ecocentric environmentalism, this response has received increased public attention among Western societies. Wilderness preservation as an ultimate goal is demanded on an international basis, regardless of cultural differences or status in development within and between countries.

Because of this radical, universalistic view of environmental protection, these environmental movements have received considerable criticism from developing countries, who are arguing that it is not possible to apply that logic, which developed in a unique social and environmental history, to utterly different societies. According to Ramachandra Guha, a scholar at the Indian Institute for Science, the deep ecological movement does not understand the 'dynamics of environmental degradation' (Guha 1993: 555) that are different from society to society. He especially points out that 'wildlife preservation has been identified with environmentalism by the state and the conservation elite' (ibid.: 556).

Moreover, these more radical movements do not consider the 'environmental problems that impinge far more directly on the lives of the poor, e.g., fuel, fodder, water shortages, soil erosion, and air and water pollution' (ibid.: 556) that are relevant in developing countries. However, the survival orientation of increasing environmental consciousness which 'emphasizes the importance of interdependent ecosystems that permit sustainable development ...' (Quinn 1993: 1), allows adequate recognition of the developing world. This point is explicitly stated in *Agenda 21*, generated by the United Nations Conference on Environment and Development in 1992. What initially criticized the modernist business policies of non-sustainable development of nature on ethical grounds, has been criticized as unethical by those who view sustainable non-development policies as an unfair burden or an undeserved benefit to the new government and business alliances between developed and developing countries.

AGENDA 21

The United Nations has recognized specifically that the achievement of *sustainable development* and thus protection of the environment to realize human survival can only be addressed in a global effort demanding partnership between government and business and co-operation between the different nations. This implies for the industrialized world, which currently consumes the major percentage of natural resources and contributes to most of the world's pollution, to assist developing countries in achieving adequate levels of development, but yet curtail industrial deterioration of the environment.

> This global deterioration has been a result of unsustainable patterns of certain kinds of consumption and production processes found especially in the industrialized countries, which are responsible for the largest proportion of the world's current pollutants, including toxic and hazardous wastes (UNCED 1992: 5).

Therefore, *Agenda 21* has identified that the main responsibility in combating further global tragedy lies within the co-operation of the governments and businesses of developed and developing countries. *Agenda 21* has also realized the close interrelationship between poverty and environmental degradation in underdeveloped countries. 'The deterioration in the developing world is of particular concern in view of the persisting and debilitating poverty which severely affects more than one billion people' (ibid.: 7). Consequently, environmental protection must be already integrated in the development process. 'All underlying causes of development failures need to be corrected if the transition to sustainability is to be effectively implemented' (ibid.: 7).

Agenda 21 has identified seven priority actions that must be considered worldwide in order to sustain human survival. Besides the major factors referring to environmental issues (sustainable development, human settlements, efficient resource use, global and regional resources, management of chemicals and waste), it also considers poverty issues, demands a change in consumption patterns to achieve what is called a 'Just World', and addresses education as well as the position of minority groups.

In stressing the global nature of environmental problems and linking them directly to development issues, *Agenda 21* explicitly targets the development gap that exists between the industrialized and developing world. This disparity was one of the major points affecting negotiations at the UNCED Summit in Rio de Janeiro which tried to address global environmental problems. Thus *Agenda 21* has offered the business world the opportunity to accept the philosophy of sustainable development as a new ethical challenge for business to correct non-sustainable development. Policies and practices and, at the same time, the opportunity to mediate and adopt the harsh criticisms of those who support a philosophy of sustainable non-development.

The Rio Conference

In June 1992, the major industrialized countries and developing nations joined the UNCED Summit on environmental issues, simply called the Rio Conference. This addressed increasing global environmental problems. The goals of the conference were to set down international principles of behaviour toward the environment, agree on *Agenda 21* to determine the implementation of such principles, as well as to achieve treaties on global warming, deforestation and biodiversity 'to be signed by heads of states and ratified by world legislative bodies' (Newton 1993: 194). Despite the major resistance of the United States at the time, the Rio Conference achieved agreements on the major issues and stressed the importance of viewing ecological problems in an international context. (This could be achieved with the co-operation of business and government in developing and developed nations.)

However, Rio also was a place that again showed the discrepancies between the industrialized and developing world. The conflict centred on the rich North wanting to impose its ideas of sustainable living—'that is without polluting and without diminishing the resource base and, incidentally, accepting a lifestyle of modest consumption' (ibid.: 196)—on the poor South which accused the North of causing the major share of the ecological problems. 'In a long indictment, the South blamed the North for exploitation of resources, for the nuclear arms race, for CFC production, and for carbon dioxide emissions and asked the North to change its overconsumptive ways' (ibid.: 196).

The notion of sustainable development became the central

framework of the conference to address issues of distributive justice. In essence, the equal distribution of resources and 'improved lifestyles for the least fortunate' (ibid.: 197), was embraced with optimism. Rio clearly showed that ecological responsibility and environmental protection is directly linked to economic growth. 'You cannot freeze people into permanent poverty while the West continues to sustain unsustainable life-styles' (ibid.: 202). As a result, the delegates signed the Rio Declaration 'to establish the link between environmental clean-up and economic development in the Third World, asserting that the first cannot occur without the second and that industrialized nations will have to help the Third World to clean up' (ibid.: 206).

Industrialized nations, however, have pursued development initiatives in Third World countries over the years to achieve economic growth. The question is, how these tasks were pursued traditionally, whether they fit into the framework of sustainable development, and whether they were successful in reducing the main source of the disparity in these nations, increasing poverty. This has resulted from the policies of international business which have emphasized dependency theory, and not modernization or bargaining power theories. The use of cheap labour without the subsequent improvement of the host country and the lack of respect for indigenous peoples and Third World governments are examples of past business practice. Moreover, one must also realize the reasons for the increasing difference in wealth and development and its implications on environmental deterioration in the Third World.

NORTH–SOUTH DISPARITY

Agenda 21 explicitly addresses the increasing poverty and lack of sufficient development in Third World countries as major contributors to the ecological problems these countries are facing. It is essential to address the main causes of these disparities to promote adequate solutions to their environmental dilemmas. It is one thing, however, to agree how to implement sustainable development in all countries, it is another to implement it in a way that emphasizes fair equality of opportunity. International practice illustrates the present disparity between the North and the South.

Protectionism

International free trade is seen as the major driving force of economic development and growth for underdeveloped countries, 'if there is an open trading environment in which countries can benefit from the comparative advantages they possess' (Ramphal 1992: 176). However, this option was not provided for developing countries as they started to take part in the international economy. Currently, Third World nations face wide-ranging restrictions on exports to the industrialized world. Most of these export restrictions are targeted against low-cost commodities like shoes, textiles, televisions, and radios and were ironically negotiated under the GATT agreement on free trade: '... the biggest "orderly" marketing arrangement of them all, the Multifiber Arrangement which regulates (and restricts) exports of developing countries' textiles and clothing' (ibid.: 179). Underdeveloped countries, therefore, must rely heavily on the export of low-priced raw materials to increase their income. Depending mainly on the export of raw materials leads to increasingly non-sustainable exploitation of natural resources and damage to the environment. 'More than 90% of developing countries' exports of sugar and cocoa, for instance, is shipped without processing; so is 70% of their meat, fish and vegetable exports. As in the case of logs, the exporting countries find that to increase their earnings they must export more of the raw product; in most cases this means using more land and water and adding more fertilizer and pesticide, all at the expense of the environment' (ibid.: 180). These countries are, therefore, entering a cycle which on the one hand does not generate sufficient capital and on the other hand reduces the sources of capital.

Commodity Prices

One reason why developing countries rely on the exploitation of natural resources can be traced back to colonial times, when many of these countries were used as suppliers of raw materials for the industrialized world (see Goldemberg et al. 1988: 20). The basic disadvantage Third World countries have is that the provision of raw materials does not sufficiently account for the value added to the end product, and that industrialized nations control the transformation processes, the marketing, and the distribution of products. Additionally, commodity prices have been very volatile over time, and have shown a continuous downward trend for raw material prices. 'Prices are peculiarly prone to fluctuation, but there was a general tendency for prices of commodities exported by developing countries to move down—unlike those of manufactured products' (Ramphal 1992: 181). The South, therefore, finds it difficult to raise its earnings and to finance its industrialization and development. Underdeveloped nations, therefore, are not capable of fighting poverty, which is one of the main factors related to environmental degradation.

Traditional Global Energy Strategies

Another reason for the increasing disparities between rich and poor countries is conventional energy strategies. Currently, 25% of the world's population living in industrialized countries accounts for an estimated energy consumption 'which is six times that in the developing countries ... ' (Goldemberg et al. 1988: 22). The result of this disparity is not only affecting the ecological balance of the planet, but also makes it makes it more and more difficult for Third World nations to achieve necessary development levels. This projected increase in energy use by the industrialized countries has driven up energy prices, especially oil prices, thereby making the development of the oil-importing developing countries all the more difficult. These factors make it difficult to implement a philosophy of sustainable development in the developing world without the co-operation of the developed world.

The Debt Crisis

According to Ramphal, the debt problem faced by a large number of developing countries is another example of how global economic arrangements are influencing the progress of the Third World (see Ramphal 1992: 183). As a reaction to the oil price shocks in the

1970s and 1980s, with the consequence of declining interest rates, Western creditors saw the chance to invest surplus funds from OPEC countries as loans to the developing world. Additionally, oil-importing underdeveloped countries saw themselves in a situation that did not allow them to continue their development programmes. 'Under such circumstances, borrowing was very attractive, and the banks made massive loans available' (Goldemberg et al. 1988: 27). However, after the surplus of petrol dollars began to diminish and capital supplies began to shrink dramatically, interest rates started to rise significantly. The result is that most of the countries in the developing world are facing tremendous amounts of interest payments which drain their capital basis. 'In 1980, the total foreign debt of developing countries was US$640 billion. By 1990 it had more than doubled, to US$1.3 trillion, which amounted to 45% of their total annual income (GNP)' (Ramphal 1992: 183). This lack of sufficient capital makes it impossible for those countries to pursue development programmes and restrain the urge to generate additional funds by exploiting natural resources. The effects on the environment and prevailing poverty are the same that were described earlier. 'Like a consumer forced to hock the family heirlooms to pay credit card bills, developing countries are plundering forests, decimating fisheries, and depleting water supplies, regardless of the long-term consequences' (ibid.: 186).

DEVELOPMENT

After addressing the major causes for the North-South conflict and describing their impact on Third World development and the global environment, it becomes necessary to describe the traditional development approaches that industrialized countries have used to compensate for the devastating situation the developing world has confronted.

Traditional Development

Traditionally, modernization initiatives were based on social theories, implying that patterns exhibited in the development of industrialized

Western nations also determine the modernization of Third World nations, regardless of cultural differences. 'Theories were used to compare the development of Third World nations with those in Europe and North America' (Melkote 1991: 39). Western cultures were implicitly used as models and ideal examples of how modern societies develop. The result was that development initiatives attempted to destroy traditional societies to achieve the ideal Western model. 'The more thorough the disintegration of traditional elements, the more able a society would "develop" continuously' (Eisenstadt 1976, in Melkote 1991: 48). Moreover, according to Max Weber, values and religion were considered pure traditionalism and incompatible with development toward modernity.

> In his studies of India, China and Asia, where he did not see anything resembling the development of European industrial capitalism, Weber reasoned that the religions of those countries lack the counterparts of a Protestant Ethic that would provide the characterological foundation for the economic motivation required. (Singer 1972, in Melkote 1991: 50).

Following these assumptions for sociological development, the models developed for the economic 'path to modernization' (Melkote 1991: 53) of Western countries. These were applied without question to underdeveloped nations.

As a result, economic growth measured by the GNP rates became the central factor to determine the success of development initiatives. Moreover, the development patterns of the industrial revolution in Europe and North America were 'considered the main route to impressive economic growth' (Melkote 1991: 57). Thus, funds were invested primarily in industrialization projects which included capital intensive technologies, like hydroelectric projects, or mining industries.

Applying Western stereotypes to development in the Third World also implied an emphasis on the importance of technological know-how for economic development. A side effect of this approach was that 'more often than not, the capital and machine intensive techniques substituted labour that was abundantly available in the Third World nations' (Melkote 1991: 58). Srinivas Melkote describes another assumption underlying what he calls the dominant paradigm of development: 'In the dominant paradigm, underdevelopment was usually attributed to internal constraints within developing countries rather than external forces acting on these nations' (Melkote 1991: 58). Therefore, development initiatives were aimed at altering these internal cultural factors to achieve optimal development in terms of economic growth. The underlying economic theories additionally complied with the private ownership of production factors and the principle of *laissez-faire* (Melkote 1991: 61) in the marketplace. The International Development Association established by the United Nations in 1960 resembles a good example of a development organization that determines the amount of aid by considering economic factors, such as creditworthiness, and economic performance (Weaver 1965: 119-55).

Another practice relevant to traditional development projects is the implicit assumption that financial means would be distributed to the benefit of the whole population in developing countries. 'The belief was that at least some of the increases in income associated with rapid growth would "trickle down" to the poor and eliminate their abject poverty' (Goldemberg et al. 1988: 30). The extensive focus on growth as a sole source of development led to the fact that the distribution of benefits was neglected. These benefits were assumed to occur automatically with increasing prosperity. 'This viewpoint may seem cold-blooded, but it was in fact motivated by the conviction that the poor would be better served in the long run if the productive capacity of the economy were rapidly built up first' (Goldemberg et al. 1988: 30).

The post-Second World War history of developing countries actually showed the success of development initiatives based on the described assumptions. The major indicator for economic growth, the GNP actually showed the improvements in a quantitatively measurable way.

> A vast number of new industries were established. At the same time, many of these countries sought to modernize their agriculture, particularly through the so-called 'Green Revolution' based on high-yielding varieties and inputs of fertilizer, pesticides, water, etc. The Gross Domestic Product ... has shown impressive increases in these

countries since the end of World War II (Goldemberg et al. 1988: 30).

How effective, however, were these traditional initiatives in terms of reducing poverty and facilitating a sustainable use of natural resources? An evaluation of development based on the increase of GNP does not provide the qualitative means to determine whether development took place to the advantage of the affected nation. The general conclusion of traditional development policies for Third World countries supports a philosophy of non-sustainable development.

Critique of the Traditional Development Approach

The old paradigm's basic negligence of history and cultural identity for developing nations has received heavy criticism from many scholars.

> Underdevelopment in Third World countries does not signify an earlier stage of European development history but instead is in large part the historical product of the past and continuing economic and other relations between the satellite underdeveloped and the now developed metropolitan countries (Melkote 1991: 101).

This development relation is basically rooted in the history of colonization of the now Third World nations. Scholars state that European countries were actually the underlying reason for the current situation. 'The underdevelopment of countries in Asia, Africa and Latin America, therefore, was not by choice' (Melkote 1991: 107). Western European development policies have not worked. Moreover, they have destroyed traditions in these countries to achieve certain degrees of modernization. This has led, however, to 'disorganization, delinquency and chaos rather than to a viable modern order' (Eisenstadt 1976, in Melkote 1991: 113). The importance of traditional roots in the process of development, therefore, has to be recognized when evaluating development projects. This sustainable development is linked to respect for the cultures of indigenous peoples.

Additionally, the assumption that underdevelopment has its roots mainly within the traditions of the developing countries can no longer be maintained without criticism. 'Thus, the sociology of development theories by relating the backwardness of the Third World nations and their peoples to internal constraints such as native cultures, religions, individual characteristics or psyche, was adding insult to grave injury' (Melkote 1991: 110).

Empirical studies have shown that the economic model used to evaluate development based on the quantitative measure of GNP as an indicator of growth had negative impacts on other more qualitative indicators of development, such as inequality, poverty, and unemployment. 'The experience of the last thirty years clearly shows that growth does not necessarily equal development. Far more pertinent ... is the structure and content of growth, and the distribution of its benefits' (Goldemberg et al. 1988: 30). Despite substantial growth of GNP, unemployment in developing countries has increased over time, resulting in even more significant levels of poverty. 'Available data indicate that the rate of increase of unemployment was concomitant with high rates of growth' (Weaver and Jameson 1978, in Melkote 1991: 126). Moreover, the development initiatives based on the dominant paradigm have led to tremendous income inequalities in Third World countries. 'In these countries, the share of national income was concentrated in the hands of a very small minority. For example, in Brazil, the top 5% cornered as much as 46% of the national income' (Melkote 1991: 127). These empirical studies clearly show that the assumption of automatic distribution, the 'trickling down' of benefits did not take place.

Following the logic of increased unemployment, partly also due to capital intensive technologies, and unequal income distribution, it becomes clear that poverty levels in developing countries also increased significantly. 'Research studies found that as economic expansion proceeded the income of the bottom 40% of people in developing countries fell not only relatively ... but in absolute terms as well' (ibid.: 129).

With increasing poverty ratios and a widening gap between the rich and the poor, negative impacts on natural resources and the environment step into the sequence of events. The lack of necessary materials and technology to maintain natural resources becomes a major source of deprivation. 'The need for food among ever-growing numbers of poor is, for example, by far the main cause of deforestation in the tropics' (Ramphal 1992: 128). 'The British ecologist Norman Myers estimated that clearance by landless peasants accounts for three-fifths of rain forest loss' (ibid.: 130). Moreover, traditional development projects themselves are not considered to have negative ecological impacts. Transnational companies have repeatedly exploited the need for development in the Third World to bypass strict environmental legislation in their own country; old and obsolete technologies have been transplanted to maximize short-term profits at the expense of the environment. 'For example, they have promoted technology that is ill-suited to the socioeconomic and environmental conditions in developing countries, sold obsolete technology and overcharged for technology' (Goldemberg et al. 1988: 21). Those practices additionally harm the development process and increase environmental problems. Consequently, the history of traditional development of Third World countries shows that the approach based on strict quantitative economic evaluation does not comply with the reduction of income inequalities, unemployment and resulting poverty levels. The discrepancy lies within the underlying assumptions of Western development patterns.

ALTERNATIVES

The previous section showed that development cannot be based simply on economic factors, as was traditionally the case. This modernist assumption, based upon the belief that nature is inexhaustible, that humans are special and apart from nature, and that nature has *only* instrumental value, has led business to non-sustainable development. The response of the developed world to the practices of traditional business has been radical. Many environmentalists have argued a philosophy of sustainable non-development as the only option that will lead to the survival of the planet. Without the recognition that all living things have intrinsic value, they will be subject to the whims of non-sustainable developmentalists. The philosophy of sustainable development with its emphasis on the balance of development and sustainability offers an option for remedying the past practices of the industrialized countries and yet it offers hope and the promise of maintaining the integrity of the earth while providing respect for present and future generations of peoples in the developing world. This part of the paper will provide an investigation of this alternative in the relationship between the industrialized nations and the developing world. These alternatives take seriously the qualitative factors mentioned above into consideration. The following section is aimed at describing some of the major alternative approaches.

Development for Basic Human Needs

The Basic Needs Approach aims directly at the poverty issue characteristic of developing countries. Basic needs are defined as 'those necessities that are absolutely essential to maintain a decent quality of life' (Melkote 1991: 197). The underlying logic of this alternative is the realization that the main reason for poverty is the insufficient satisfaction of the basic needs of the bulk of the population. Goldemberg concludes, therefore, that 'the satisfaction [of these needs] must be made a direct and immediate economic objective in development strategy' (Goldemberg et al. 1988: 31). In this context, employment is also considered one of the basic needs that must be available to human beings (ibid.: 31). In order to affect the existing inequalities of income distribution effectively, this approach demands a shift in production priority toward fundamental products. Summarizing the main objectives of this alternative leads to seven requirements, which were reviewed by Paul Streeten in 1979:

1. provide adequate food and clean drinking water;
2. provide decent shelter;
3. provide education;
4. provide security of livelihood;
5. provide adequate transport;
6. help people participate in decision-making; and
7. uphold a person's dignity and self-respect (Melkote 1991: 198).

It can be concluded that, by directly tackling poverty in developing nations, the Basic Needs approach also implicitly does consider the ecological problems associated with the poverty issue as it is recognized in *Agenda 21*. 'The deterioration in the developing world is of particular concern in view of the persisting debilitating poverty which severely affects more than one billion people' (UNCED 1992: 7). This option requires the partnership of business and government for its success.

Intermediate Technology

One way to address the socio-economic conditions gap in underdeveloped countries focuses on the problems of unemployment. Traditional development utilized mainly capital-intensive technologies that disregard the ample labour available in the Third World. As a reaction to this approach and to achieve higher levels of employment in the heavily occupied rural areas, developers call for the use of intermediate technologies to utilize local know-how, resources, and techniques. This alternative, however must not lead to the promotion of labour-intensive, low-productivity employment that is not capable of producing sufficient income levels. 'The roots of poverty spring not only from unemployment and underdevelopment but also from the low-productivity of employment' (Goldemberg et al. 1988: 31).

Moreover, according to the British economist Schumacher, the appropriate technology approach demands to:
1. create employment in rural areas where most of the people live;
2. use local skills, material, and financial resources, thus leading to lesser dependence on external sources;
3. maximize use of renewable resources;
4. be compatible with local cultures and practices; and
5. satisfy local needs and wishes (Dunn, in Melkote 1991: 197).

This approach respects indigenous people and tries to incorporate their traditional know-how into development. The degree to which these practices respect and sustain the environment is as great as the degree to which they can be incorporated into business practices. Biodiversity and cultural diversity are inextricably intertwined. Opposing the traditional way to development, this alternative explicitly considers local factors such as culture and tradition. Moreover, by promoting the use of renewable resources, development in this context fosters *Agenda 21*'s request for development which sustains natural resources and the environment.

Local Organization of Development and Participation

One reason given to explain why the rural population of developing countries suffers increasing poverty is the lack of power to influence development efforts. A solution to these problems can be achieved by the 'formation at the grassroots of strong organizations capable of articulating and protecting the interests of the peasants and others residing on the periphery' (Melkote 1991: 200). Organizing development on a local basis, therefore, requires development from the bottom-up instead of simply dumping development funds and assuming that the distribution and coordination would take place automatically. The achievements that can be gained through the establishment of small-scale self-help development projects have been discussed and summarized by Barkan et al. in 1979 (see Melkote 1991: 201):

1. They produced a net transfer of resources from the centre to the rural areas.
2. They appeared to foster a more equitable distribution of wealth within local communities.
3. They marshalled local initiative and entrepreneurial skills in ways the state could not do by itself.
4. Most importantly, they provided an organizational infrastructure at the grassroots without which development of the rural poor was unlikely to proceed.

I should point out that this alternative also bears the danger of producing greater inequalities, especially when control mechanisms are neglected and development is left without proper supervision. The success of local development initiatives is closely linked to the commitment from the government of the country itself to work with business. As Uphoff and Esman (1974, in Melkote 1991: 202) caution, 'the governments must be committed to the idea of equitable rural development through local organizations which would entail significant transfer of resources from the centre to the periphery.' Moreover, participation in development must not be associated with a simple means to assist initiatives, but treated as an end in itself. 'Participation as a process of empowering the people, though politically quite risky to higher authorities, is the ideal consequence of participation. Here, the individuals are active in the development programmes and process' (Melkote 1991: 237). This shift from the use of hierarchical power to manage workers to a more vertical, participatory empowerment of workers has been working successfully in developed countries, and it promises to be even more successful in underdeveloped countries. If participation is used under these assumptions, an international approach to the problems of development and the closely linked ecological problems become more manageable.

> The achievement of sustainable development and enhancement of the environment are priority issues that affect economic growth and the well-being of peoples throughout the world ... This would involve channelling new and additional financial resources and providing favorable access to science and technology to all developing countries to ensure their full participation ... (UNCED 1992: 5).

The participative approach to development, however, does rely heavily on the willingness of political organizations and business in developing as well as developed countries to promote these values. Some of the limitations refer to the political climate in the host society, the authoritarian structure that prevents democratic decision making, or unequal access to factors of production (see Alamgir, 1988, in Melkote 1991: 244). Ann Seidman and Frederick Anang outline, in their book *21st Century Africa*, an approach to participatory problem solving. They conclude that the involvement of community representative, especially business, together with politicians and researchers can

> help to find the information necessary to resolve the core debates raised by the reviews of each of the key problem areas ... by involving those affected in the research process, help them to acquire the skills and confidence essential to self-reliant sustainable development (Seidman and Anang 1992: 19).

Following a participative method to promote development in

Third World countries also ultimately addresses the issues of women positions in the different societies. Since, development concerning the discussion of women's position in the process includes 'a non-manipulative process at all stages, open dialogue at all levels, and a willingness to analyse in-depth both success and failures of past approaches to enable poor women to move out of poverty into sustainable development' (Wignaraja 1990: 211). The participative approach seems the most appropriate to address these issues of development and sustainability of the environment.

CONCLUSION

Sustainable development as a new strategy to conduct business is more than a new way for the industrialized world to increase productivity while respecting nature, it is also a fundamentally different approach to the relationship between the developed and the developing world. I believe that the agreement between the United States, Canada and Mexico, the North American Free Trade Agreement, is such an effort. It is based not upon dependency but the modernization of Mexico, a developing country. This was legally guaranteed by the side agreements on labour and the environment, which will be enforced through the co-operation of a Joint Council of government and business representatives from all three countries.

With the formulation of the United Nations' *Agenda 21*, the world community has realized that sustainable development initiatives, necessary to maintain human survival on Earth, are closely linked to the situation of developing countries and their relationship to developed countries. *Agenda 21* also recognizes the responsibility of Western businesses to assist underdeveloped countries in achieving sufficient and sustainable levels of development. A major concern articulated in the proposal is to tackle the increasing poverty levels in the Third World which are closely related to environmental degradation.

Moreover, simple protectionist approaches to environmental preservation have received increasing criticism from developing countries. The notion of 'We want our turn and when we're rich, we can start worrying about the environment' (Newton 1993: 197) puts increasing pressures toward the North to assist the South in development and not in preservation. The reasons for the increasing disparity between the North and the South have their roots mainly in Western ways of controlling the world market. Low prices for raw materials, increasing debt, and protectionist trade agreements contribute to the desolate situation of underdeveloped nations and their poverty problems.

Moreover, traditional development initiatives, by neglecting cultural and historical differences and solely concentrating on top-down standard economic development, have actually helped to create more inequalities, unemployment and poverty. Traditional development is not in compliance with the requirements of sustainable world business practices as articulated in the literature of sustainable development.

New, alternative development initiatives, on the other hand, foster cultural identity and directly attack poverty by focusing on the satisfaction of basic human needs that are necessary to achieve levels of sustainable development. By using intermediate technologies and local know-how, it becomes possible to promote the use of renewable resources, create employment in impoverished areas, and satisfy local needs.

Moreover, the local and participative organization of development creates the possibility of joint efforts to tackle development problems in addition to equal distribution of funds and decreasing poverty levels. Although this approach seems most difficult to implement, since it relies heavily on political willingness to give up central power, it aligns with *Agenda 21* and the requirement of international and local co-operation between governments and businesses.

REFERENCES

Goldemberg, J., et al. 1988. *Energy for a Sustainable World.* New Delhi: John Wiley.

Guha, R. 1993. Radical Environmentalism and Wilderness Preservation: A Third World Critique. In *Environmental Ethics, Divergence and Convergence,* 552-61. Ed. Armstrong and Botzler. New York: McGraw Hill.

Melkote, S.R. 1991. *Communication for Development in the Third World: Theory and Practice.* New Delhi: Sage.

Newton, L.H. 1993. *Watersheds, Classic Cases in Environmental Ethics.* Belmont, CA: Wadsworth.

Quinn, F.J. 1993. *Agenda 21: Biodiversity and Responsible Land Use, Planning and Management: Economic, Political, Legal, Scientific and Ethical Implications of Modernist, Universalist, and Post-Modernist Environmental Philosophies.* Paper presented at United Nations Conference on Earth Ethics (October).

Ramphal, S. 1992. *Our Country The Planet: Forging a Partnership for Survival.* Washington, D.C.: Island Press.

Seidman, A. and F. Anang (eds.). 1992. *21st Century Africa: Towards a New Vision of Self-Sustainable Development.* Trenton, NJ: Africa World Press.

United Nations Conference on Environment and Development (UNCED). 1992. *The Global Partnership For Environment and Development: A Guide to Agenda 21.* New York: UN.

Weaver, J.H. 1965. *The International Development Association: A New Approach to Foreign Aid.* New York: Praeger.

Wignaraja, P. 1990. *Women, Poverty and Resources.* New Delhi: Sage. Copyright UNICEF 1990.

CONCLUSION: WHOSE BUSINESS VALUES?

Sally Stewart and William White

The study of business values is a relatively new academic discipline; the first real debate on business values is usually considered to have taken place as late as 1904 with the Barbara Weinstock series of lectures, on the 'Morals of Trade', closely followed in 1908 by the Page Lectures at the Sheffield Scientific School, which purported to identify the main areas of the development of business which were in need of some form of ethical input. Commercial transactions and a concern for acceptable behaviour when undertaking them, however, undoubtedly characterized the earliest human societies. The penalties demanded for cheating in business were, moreover, almost certainly greater in early societies than they are now. For instance, Plato, writing in about 500 B.C., proposes that in an ideal society:

> Anyone discovered selling such adulterated merchandise, apart from being deprived of it, must be whipped (one lash for every drachma of the asking price of the object he was selling), after a herald has announced in the marketplace the reason why the culprit is going to be flogged (Plato 1970: 456).

Obeying the law is not sufficient for a business person to be regarded as someone acting ethically. A study of the regulations governing business in a particular place or period does, on the other hand, throw some light on what behaviour society expected from those engaged in commerce and also on what malpractices were common.

This chapter is not, however, centrally concerned with the rules, but rather the sources of the value systems which have underpinned the societies in which business people have operated. In any attempt to discover the origins of how people should behave, religious beliefs are an obvious starting point, since they both reflect and mould ethical practices, and the following section deals first with the three major 'religions of the book', as Muhammad described them, and then turns to the Eastern religions. The chapter then attempts to draw some conclusions as to how business values in Asia might progress.

RELIGION AND BUSINESS

While Judaism and Christianity have both traditionally condemned usury, only Islam maintains that prohibition today. Fair trading is, however, encouraged, and Muhammad himself, who ran a trading enterprise together with his wife, said 'Wealth, properly employed, is a blessing; and a man may lawfully endeavour to increase it by honest means.' (Muhammad 1954: 110). The Koran stipulates,

> O ye who believe!
> Eat not up your property
> Among yourselves in vanities;
> But let there be amongst you
> Traffic and Trade
> By mutual good-will (Koran, Sura 4, 29)

Honesty and fair treatment in business transactions were enjoined by Muhammad who preached:

> Woe to those
> That deal in fraud,
> Those who, when they
> Have to receive by measure
> From men, exact full measure
> But when they have
> To give by measure
> Or weight to men,
> Give less than due (Koran, Sura 83, 1–3)

It is to be hoped that more Muslim scholars will enter the debate about ethics in business and contribute their insights to the search for codes of behaviour founded on high ethical standards.

The Jewish Talmud laid out rules regarding profits, prices and quality; one of its minor tracts dictates that riches are one of the seven things which 'in large quantity are harmful but in small quantity are beneficial.' (Talmud: 153, see also Friedman 1980). Regarding the principles of Judaism, the German sociologist Max

Weber adds,

> To escape the temptations of wealth is not easy, but is for this reason all the more meritorious. 'Hail to the man of wealth who has been found to be blameless' (Weber 1922: 247).

These matters were regulated according to ethical principles by Jewish magistrates, and the same principles travelled with those Jews who came to dominate the financial world of Europe in the Middle Ages.

The Christian Church at that time exercised a strict prohibition on usury, restricting money-lending to non-Christians; it regarded business as a morally acceptable activity as long as the sins of avarice, fraud and luxury were avoided. Its enormous power and reliance on ancient, immutable codes tended, however, to prevent the debate from moving further than the usury issue, if there was any debate at all. Figures such as St Antonino, an expert on medieval economic life, were universally critical of traders, their objections extending even to ideas taken for granted in the present day, such as making a profit, which St Thomas Aquinas (1225-74) describes as 'justly deserving of blame, because, considered in itself, it satisfies the greed for gain, which knows no limit and tends to infinity' (Aquinas 1925: 327). This condemnation is, nevertheless, qualified; he does admit that 'gain which is the end of trading ... does not, in itself, connote anything sinful or contrary to virtue' (ibid.). In general, however, the attitudes of the medieval Church tended towards the first half of Aquinas' view, in spite of the parable in which a servant who trades with his master's money and doubles it is rewarded, but the man who buries his master's money in the ground to safeguard it is castigated by Christ as a 'wicked and slothful servant' (Matt. 25: 14-30). The earlier account in the same gospel of how

> Jesus entered the temple of God and drove out all who sold and bought in the temple, and he overturned the tables of the money-changers and the seats of those who sold pigeons. He said to them, 'It is written, "My house shall be called a house of prayer"; but you make it a den of robbers' (Matt. 21: 12-13).

was, however, used to justify the distancing of the Church, which had a virtual monopoly of education, from commerce.[1]

The Protestant Reformation failed to change the Church's hard-line attitude in this sphere: 'Luther resisted ... stoutly the concessions that were being made in response to the demands of the new commerce spreading across Europe' (Childs and Cater 1954: 23). In the late eighteenth century, however, the power of religious authorities started to wane, and the accepted position began to be challenged, most notably in Jeremy Bentham's *Defence of Usury* (1787). Weber famously argued, on the other hand, in 1904 that Protestantism laid the foundations for modern capitalism:

> ... when asceticism was carried out of monastic cells into everyday life, and began to dominate worldly morality, it did its part in building the tremendous cosmos of the modern economic order (Weber 1904: 181).

A significant example of the influence of religious values in business is the impact of Quakerism on the management ethics of Britain from the seventeenth century onwards: 'In an attempt to reconcile conscience and practice, these employers formulated new approaches to a wide range of industrial problems, and ... exerted considerable influence on the overall development of British managerial thought' (Child 1964: 293). Firms such as Cadbury and Rowntree (now, respectively, Cadbury-Schweppes and Nestlé-Rowntree) helped to pioneer the idea of business with a social conscience, basing their practices on certain principles of their religion, summarized as follows:

> (i) a dislike of the exploitation and profit of one man at the expense of another, (ii) a traditionally puritan view of the 'stewardship of talents', stressing the value of hard work, lack of waste, the careful organization of resources, and a personal renunciation, all for the service of others, (iii) a tradition of egalitarianism and democratic relationships, and (iv) an abhorrence of conflict between men (ibid.: 294).

EASTERN RELIGIONS

It is difficult to generalize about the teachings of Hinduism since there is no one accepted text as there is for the people of the books. It would appear, however, that most teachers place more emphasis on spiritual rather than practical matters. Hinduism defines the second lowest of four caste groups as the *vaisyas* (farmers and traders) and holds that farming and trading are their natural duties, but makes no moral comment on either of these activities. The Parsees, on the other hand, related business to Zoroastrianism's principles of good thoughts, good words and good deeds, gaining its followers an elevated position when they came to India from their native Persia, especially after the British takeover of the country, when they rose to high positions in colonial administration and business (Kulke 1974).

The principles of Buddhism meant that the 'morality of inclusion' described in Georges Enderle's chapter in this volume 'An Outsider's View of the East Asian Miracle' has always been the case in its societies. The *Mahayana* ('greater vehicle') school of Buddhism, which encourages the pursuit of collective advance as opposed to individual nirvana, embodies this principle implicitly almost from the first word: 'all entities are seen to be ... lacking a truly separate individuality or "self"' (Blofeld 1971: 6). Mahayana Buddhism is the predominant strain of Buddhism among the Overseas Chinese, who have been the driving force behind the economic development of Southeast Asia (Stewart et al. 1992: 34–5); Blofeld (1971: 4) says, of Malaysia and Singapore, 'There, more than anywhere else, means have been found of integrating Buddhism with modern life.' Principles of business values are thus deeply rooted in Buddhism:

> The Buddha gave five reasons why a moral person should desire to be possessed of means. Firstly, by his work, diligence and clear-sightedness he could make happy himself, his parents, wife and children, servants and workpeople ... At the same time, whether his wealth increases or whether it does not, he should not be disturbed in his mind if he knows that his reasons for trying to amass it were good. In the meantime the householder successfully amassing wealth by lawful and honourable means, by his own energy and effort, enjoys ... well-being ... and blamelessness ... There are, however, certain trades and pursuits which the householder should not follow since these are not in accord with the Precepts ...: trade in weapons, trade in human beings, in flesh, intoxicants, and trade in poison (Saddhatissa 1970: 129-30).

Even *Theravada* ('way of the elders') Buddhism, the strain of the more conservative *Hinayana* ('inferior vehicle') Buddhism predominant in Thailand and elsewhere, with its emphasis on each individual striving towards attaining nirvana for themselves, has something to offer; its emphasis on 'merit-making' institutionalizes making the best possible use of wealth from the point of view of society as well as of the self:

> Implicit in the ethic of individual self-discipline is a social, economic and political ethic. The 'Middle Way' of the Buddha is neither total renunciation of the world nor simple materialism, but the way of the welfare of all beings through reciprocal action ... The merit of the individual ... is dependent on compassionate giving (Lester 1973: 156).

The texts of the Daoist religion provide a plethora of information on business. In a lengthy description of evil-doers, Laozi identifies the following practices:

— Disregarders of law they are, and bribe-takers (Lao Tze [Laozi] 1950: 415–8).

— They impoverish others for their own gain. For worthless things they exchange what is valuable. For private ends they neglect public duties (ibid.: 507–18).

— They shorten the foot, they narrow the measure, they lighten the scales, they reduce the peck. They adulterate the genuine, and they seek profit in illegitimate business (ibid.: 879–94).

In the present day, few businessmen are seen as being deeply religious; Silvio Berlusconi often claimed to be a fervent, practising Catholic, but the lavish tomb which has been built for him and his empire's inner circle contains no religious insignia. If any deontology is claimed to be the guiding principle of a businessmen claiming to be 'ethical', it is usually 'green' values; witness the ethical stance of The Body Shop, based on a well-documented image of environmental responsibility both chemically and socially.

It may be argued that religion underpins values, but it does not seem that the classical philosophers of both East and West appealed to a higher power when proposing their codes of right behaviour; they were more concerned with rules for society than with theology.

PHILOSOPHERS AND BUSINESS ETHICS

Common to both of the world's first two great philosophers, as pointed out in the Foreword, was the idea that people should base all their actions on a spirit of mutuality, or an idea of the common good: Confucius' term was *ren* and Aristotle expressed exactly the same idea with his notion of *philia*. Comments from early writings are discussed below.

Early Philosophy—Ancient Greece

Athens' most famous historian, Xenophon, seemed supportive of the exclusion of all hawkers from the *agora*:

> The Persian laws, however, begin at the beginning and take care that from the first their citizens shall not be of such a character as ever to desire anything improper or immoral; and the measures they take are as follows. They have their so-called 'Free Square' ... The hucksters with their wares, their cries and their vulgarities are excluded from this and relegated to another part of the city, in order that their tumult may not intrude upon the orderly life of the cultured (Xenophon 1914: 11–3).

He did, on the other hand, recognize the necessity and usefulness of traders to the economy of Athens and in his pamphlet *The Ways and Means* proposed removal of restrictions against, and preferential treatment of, the *metics* (resident traders) (Finley 1970: 24).

Plato, renowned as the first person to suggest a form of 'communism', envisaged in the ideal situation described in *The Republic*, a society free from traders: 'just as men escape from prison to take sanctuary in temples, so these gentlemen joyously bound away from the mechanical arts to philosophy' (Plato 1935: 49). He takes a realistic and balanced attitude in *The Laws*, however, which describes how to create a good society from imperfect people, through use of rules:

> The natural function in the state of retail trading in general is not to do harm, but quite the opposite. ... Why has it come to be so abused? Let's see if we can discover the reason, so that we can use our legislation to reform at any rate some branches of commerce, even if not the whole institution (Plato 1970: 457).

Aristotle appears to take a sceptical line on even the possibility of business values; he numbers among the many who, over the millennia, have condemned loans at interest from an ethical standpoint:

> the most hated sort [of wealth-getting], and with the greatest reason, is usury, which makes a gain out of money itself, and not from the natural object of it. For money was intended to be used in exchange, but not to increase at interest (Aristotle 1941: 1141).

M.I. Finley demonstrates that Aristotle also tended towards the *caveat emptor* maxim:

> Under what conditions did Aristotle envisage an injustice, an unjust gain, in a voluntary transaction, especially in a sale? The answer is, I think, beyond dispute that he had in mind fraud or breach of contract, but not an 'unjust' price (Finley 1970: 6).

However, Aristotle rejects the notion that trade corrupts morals through the influence of foreigners (Aristotle 1914: 1285). He also suggests that exchange relations within the framework of the community are natural to society and advocates the principle of *philia* (friendship/benevolence/mutuality), which, as pointed out in the Foreword, is almost exactly similar to the Confucian notion of *ren*, as a guiding principle for this type of trade (Finley 1970: 8). It may thus be claimed that, far from spreading scepticism, Aristotle was sowing the seeds of business values.

Early Philosophy—China[2]

An understanding of Confucianism is important for anyone studying present-day business among PRC citizens and overseas Chinese (Stewart 1995). Although Confucius (551-479 B.C.) did say that: 'A gentleman is conscious only of justice, a petty man only of self-interest' (Confucius 1991: 48-9), he also praised his pupil Duanmu Ci thus: 'Duanmu Ci is discontented with his lot, he goes to do business and he often hits the mark in his calculations.' (ibid.: 163). The Confucian *rujia* school emphasized many concepts fundamental to business ethics, such as *ren* (benevolence), *yi* (righteousness), *li* (rules/rites), *cheng* (sincerity), *xin* (trustworthiness) and *zhong* (loyalty, honesty). The Chinese historian Sima Qian

(205-154 B.C.) analysed figures from sages and honest traders to gamblers and bribe-taking officials and concluded that 20% was a reasonable profit but wartime usury of 200% was not (Hu 1988: 250). Later on, the reformist prime minister Wang Anshi (1021-86) was immensely concerned about corruption, as shown by his poem 'The Monopolists':

> Holes from which lucre flows appear by hundreds,
> Mean men open and shut them on their own:
> The state's officials with those mean men vie!
> Are not the people to be pitied then? (Williamson 1937: 122)

It was against the so-called 'Monopolists' in particular that Wang Anshi implemented his Trade and Barter Measure; their practices consisted of loan-sharking, and of abusing their powerful market position to buy farmers' surplus stocks cheaply, storing them until there was a shortage of the same, and then re-selling them at vastly inflated prices. His measure was intended, however, not only to clamp down on these unfair practices but also to stimulate commerce, to which on its own Wang had no objection:

> Wang An-Shih's [Wang Anshi] main idea in promoting it [the Trade and Barter Measure] was ... that the poor should be relieved of the exorbitant demands of the wealthy monopolists; and *that trade should be stimulated* by relieving the farmer and artisan of surplus stocks (Williamson 1937: 250) (italics added).

It must be noted that these three leaders in Chinese thought only exemplify major influences in Chinese thinking; they do not produce any consensus, for as David Ralston *et alia* rightly point out,

> ... it appears that regional differences in China are most likely influenced by historic precedence, geographic location, economic development, educational level, and technological sophistication. ... To understand Chinese values, we need to go beyond Confucianism and to explore these influences in order to pinpoint subcultural differences within the diverse Chinese culture (Ralston et al. 1994: 6).

Laozi provides one more piece of wisdom: 'They [evil-doers] take up the new and forget the old' (Lao Tze [Laozi] 1950: 793-6). As people move into the relatively new sphere of business, it is important that they do not forget the principles applicable to it which are contained in most of the world's old religions and philosophies. One example of a successful business value system that was firmly rooted in old beliefs but adapted to changing circumstances was that of the 'British Gentleman'.

BRITISH BUSINESS VALUES IN THE NINETEENTH CENTURY

The values of some major professions in the world today owe much to the nineteenth century concept of the gentleman. Professional people, such as lawyers and accountants, are still expected to keep their word, to be honest and generally behave according to an unwritten but clear code of gentlemanly behaviour inculcated in childhood. 'Conduct unbecoming a gentleman' is still enough to have someone dismissed as an army officer; even if not stated in exactly these words, it may also debar people from membership of a profession.

The origins of this code can be traced back to the Victorian acceptance of chivalry and the Middle Ages and their admiration for Chaucer's 'parfit gentil knight'. It provided a clear basis for the large professional class which came into existence in the nineteenth century and established the 'service industries' that are now so vital everywhere in the world (Stewart et al. 1994).

Cain and Hopkins (1991-92) have emphasized the importance of this sector to Britain and its growth was undoubtedly due to the shared values of the upper middle-class which spearheaded it. The British 'gentlemanly class' consisted of people who emulated those already rich not merely through pretension but also by acquiring the status of a 'gentleman' through trustworthiness. These values were paramount in the success of the British service industries, which in turn contributed to the rise of the British economy in the Victorian era.

An external view of a Victorian gentleman is given by the French writer Jules Verne, whose character Phileas Fogg is a London gentleman:

> The way in which he got admission to this exclusive club was simple enough. He was recommended by the Barings Brothers, with whom

he had an open credit ... his account ... was always flush ... He was not lavish, nor, on the contrary, stingy; for whenever he knew that money was needed for a noble, useful or benevolent purpose, he supplied it quietly, and sometimes benevolently (Verne 1991: 10).

It may be worth pointing out that while the British schools reinforced this code of values, the old saying that 'Public schools exist not to make gentlemen but the fathers of gentlemen' would seem to acknowledge the importance of early conditioning in line with Hofstede's (1991) belief that values are fixed by the age of puberty.

The economic success of those in the learned professions can be attributed largely to the trust earned by adherence to a rigid code of ethics and it thus provides comfort to those who wish to maintain that high standards can lead to business success.

CONCLUSION

Two leitmotifs appear in the teachings of ancient philosophy and religion regarding business. The first, avoidance of fraud and greed, was to be expected. The second is both deeper and more significant for business ethics worldwide. What Confucius names *ren* and Aristotle *philia* is described in the *Koran* as 'mutual good-will' (Koran, Sura 4, 29) and by Lester, talking of *Hinayana* Buddhism, as 'the way of the welfare of all beings through reciprocal action' (Lester 1973: 156). Business values thus has worldwide potential, arising from its firm foundations in commerce and religion.

The growing significance of business values is indicated by the proliferation of dedicated institutions in the United States; as long ago as 1986, there were twenty-nine dedicated American institutions (Bennett and Jones 1986: xiii-xv). The European Business Ethics Network now has units in the Netherlands, Switzerland, Germany, Spain, Italy and the United Kingdom, and held its seventh European Conference from 14-16 November 1994 at St Gallen. Jack Mahoney (see Chapter 11 in this volume) is the London Business School's first Dixons Professor of Business Ethics and Societal Responsibility. Business ethics has at least two dedicated periodicals, in the form of America's *Journal of Business Ethics* and Europe's *Business Ethics: A European Review* (edited by Jack Mahoney).

Deficiencies

The comparative youth of the concept of 'business values' as a concrete, academic subject is illustrated by the numerous misconceptions and cynicism surrounding it: see the reaction, referred to in Klaus M. Leisinger's chapter in this volume 'Corporate Ethics and International Business', of the Austrian satirist Karl Kraus (1874-1936), namely 'business ethics' was a contradiction in terms. Admittedly, this example may be a little extreme, but in many environments, age-old dilemmas are recurring in new environments, long after solutions to them have been found elsewhere. For example, it took a great deal of effort and argument to end the exploitation of child labour in 1830s industrial Britain and to establish that this was morally wrong, with the Factories Act, yet child labour is being used in other rapidly industrializing areas today such as the Philippines, India, Indonesia and Thailand. Hong Kong is especially relevant to this ethical crisis as it is credited as having solved the problem of child exploitation. Enterprises from developed countries with certain developed ideas in business standards are relocating to newly industrializing areas such as China and Mexico to avoid them. An editorial in *Eastern Express* concludes:

> ... the Chinese authorities must turn over this Dickensian page as soon as possible and define a new set of ideological values for its people so that there is a greater awareness among businessmen of the need for a more humane society (*Eastern Express* 1994: 15).

Regional or Global Values?

If the idea of business values is spread, dilemmas and disasters can be prevented; Hong Kong has particular potential given its influence as an international business centre. In this domain it could serve as leader of the region: not only is the city what other industrializing Asian states for the most part aspire to, but these states are naturally far more ready to learn from a neighbour than from a civilization on the other side of the world. Hong Kong has its own fair share of lessons for others, notably how to combat endemic corruption, as Jack Mahoney demonstrates in 'Ethical Attitudes to Bribery and Extortion' in this volume. If mainland China is to learn how to resolve its own problems in that domain, its easiest option is to learn from its prodigal child, before or after the territory reverts to Chinese rule.

It may seem to some that it is being alleged that the business giants of the United States and Europe are, due to experience, paragons of virtue, and that backward Asia must copy their ways as soon as possible. Such an outlook is myopic. As business and the power of business develop in the United States and Europe, new ethical problems arise to which new solutions must be found. As business develops in Asia, local societies are re-examining the problems of corruption and prevalent market distortion. In order fully to contribute to world economic development, Asia, including less developed Asian economies, will need to play its part in establishing a global dialogue on ethics.

As Confucian influenced areas such as the 'little dragons'[3] and the 'tigers'[4] emerge from a former 'Third World' status to acquire a position around the table of countries considered 'developed', it is inevitable in each case that the state will gradually have less dictating power over the economy and the workforce; Taiwan began its shift from military dictatorship to pluralist democracy in 1986, and South Korea has had its first ever civilian head of state since the early 1980s. As economic power shifts from the state to business people, so does the potential for abuse, and a shift in mentality becomes necessary.

This may seem little more than idealism; the concept of business values has yet to establish global credibility and to overcome reactions of ignorance and fatalism. If its pace of development begins to approach that of development in business, that credibility can easily be established, given the cross-cultural foundations upon which the subject is built. We must now look ahead.

NOTES

1. A dubious interpretation, at any rate; the traders were in the temple to sell ritually pure animals for sacrifice, and other artifacts. Most theologians nowadays would argue that the story is an attack on commercial exploitation of religion, not on commerce itself. The previous extract reinforces this view.

2.   For a fuller treatment of this area, see Stewart et al. (1994).
3.   The 'dragons' are the Asian Newly Industrializing Economies (NIEs): Hong Kong, Singapore, Taiwan and South Korea (see Stewart et al., 1992: 34–5).
4.   The 'tigers' include Vietnam, Malaysia, Thailand and Indonesia, which all have influential overseas Chinese business communities.

REFERENCES

Aquinas, St Thomas. 1925. *Summa Theologica.* (tr. Fathers of the English Dominican province, 1911-1925) London: Burns, Oates & Washbourne.

Aristotle. 1941. *The Basic Works of Aristotle.* New York: Random House.

Bennett, P.I. and D.G. Jones. 1986. *Bibliography of Business Ethics, 1981-1985.* Lewiston, NY: E. Mellen Press.

Bentham, J. 1952. Defence of Usury. In *Economics Writings* [1787]. London: Allen & Unwin.

The Holy Bible (Catholic Edition). 1966. London: Nelson.

Blofeld, J. 1971. *Mahayana Buddhism in South East Asia.* Singapore: Asia Pacific Press.

Cain, P.J. and A.G.Hopkins. 1991–92. *British Imperialism: Innovation and Expansion, 1688-1914.* London: Longman.

Child, J. 1964. Quaker Employers and Industrial Relations. *The Sociological Review* 12(3).

Childs, M.W. and D. Cater. 1954. *Ethics in a Business Society.* New York: New American Library.

Confucius (Kung Fu Jia). 1991. *Analects of Confucius* (tr. Li Tianchen et al.). Jinan: Shandong University Press.

Eastern Express, 1994 (Dec 1), p. 15: The Hard Lessons of Catastrophe (editorial).

Finley, M.I. 1970. Aristotle and Economic Analysis. *Past and Present* 47: 3–25

Friedman, H.H. 1980. Talmudic Business Ethics: an historical perspective. *Akron Business & Economic Review* 11(4): 45–9.

Hofstede, G. 1991. *Cultures and Organisations: Software of the Mind.* London: McGraw Hill.

Hu, J.C. 1988. *Concise History of Chinese Economic Thought.* Beijing:

Foreign Languages Press.

The Koran. 1968. (tr. A. Yusuf Ali). Beirut: Dar Al Arabia.

Kulke, E. 1974. *The Parsees in India.* New Delhi: Vikas.

Lao Tze. 1950. *Treatise of the exalted one on response and retribution (T'ai-Shang Kan-Ying P'ien).* (tr. D.T. Suzuki & Paul Carus). La Salle, Il: Open Court Publishing.

Lester, R.C. 1973. *Theravada Buddhism in Southeast Asia.* Ann Arbor: The University of Michigan Press.

Muhammad. 1954. *The Sayings of Muhammad.* (ed./tr. Allama Sir Abdullah al-Mamun al-Suhrawardy). London: John Murray.

Plato. 1970. *The Laws.* (tr. Trevor J. Saunders). London: Penguin.

Plato. 1935. The Republic. In *Plato: Complete Works,* vol. 6. (tr. various). London: William Heinemann.

Ralston, D.A., K.C. Yu, Xun Wang, R.H. Terpstra and He Wei. 1994. *An Analysis of Managerial Work Values Across the Six Regions of China* (working paper).

Saddhatissa, H. 1970. *Buddhist Ethics: The Path to Nirvana.* London: George Allen & Unwin.

Stewart, S.E.A. 1995. Return of the Prodigals: The Overseas Chinese and Southern China's Economic Boom. In *Natural Economic Territories and Challenges to the Nation-State.* Ed. Khanna. Washington, DC: CSIS/Westview Press.

Stewart, S.E.A., M.T. Cheung and D.W.K. Yeung. 1992. The Latest Asian Newly Industrialized Economy (NIE) Emerges: The South China Booming Boomerang. *Columbia Journal of World Business* 27(2): 30–7.

Stewart, S.E.A., E.K.C. Chiu and D.W.S. Wong. 1995. *Business Values and China's Traditions* (working paper).

Talmud: Minor Tractates – The Fathers According to Rabbi Nathan. 1956. (tr. Judah Goldin). New Haven: Yale University Press.

Verne, J. 1991. *Around the World in Eighty days [Tour du Monde en Quatre-vingt Jours].* (tr. Jacqueline Rogers). New York: Signet Classics.

Weber, M. 1965. *The Sociology of Religion (Religionssoziologie) [1922].* (tr. Ephraim Fischoff). London: Methuen.

Weber, M. 1985. *The Protestant Ethic and the Spirit of Capitalism (Protestantische Ethik und der Geist des Kapitalismus) [1904].* (tr. Talcott Parsons). London: Unwin University Books.

Williamson, H.R. 1937. *Wang An Shih: a Chinese Statesman and Educationalist of the Sung Dynasty*, vol. 1. London: Arthur Probsthain.

Xenophon. 1914. *Cyropaedia. Volume I.* (tr. Walter Miller). London: William Heinemann.

INDEX